PRAISE FOR

Yanks

"A rousing military history of an older, and in some ways better, America. The pen portraits of America's heroes in the First World War—whose fame in many cases extends beyond, like Patton, MacArthur, and Truman—are terrific!"

> —William Peter Blatty, Academy Award–winning screenwriter and bestselling novelist, author of *The Exorcist,* and co-screenwriter (with Blake Edwards) of the World War I comedy-drama *Darling Lili*

"Harry Crocker presents a very readable, lively, and historically rich account of America's involvement in World War I, from strategic-level power politics to the blood and grime of the trenches. The war narrative is complemented with short, incisive biographies of prominent leaders—Pershing, Mitchell, and Lejeune, among others—and the 'Young Lions' such as George Patton, Eddie Rickenbacker, Alvin York, and 'Wild Bill' Donovan. This is an outstanding and enjoyable volume for both seasoned military history buffs and readers who want to know more about the dramatic events that were shaping our present day a century ago."

> —James S. Robbins, author of *The Real Custer*

"A brilliant book. Crocker is the absolute master at creating readable history—and on few subjects is his clarity more needed than on America's involvement in World War I, helping readers to understand and appreciate our commitment and sacrifice. *Yanks* is a great book—highly recommended for anyone interested in American military history."

— Phillip Jennings, former Marine Corps combat pilot
and author of *Nam-A-Rama* and *The Politically Incorrect Guide*™ *to the Vietnam War*

"A great story has met a great writer! Historian Harry Crocker skillfully records the important but often overlooked story of America's pivotal role in winning World War I. Peopled by a fascinating historical cast of characters, *Yanks* puts the reader on the front lines with the American doughboys with a you-are-there sense of immediacy. It is a memorable story of American courage and sacrifice, and the author's insightful, fast-paced narrative enlivens it anew. First-rate!"

— Rod Gragg, author of *The Illustrated Gettysburg Reader*
and *The Pilgrim Chronicles*

"Harry Crocker has tackled one of the most perplexing major wars of modern history, untangling the confusion to deliver a narrative that is not only easy to follow, but a joy to read. Unlike so many histories of the Great War, which draw readers into the snarl of the war's complexity, Crocker's unwinds the sinews, laying them out in plain sight. It is a rare book that can be truly described as hard to put down. If a person was to read just one book about the Great War, there is no better one than this."

— Bill Yenne, author of *Hap Arnold: The General Who Invented the U.S. Air Force* and a contributor to encyclopedias of both world wars

Yanks

YANKS

THE HEROES WHO WON
THE FIRST WORLD WAR AND MADE
THE AMERICAN CENTURY

H. W. CROCKER III

REGNERY
HISTORY

Regnery History™ is a trademark of Salem Communications Holding Corporation; Regnery® is a registered trademark of Salem Communications Holding Corporation

First paperback edition published 2017; ISBN 978-1-62157-624-2
First hardcover edition published 2014 under the title *The Yanks Are Coming!*; cataloging information below

Library of Congress Cataloging-in-Publication Data

Crocker, H. W.
  The Yanks are coming : a military history of the United States in World War I / H. W. Crocker III.
     pages cm
  ISBN 978-1-62157-262-6
  1. World War, 1914-1918--United States. 2. United States. Army. American Expeditionary Forces. 3. World War, 1914-1918--Biography. I. Title.
  D570.C68 2014
  940.4'0973--dc23
                                    2014011621
Published in the United States by
Regnery History
An imprint of Regnery Publishing
A Division of Salem Media Group
300 New Jersey Ave NW
Washington, DC 20001
www.RegneryHistory.com

Manufactured in the United States of America

10 9 8 7 6 5 4 3 2 1

Books are available in quantity for promotional or premium use. For information on discounts and terms, please visit our website: www.Regnery.com.

Distributed to the trade by
Perseus Distribution
www.perseusdistribution.com

For the VMI Keydets, class of '17

and

Scott E. Belliveau, class of '83

CONTENTS

"WELL, YORK, I HEAR YOU'VE CAPTURED THE WHOLE DAMN GERMAN ARMY"

It was cold, wet, and dreary—8 October 1918—the Meuse-Argonne Campaign. A miasmic mist drifted through the early morning sky from exploded artillery shells and gas canisters; men clung to clumps of damp earth as bullets spat toward them from sporadic machine gun and rifle fire. On the far left of the American line was squad leader Sergeant Alvin York. In the course of his thirty years, York had grown from a sharpshooting, hard-drinking mountain brawler into a Christian pacifist, and then, once he was drafted, into a Christian soldier. He wasn't an educated man or a cosmopolitan one—he'd had a hard time taking his eyes off the French-speaking Vietnamese truck drivers ("Chinamen," he called them) who had rocketed him to the front, driving like drunken fiends—but he had superb instincts in the field.

The Germans had a well-earned reputation for being tenacious, superb infantrymen, but it was one of the virtues of the Americans that they weren't much impressed by reputations. The Germans were entrenched on forested high ground around a valley, about five hundred yards long, that the Americans were trying to cross, having taken Hill 223 at the opening of the arc the night before. If the Germans were battle weary—intelligence reports promised that the units in front of the Americans were of low caliber, their morale used up—they were still in an excellent position to hit the Americans on three sides; in fact, the advanced American platoons were already pinned down, fenced in by German mortar and machine gun fire.

York's company on the far left of the American line was moving in support of the trapped units. Sergeant Harry M. Parsons sent three squads, including York's, a total of about seventeen men, on what he feared was a suicide mission: flank the German machine guns enfilading the American platoons.

Sergeant Bernard Early led the doughboys[1] into the forest. Their first contact with the enemy was two Germans who wore Red Cross armbands and were shocked to see the Americans. One surrendered; the other plunged into the forest like a high-tailing deer, York and his comrades in pursuit.

The Americans weaved through the forest, finally stumbling on a detachment of tired German soldiers who had dropped their packs and were sitting down eating breakfast. Stunned at being flanked, the Germans surrendered. Except for one, who fired at York: the German missed; York didn't.

The Americans, having surprised the enemy, were now surprised in turn. German machine gunners, hidden on a covering hill, suddenly opened fire, raking the Americans, hitting one poor corporal with, York estimated, a hundred bullets, practically shredding the uniform from his body. Nine of York's colleagues—more than half the unit's strength—fell dead or wounded. York was on the ground too—unhurt, though bullets had sliced the dirt in front of him and left a stray helmet "all sorter sieved, jes like the top of a pepper box."[2] He guessed there were more than twenty machine guns ahead of him; occasionally he saw German heads over the barrels.

Lying prone, York treated the German heads popping over the parapets to old-fashioned target practice. Machine gun bullets whipped past him, the gunners apparently unable to depress the barrels far enough to nail him to the ground. York's relentlessly accurate shooting suppressed the German fire to the point he could stand up and advance. As he did so, a German officer and five soldiers with fixed bayonets charged from about twenty-five yards. The magazine in York's rifle was down to its final rounds, so he flipped out his pistol, a Colt .45 automatic, and shot his attackers as he would have shot wild turkeys—hitting the last one first and working his way up the line. It worked with turkeys because they didn't see their fellows getting blasted, and it worked with Germans on the same principle. He intuited—he didn't have time to think—that if he shot the lead man, the others would fall to the prone position and pick him off. But they didn't. He shot them each in succession. Then he advanced again with his rifle, shouting at the machine gunners to surrender. He figured he had them now—between foiling the bayonet charge and knocking bullets into German heads, York had killed about twenty men.

The German officer in command, Lieutenant Paul Jürgen Vollmer, emptied his pistol at the advancing Tennessean. Every shot missed; there was no getting at such an invulnerable foe.

"English?"

"No, not English."

"What?"

"American."

"Good Lord! If you won't shoot any more I will make them give up."

York agreed; as he recounted later, "I didn't want to kill any more 'n I had to."

He did have to kill one more. A surrendering German threw a grenade at him. Inevitably, it missed. York didn't. York and his comrades suddenly found themselves the captors of about fifty German soldiers. When Vollmer asked York how many men he had, York said, "A plenty."[3] York's men weren't so sure. York was: he kept his pistol on Vollmer.

York's march back became a sort of forcible conga line of captured Germans as he rolled up one unit after another with minimal fuss, shooting only one recalcitrant German machine gunner. By this time York had gathered so many prisoners—4 German officers and 128 other ranks—that he was turned away from both the battalion and regimental headquarters as having too many for them to handle. At his third stop, division headquarters, York's brigade commander said, "Well, York, I hear you've captured the whole damn German army."

"No," replied York, saluting. "Only 132."[4]

THE WAR THAT MADE THE MODERN WORLD

Most Americans are probably equally humble when they think about their country's contribution to victory in World War I. They figure we entered the conflict too late to claim much credit, or maybe they think our intervention was discreditable. Some say we had no compelling national interest to enter the Great War; worse, our intervention allowed Britain and France to force on Germany an unjust, punitive peace that made the rise of Adolf Hitler's National Socialist German Workers Party inevitable. Had we stayed out of the war, the argument goes, the Europeans would have been compelled to make a reasonable, negotiated peace, and postwar animosity would have been lessened.

Part of Americans' disillusionment with World War I can be blamed on Woodrow Wilson. After preaching strict neutrality and campaigning on how his deft diplomacy "kept us out of war," Wilson changed his tune in April 1917 and said the United States had to enter the war because the "world must be made safe for democracy"[5]—though that was never really the issue. He embraced the idea, even if he did not invent it, that this was a war to end all war—an expectation sure to be disappointed. Some, no doubt, think of the war in terms of the cynical "lost generation"—men like Ernest Hemingway and F. Scott Fitzgerald—getting sozzled in postwar Europe, pickling their former ideals, thinking, perhaps, that abstract "words like glory, honor, courage, or hallow were obscene."[6]

Americans are easily forgetful of history, but we should not forget the First World War or our far from discreditable role in it. American intervention was decisive in the Anglo-French victory, a victory that deserves celebrating. Even if, as is obviously the case, the Second Reich was not as evil as the Third, and Germany's initial decision to back its ally Austria-Hungary against Serbia was justified, its ambition to dominate the continent through force of arms—and its often brutal occupation of France and Belgium—was in no less need of rejection.

The war shaped the lives of some of America's greatest soldiers and statesmen—including George Patton, Douglas MacArthur, Dwight Eisenhower, George Marshall, and Harry Truman—and was hugely consequential. Without exaggeration one can say that it was the war that made the modern world. It was the war that set the boundaries of the modern Middle East out of the ruins of the Ottoman Empire. It was the war that saw the collapse of the Austro-Hungarian Empire, which had held together *Mitteleuropa*. It was a war that rewarded nationalism, which, perversely, had been the war's original cause. It was the war that ended the Second Reich in Germany and witnessed the Bolshevik Revolution in Russia. It was a war that moved into the skies and under the seas. Men were set alight with flamethrowers and choked by poison gas. Infantry officers wore wristwatches to coordinate attacks. Trench coats became a military fashion accessory. And a Europe that could still see angels hovering over battlefields in 1914 was shell-shocked by 1919, full of doubts about the old chivalric ideals, prey to callow superstitions and pagan political movements.

It was the apparent collapse of the old ideals that helps explain what has become the popular view of the First World War—that it was a senseless, stupid struggle, the ultimate charnel house, a watchword for the obscenity and absurdity of war. The casualty lists were indeed horribly long. The victory that was won was indeed horribly mismanaged. But such casualty lists were inevitable in a modern war of European empires; and the mismanagement of the peace was not the soldier's folly.

Part of the problem is a misguided, jejune nostalgia. Before the war, it is often said, was a graceful Edwardian summer absorbing the warmth of a Western civilization that had found—in its empires and global dominance, in its booming economies and steady social progress, in its stable institutions and its music, art, and literature— "its place in the sun," to use Kaiser Wilhelm II's phrase about Germany's prewar empire. If the First World War had not happened, the story goes, Europe would have carried on in some sort of blissful stasis, progressive yet stable and pacific, and no terrible calamities would have occurred. This theme, common among liberals even before the war, was most famously articulated by Norman Angell, who published *The Great Illusion* in 1910. Angell believed that Europe's international trade and its modern industrial economies meant the abolition of war, because conquest now brought no economic advantage—an argument that has been repeated many times over the decades, though reality never seems to cooperate.

THE REASONS WHY

Those who class every modern evil as a consequence of the First World War seem to forget that Marx, Nietzsche, "Dover Beach" with its receding sea of faith, social Darwinism, nationalism, racism in Eastern Europe (Slav versus Teuton), militarism, Slavic terrorism, the Franco-Prussian War, the Balkan Wars, a crumbling Ottoman Empire, Russian designs on Constantinople, and the German Schlieffen Plan that envisioned the violation of neutral Belgium and an aggressive war against France as a military necessity in case of war against Russia (with such a two-front war considered inevitable) all preceded the guns of August 1914.

It is true that National Socialists (eventually) and Communists came to power in the wake of the First World War. It is equally true that National Socialism and Communism were already seeded in Europe. Europe had been roiled by revolutions in 1848, of a mostly nationalist, liberal variety, though sometimes socialist in intent. Communards under the red flag had held Paris in 1871; the Russian government had squashed a socialist revolution (in which Leon Trotsky had a role) in 1905. Germany, France, and Russia all had large socialist parties, and indeed much of the thrust of left-liberal thought on the Continent since the Reformation and the Enlightenment had been about rationalizing and centralizing power in the state. Otto von Bismarck, chancellor of the German Reich, often regarded as a conservative, had shown this very same tendency when he waged a *Kulturkampf* against the Catholic Church (which, unlike the state Lutheran church, was an intolerably supranational institution). He dropped his culture war only after he belatedly realized that the Church was a useful ally against socialism, which he opposed but hoped to appease by reforms.

One of Bismarck's ardent political supporters was Heinrich von Treitschke, a German liberal nationalist (with an ever-increasing emphasis on the latter). Treitschke, who died in 1896, was one of the most influential German historians of the late nineteenth century. He was an anti-Semite and a social Darwinist (much quoted by the later National Socialists) who praised war for its "utter annihilation of puny man in the great conception of the State."[7]

Adolf Hitler himself avoided serving in the armed forces of conservative, reactionary Habsburg Austria in the First World War, preferring what he saw as nationalist, progressive Germany; and one of his early political patrons after the war was General Erich von Ludendorff, who, along with General Paul von Hindenburg, had practically led the Second Reich in its final two years, practiced "war socialism" during the war, believed in German colonization of Eastern Europe, and was a social Darwinist and pagan who blamed weak-kneed Christianity for much that was wrong with the world. In postwar, post-monarchical Germany, National Socialism was only the logical extension of what Ludendorff already believed; and, in due course, it was Hindenburg who reluctantly made Hitler chancellor of Germany.

WHAT THE WAR ACHIEVED

The evil that followed the war was no more inevitable than the good—and preventing the Second Reich's forcible subjugation of the Continent to the likes of Ludendorff was indeed a good thing. The First World War was not pointless. On the Western Front—that European scar that came to epitomize the war's futility—France, Britain, and the United States successfully repelled an aggressor who had violated Belgian neutrality and planned to impose a not so very gentle domination on the Continent. The generals who achieved this feat were not insensate brutes who callously ignored the hecatombs on the battlefield. Few people believe the Second World War was a senseless war or that it was fought by idiotic generals. Yet far more lives were lost in the Second World War than in the First (more than 60 million versus about 17 million). The First World War generals of the Western powers achieved their victory in four years; the Allied generals of the Second World War took six. And if the First World War witnessed the collapse of the monarchies of Central Europe and saw the Bolsheviks seize power in Russia, at least the Western powers kept the Bolsheviks, preachers of world revolution, penned up within Russia's borders. The Second World War ended with Eastern Europe in the hands of the Soviet Communists—Hitler's former allies and the West's adversaries in the subsequent decades-long Cold War. In other words, the imperfect outcome of the First World War was no worse than the imperfect outcome of the Second, and both were better than if the Central Powers or the Fascist powers had won.

The doughboys of the American Expeditionary Force helped win a great victory for the United States and, of course, for Britain and France. From his initial pacifism, Alvin York had convinced himself that the war was just—and it was. It was also, in its scope and in its consequences, no small war, and though the first Americans would not arrive in France until 1917, they would play no small part in winning it.

In the pages that follow, we will see how the war began, how it was conducted, how the United States came to enter the war, and how it was won. We will look at some of the men who fought it, from the generals like "Black Jack" Pershing, commander of the American Expeditionary Forces, to young Brigadier General Douglas MacArthur. We will see the young lions who were finding their way, men like "Wild Bill" Donovan and George S. Patton. In the process, we will see in outline the arc of the American Century, which took American soldiers from fighting Indians to the Great War to World War II and made America the paramount superpower in an atomic age.

PART I

ARMAGEDDON FAR AWAY

CHAPTER ONE

THE CLASH OF EMPIRES

At first it all seemed very far away.

On 28 June 1914 the Archduke Franz Ferdinand and his wife, Countess Sophie, were assassinated in Sarajevo, Bosnia. It was the couple's fourteenth wedding anniversary. They were utterly devoted; indeed it sometimes seemed Sophie was Ferdinand's only friend. Politically liberal and personally difficult, Ferdinand had married against the wishes of his uncle, Austria's emperor Franz Joseph. As a result, his children were removed from any right to succession, but he was still next in line to the throne of the Austro-Hungarian Empire.

An empire it surely was, even if its welter of nationalities were only tenuously welded together. Ferdinand was an Austrian, skeptical of Hungarians, married to a Czech, and inclined to be indulgent with Croats and Serbs. His reputation for liberalism—in what was a tolerant, cosmopolitan, fatalistic, conservative-reactionary empire, which regarded itself, in the famous Viennese phrase, as being in a situation that was hopeless but not serious—came largely from his support for expanding the dual monarchy of the Austro-Hungarian Empire into a tripartite monarchy that would have given greater autonomy to the Slavs.

It was not a popular position. Austrian hardliners saw no reason for change, Hungarians feared it would lessen their influence, and Slavic nationalists did not want their people reconciled to Austrian rule; they wanted violence, bloodshed, and nationalist revolution. On 28 June 1914, one of their number—Gavrilo Princip, a tubercular student, an atheist in a famously Catholic if multireligious empire, and a member of the Black Hand, a Serbian terrorist movement—committed the murders that eventually created an independent Yugoslavia, all at the cost of a cataclysmic world war and 17 million dead.

The assassination was a bungled affair that succeeded only because of the typically lax security of the Austrians. There were seven conspirators, all perfervid terrorists sick with tuberculosis, lining the Archduke's route through the city. The first never threw his bomb; the second threw his bomb, but it was deftly deflected by the Archduke (though it wounded his wife, slightly, and several others, more seriously); the third, fourth, fifth, and sixth would-be assassins did nothing, and even those who tried to commit suicide with their cyanide pills failed; but Princip got his chance when the Archduke insisted on visiting the wounded in hospital and his wife insisted on accompanying him—and even then, it was only because the Archduke's driver got lost and turned down the wrong street. It was sheer bad luck that, putting the car in reverse, he paused five feet from Princip, who fired two fatal shots.

The Archduke and his duchess died true to their aristocratic birth, at first ignoring the bullets that had penetrated them. The duchess's concern was for her husband. As blood spilled over his lips she asked, "For heaven's sake, what's happened to you?" He, in turn, feared for his wife: "Sophie dear, Sophie dear, don't die! Stay alive for our children!" His last words dismissed his wounds: "It is nothing."[1] But in the chancelleries of Europe, aristocratic phlegm soon gave way to the demands of honor, geopolitical ambition, revanchism, and fear.

GOING TO WAR TO HOLD THE EMPIRE TOGETHER

Austria-Hungary's statesmen knew just how vulnerable they were as a multinational empire. Avenging Franz Ferdinand's death—even if he was not much liked—was necessary to affirm the dual monarchy's staying power. Heirs to the throne simply could not be picked off by Slavic nationalists at will and without consequences. While the reaction throughout much of Europe was measured, shock mingling with the assumption that this was a local affair—there was always something new out of Austria-Hungary—Austria's foreign minister, Count Leopold von Berchtold, advocated "a final and fundamental reckoning with Serbia,"[2] a terror-sponsoring state, the power behind the assassins. He was supported by the hawkish chief of the Austrian general staff, Count Franz Conrad von Hötzendorf, who recognized the danger of Slavic nationalism if it were led by Serbia rather than contained within the Habsburg Empire.

If the war were limited to Serbia, the empire could fight it successfully. But of Europe's five great powers—Austria-Hungary, Germany, France, Russia, and Britain—Austria-Hungary was by far the weakest; it could make no pretense to dominate Europe; defending itself in the Balkans was challenge enough. Barely a quarter of its army was Austrian, another near quarter was Hungarian, and the rest, the majority, was a motley of Czechs, Italians, and Slavs whose devotion to the dual monarchy was open to question. Germany was Austria's necessary ally to keep the Russian bear from mauling the Austrian eagle—especially as the Russian bear made a pretense of looking on the Balkan states as her lost cubs. What the Russian bear wanted most of all was to splash in the warm water port of Constantinople, the gateway from the Black Sea to the Aegean Sea and the Mediterranean, and her cubs could lead her there.

THE GERMAN BLUNDERBUSS

The Austrians took the position that one was either with the dual monarchy or with the terrorists. Germany was with the dual monarchy. But despite Prussian stereotypes to the contrary, turmoil in the Balkans potentially pitting Austria-Hungary against Russia had for decades made Germany the peacemaker of Central Europe. In the famous formulation of Otto von Bismarck, chancellor of the German Reich from 1871 to 1890, "The whole Eastern question"—by which he meant the Balkans—"is not worth the healthy bones of a Pomeranian musketeer."[3]

Germany was Europe's most powerful state. United only since 1871 (before that it had been a congeries of kingdoms, principalities, duchies, free cities, and confederations), Germany was an industrial superpower, with the second-largest manufacturing economy in the world (behind the United States), double the steel production of Britain, and world leadership in fields from applied chemistry to electrical engineering. Germany's industrious population was growing—to 65 million in 1913—casting an ominous shadow over the French, who, for all their reputation as lovers, were not having babies; France boasted a population of only 39 million.

The German education system was broad, deep, and effective, stamping out engineers, physicists, and highly trained specialists in every academic and technical field—including the profession of arms, where even the lowliest private was literate. So professional, well-trained, and highly educated was the German army—and so politically dominant was militaristic Prussia within Germany—that the Second Reich was really the kingdom of the German general staff.

But Bismarck knew how important it was for Germany, having forged itself through "blood and iron," to reassure Europe that it was a "contented" power. His chief foreign policy goal was to isolate France and keep Germany allied with Austria and Russia. As Bismarck said, "I am holding two powerful heraldic beasts by their collars, and am keeping them apart for two reasons: first of all, lest they should tear each other to pieces; and secondly, lest they should come to an understanding at our expense."[4]

All this changed with the arrival of Kaiser Wilhelm II, who assumed the throne in 1888 and dismissed Bismarck two years later. The Kaiser did not follow Theodore Roosevelt's foreign policy admonition about speaking softly and carrying a big stick. Instead, he spoke like an exploding blunderbuss while insisting on having the biggest stick possible and waving it furiously. He practiced diplomatic brinksmanship, thrusting himself forward, asserting German rights—and then almost invariably backing down, grumbling about the lack of respect granted to his empire.

In the process, he forfeited Germany's alliance with Russia, though he maintained a friendly correspondence with his cousin Nicky, Czar Nicholas II. Not content with being militarily dominant on the Continent, the Kaiser decided that German pride, prestige, and power demanded a navy to rival Great Britain's and built the second-largest navy in the world, thus alienating the British. He was half-English himself[5]—no less than a grandchild of Queen Victoria—though he seemed intent on proving himself more belligerent than the most bullet-headed Prussian martinet, and harbored a special dislike for Britain, the land of his mother. Among other things, he blamed the English doctors who had attended his birth for his withered left arm, which he often tried to disguise by gripping the pommel of a sword with his left hand.

He twisted the lion's tail when he could. About a third of the world's Muslim population lived under the Union Jack, so the Kaiser made a trip to Damascus in 1898 and declared himself a Teutonic Saladin: "The [Ottoman] sultan and the 300 million Muslims who revere him as their spiritual leader should know that the German Emperor is their friend forever."[6] German railroad engineers backed his boast by helping to build the Berlin-to-Baghdad railway and the Hijaz Railway from Damascus to Medina—neither of which was completed before the war, but both of which Britain saw as potential threats to India.

During the Boer War (1899–1902), the Kaiser publicly expressed sympathy for Britain's enemies, and twice in North Africa he tried to divide British and French imperial interests but only united them in consternation at his own belligerence. In the First Moroccan Crisis of 1905–1906, the Kaiser visited Tangier and declared his support for Moroccan independence against the expanding influence of France. An international conference resolved the dispute in

France's favor—but not before French and German troops were mobilized. In 1911 Germany sent a gunboat to Agadir, after a rebellion against the Moroccan sultan and a subsequent deployment of French troops. In return for accepting a French Morocco, Germany demanded an expanded German Cameroon (at French territorial expense) in central Africa. The Kaiser's bullying manner convinced the British government that Germany was not quite the contented power that Bismarck had made it out to be. Indeed, since Bismarck's dismissal, Germany had embarked on a foreign policy of *Weltpolitik*, making Germany a player in the game of global power politics.

Germany's diplomatic sabre-rattling had inspired some odd alliances. Since 1892 anti-clerical republican France had been allied with Orthodox czarist Russia. Russia was notoriously weak—her armed forces had been humiliated in the Russo-Japanese War of 1904–1905[7]—but the German general staff could not discount her size (170 million people) or her potential to cause trouble in the Balkans. In the west, Britain's John Bull became the unlikely escort of the French Marianne in 1904 with the Entente Cordiale. On its face the entente simply resolved imperial issues, but de facto it made Britain an ally of France. It was followed in 1912 by an Anglo-French naval agreement committing the Royal Navy to defend France's Atlantic coast.[8] In 1907, Britain even agreed to an entente with Russia, which had long been regarded as the great imperial threat to British India. In British eyes the railroad-building, battleship-constructing, Boer-supporting, philo-Islamic German Kaiser had become the greater threat; and the Russians were equally worried that Germany's increasingly friendly relationship with the Ottoman Turks could block their dream of acquiring Constantinople. Bismarck's goal had been to isolate France and conciliate

Russia; the Kaiser had successfully, if unintentionally, made France the anchor of an anti-German coalition that included Russia.

AUSTRIA DECLARES A SMALL WAR;
FRANCE, RUSSIA, AND GERMANY MAKE IT A BIGGER ONE

On 23 July, Austria delivered an ultimatum to Serbia. The assassination of the Archduke had put an end to Austrian tolerance. Austria demanded that Serbia ban all propaganda directed against the Habsburg Empire, shut down the nationalist organizations that fanned it, allow Austrian officials to help suppress anti-imperial groups in Serbia, sack Serbian officers as specified by Austria, and allow imperial investigators to bring the terrorists who had conspired against the Archduke to justice. The Serbians were given forty-eight hours to respond. To the Austrians' surprise, the Serbians agreed to almost everything, quibbling only at allowing Austrian police onto Serbian territory, which the Serbs considered an unacceptable violation of their sovereignty. Even the Kaiser thought Serbia's response was a "capitulation of the most humiliating character. Now that Serbia has given in, all grounds for war have disappeared."[9] For the Austrians the point had been to establish the pretext for war, not to get Serbian agreement, and Austria decided Serbia's response was insufficient. On 28 July, the Habsburg Empire declared war on Serbia.

The Austrians' declaration of war put the cat among the pigeons, or the Teutons among the Slavs. But the first major power to go on full mobilization for what could be a wider war was not Austria or Germany,[10] it was Russia. Russia's foreign minister Sergei Sazonov saw the Austrian ultimatum as a starting pistol—*"c'est la guerre européene!"*—that provided Russia cover (and allies) for a strategic lunge at Constantinople.[11]

Encouraging Russian belligerence was France, which had its own territorial designs if Russia could tie down German armies on an eastern front. For more than forty years, the French had wanted to regain the territory of Alsace-Lorraine in southwestern Germany. It had been lost to the Germans when the hapless Napoleon III declared war on Prussia in the Franco-Prussian War (1870–1871). That war, disastrous for France, had led to Napoleon's abdication, the creation of a new French republic, and the crowning of a Second German Reich at Versailles. Virtually every Frenchman—republican or monarchist, socialist or Catholic—was passionate about recovering Alsace-Lorraine.[12] The French knew they could not regain the territory by diplomacy or by fighting Germany on their own. The French could never instigate a war; they could only hope for one in which they had surrounded Germany with enemies and strengthened themselves with allies. And now they had done just that. French finance of Russia's railways threatened to deposit the Czar's enormous if ramshackle army on Germany's eastern border. With the Entente Cordiale, the French believed they had seduced Britain from her previous policy of "splendid isolation" from the Continent. The "Triple Entente" had put the Russian steamroller in the East on the side of *la belle France*, and in the West procured her the tacit support of the world's largest navy, backed by the resources of the world's largest empire.

While Europe's diplomats and statesmen talked peace, more than a few wanted war. All the major belligerents in the First World War, with the exception of the British Empire and the United States, entered the war thinking they had something to gain.[13] All had made fatal miscalculations. Austria, in its desire to punish the Serbs, had misjudged the possibility of a greater war. The Russians, with their eyes on seizing Constantinople, failed to recognize how vulnerable their society was to the shock of a European conflagration.[14] French revanchists misjudged the price of glory.

The Russians turned what should have been a limited punitive war into *la guerre européene*. The Germans had an equally belligerent faction who thought war was inevitable—and better to defeat Germany's enemies now than wait until they were stronger. Had the Germans focused entirely on the war in the East, not only would they have been victorious, but a credible case could have been made that theirs was a just war, a war of defense against Slavic aggression, sparked by the Slavic terrorists in Sarajevo. But the German general staff, for all its superlative professionalism, proved singularly inept at larger strategic questions that went beyond military necessity.

Germany military planning was for a two-front war. The Schlieffen Plan, drawn up by Field Marshal Alfred Graf von Schlieffen in 1905—and implemented in 1914 by General Helmuth von Moltke the Younger,[15] chief of the German general staff—was to knock out France in six weeks with one enormous blow and then turn Germany's full strength against the lumbering Russians. Schlieffen polished his plan until the end of his life in 1913. From a purely military point of view, it was a plan of genius, and had it been implemented as designed it might very well have achieved its aims. But the Achilles' heel of the plan was its amorality. It utterly disregarded the rights of neutral Belgium, the Netherlands, and Luxembourg—rights that Germany was pledged to uphold. While to the German general staff these rights were insignificant, they became the direct cause of British intervention in the war.[16]

While in the Franco-Prussian War Bismarck had cleverly led the French to fire the first shot, at the outset of World War I the French pulled back from their borders to avoid any chance of instigating the conflict. The German general staff—wedded so completely to the

Schlieffen Plan and the need to act quickly—did not fully consider that the Gallic rooster, however devoted to *l'offensive à outrance*, might not let its *élan vital* overrule its sense of self-preservation. If Germany was culpable for the war—a burden placed on the Germans by the postwar Treaty of Versailles in Article 231, written by two Americans, Norman Davis and John Foster Dulles[17]—it was not because of the war against Russia, but because Germany enlarged that war by attacking Russia's ally France. Germany did France the favor—though it hardly seemed that after its deadly toll—of launching a war France wanted but was loath to start.

On 1 August, the Germans declared war on Russia; two days later they declared war on France; and on 4 August, they invaded Belgium, which had rejected Germany's ultimatum for free passage of its troops. Britain then declared war on Germany. German chancellor Bethmann-Hollweg rebuked Britain's ambassador to Berlin: "Just for a scrap of paper, Britain is going to make war on a kindred nation."[18] That amoral disregard for scraps of paper was one reason Europe's Armageddon had begun.

When Sir Edward Grey, Britain's foreign secretary, received word that Germany had declared war on France, he was watching the street lamps being lit below his office window. He remarked to a friend, "The lamps are going out all over Europe; we shall not see them lit again in our lifetime."[19] In the United States, the lamps would continue to burn brightly, and they would be lit again in Europe, but only after the New World came to redress the balance in the Old.

CHAPTER TWO

TWO AND A HALF YEARS HARD

Belgium was more than overrun, it was terrorized. While propagandists exaggerated German atrocities in Belgium, the reality was striking enough. The Germans razed Belgian villages and executed villagers—men, women, and children, eventually numbering into the thousands—*en masse*. Priests, as authority figures and potential symbols of resistance, were particular targets. If that outraged some, even more were outraged by the burning and looting of the famous university town of Louvain. Over the course of five days, beginning on 25 August 1914, the Germans pillaged the city. Its celebrated library, with its collection of medieval manuscripts, was put to the torch; its townspeople were driven out as refugees. Hugh

Gibson, an American diplomat arriving at Louvain three days into its sacking, was told by a German officer, "We shall wipe it out, not one stone will stand upon another! Not one, I tell you. We will teach them to respect Germany. For generations people will come here to see what we have done!"[1]

The officer was unconsciously echoing earlier words of the Kaiser, who at Bremerhaven on 27 July 1900 had told German troops embarking for China to put down the Boxer Rebellion, "When you come upon the enemy, smite him. Pardon will not be given. Prisoners will not be taken. Whoever falls into your hands is forfeit. Once, a thousand years ago, the Huns under their King Attila made a name for themselves, one still potent in legend and tradition. May you in this way make the name German remembered in China for a thousand years so that no Chinaman will ever again dare to *even squint at a German!*"[2] Kaiser Wilhelm II, with his unerring ability to be his own worst enemy, had thus established the image of the savage German Hun—which the German army appeared to fulfill. The Allies came up with the word *schrecklichkeit* (frightfulness) to describe the Germans' use of terrorism to cow civilians.

"NECESSITY KNOWS NO LAW"

The Germans, however, believed they were fighting a war for civilization—for German *Kultur* against Latin decadence and Slavic barbarism.[3] But that *Kultur* put necessity and progress beyond traditional categories of good and evil. Necessity mandated the violation of Belgian neutrality. "Necessity," said Chancellor Bethmann-Hollweg, who was less of a militarist than his colleagues, "knows no law."[4] Necessity mandated lining up and executing civilians to intimidate others from resisting.

The highly educated German general staff had readily adopted social Darwinist ideas and applied them to the conduct of war—for example, in General Friedrich von Bernhardi's book *Germany and the Next War* (published in 1911).[5] He called war "a biological necessity" in the struggle for existence, adding that war "is not merely a necessary element in the life of nations, but an indispensable factor of culture, in which a true civilized nation finds the highest expression of strength and vitality." Indeed, "Struggle is ... a universal law of nature" and "Without war, inferior or decaying races would easily choke the growth of healthy budding elements, and a universal decadence would follow."[6] Bernhardi's was hardly a lone voice; he quoted many other celebrated German thinkers who agreed with him; and while Germany was, obviously, not the sole repository for these ideas—they could be found in varying degrees throughout the educated classes of the Western world—nowhere had they gained such a concentrated hold in military policy as in the German general staff.[7]

Beyond this, the German army had prosaic reasons for treating Belgian civilians with suspicion, if not hostility. The army had drilled into it a fear of *francs-tireurs*, irregular sharpshooters not in military uniform who had harassed German troops in the Franco-Prussian War. Such *francs-tireurs* were to be given no quarter this time round. German officers were also pressured by the relentless timetable of the Schlieffen Plan to blitzkrieg to victory in France. Impediments had to be cleared away, and that included recalcitrant or untrustworthy civilians. In the words of General Helmuth von Moltke, "Our advance in Belgium is certainly brutal, but we are fighting for our lives and all who get in the way must take the consequences."[8] The Germans were frustrated by unexpectedly stiff Belgian resistance—and that frustration led to civilians being sent to the wall.

It was not just the Germans. Moltke's remarks justifying the army's brutal advance through Belgium were addressed to General Conrad von Hötzendorff, chief of the Austrian general staff, whose own army was behaving in similar fashion in Serbia. In Austria's view Serbia had endorsed terrorism, so it was taken for granted that reprisals against civilians were justified. It was now, for the Austrians as much as for the Germans, a war of national survival. The idea of a limited war was utterly kaput.

Unfortunately for the Germans, so was the Schlieffen Plan, which had been fatally compromised by Helmuth von Moltke the Younger. Schlieffen had warned, up to his deathbed, that everything must be done to strengthen Germany's right hook slicing through Belgium and into France. He wanted the German attack to swing all the way to the coast: "When you march into France, let the last man on the right brush the Channel with his sleeve." He insisted (in 1913, allegedly, these were his dying words): "It must come to a fight. Only make the right wing strong."[9] Moltke was as certain as Schlieffen that it must come to a fight—and the sooner the better—but unlike Schlieffen, he preferred not to risk everything on the knockout punch into France. He diverted troops to block the French from Alsace-Lorraine and, with war under way, sent two corps on an unnecessary mission to defend East Prussia from the Russians. Moltke feared a French invasion of German territory, and guarded against it, while Schlieffen had welcomed the possibility because it would trap the French army in a crushing German envelopment. Schlieffen's audacity might have succeeded; Moltke's caution certainly did not.

The first problem was the Belgians. They refused to capitulate, blunting the initial German assault, inflicting heavy casualties, and withdrawing only when the German army's determination to stay on schedule at any price was backed by heavy guns. Despite gallant

Belgian resistance, the German juggernaut bombarded its way through the country: the Germans took Brussels on 20 August and sped to France.

The French, meanwhile, in traditional finery—blue coats, red trousers, officers in white gloves, all of which gave courage to their hearts if not concealment from the enemy—stormed into Lorraine and the forest of the Ardennes to be met by Germans in field grey manning entrenched machine guns and artillery. The results were what might be expected: a grand sacrifice *pour la patrie*. In the single month of August, 10 percent of the French officer corps fell as casualties.[10]

As the Germans made their great wide sweep through Belgium and into France, they stubbed their toe on the British Expeditionary Force (BEF) on the far left of the French line at the Belgian city of Mons. At the war's commencement, Kaiser Wilhelm had ordered the BEF destroyed, dismissing it as a "contemptibly small army."[11] Small it was, at least in the context of the Great War. About eighty thousand men of the BEF were at the Battle of Mons on 23 August. Contemptible it was not, as the British regulars stopped the German advance before being ordered to withdraw against an enemy that had twice their number of men and guns. The Battle of Mons was the sort of thing the British specialize in—heroic withdrawals, which if they do not win wars at least exemplify the bulldog spirit. The Battle of Mons inspired a legend about the Angels of Mons, where St. George and the Bowmen of Agincourt were said to have descended from the heavens to help the British.[12]

In the East, Austria had to divert troops from its Serbian offensive to fend off the Russians, and a worried Moltke reinforced East Prussia. Before those reinforcements arrived, the German Eighth Army, under Generals Paul von Hindenburg (called out of retirement to meet the crisis) and Erich von Ludendorff, had knocked the wheels off the Russian steamroller, destroying its Second Army at the Battle of Tannenberg (26–30 August). Russian losses (170,000 casualties, more than 90,000 of them surrendering) were greater in size than the entire German Eighth Army, which suffered 12,000 casualties. The stolid, determined Hindenburg, the embodiment of the tough, dutiful virtues of the Prussian aristocracy, became a hero, as did the emotionally tempestuous and not quite as well-born Ludendorff. Ludendorff, brilliant and aggressive, had already made his name and been awarded the Blue Max for his conduct in Belgium, where he had taken a sword and pounded on the gates of the citadel at Liège, and accepted the surrender of hundreds of Belgian soldiers.

Though impeded in the West and outnumbered in the East, the Germans were crushing their enemies, proving themselves the best soldiers in Europe. The Austrians, however, were taking a pounding. The Austrian Field Marshal Conrad von Hötzendorff was as aggressive as Ludendorff but with an army incapable of carrying out his ambitious plans. By the end of 1914, the Habsburg Empire had suffered an astonishing number of casualties—more than six hundred thousand men—and was in constant need of German support. Many German officers felt that being allied to the Habsburg Empire was, in the famous phrase, like being "shackled to a corpse."[13]

While the Austrians were struggling, the Germans had blown through Belgium and now appeared almost unstoppable: the French government felt compelled to evacuate Paris on 2 September. One very important Frenchman, however, retained his *savoir faire*. The French commander General Joseph Joffre—walrus-moustached, imposing, imperturbable—rallied his army for what became "the miracle of the Marne." French troops, still in their prideful blue coats and pantaloons *rouge*, came ferried to the front in an armada of French taxis pressed into emergency service. The French hit the exhausted German First and Second Armies, surrounding them on three sides and bringing them to a shuddering halt; Moltke had a nervous breakdown, fearing he had stumbled into a disaster (though the Germans were able to extricate themselves); and the Schlieffen Plan fell to pieces. Two million men fought at the First Battle of the Marne (5–12 September 1914), and the consequence of this epic battle was not just an Anglo-French parrying of the German slash and thrust, it was a stalemated war of trenches from which there appeared no escape.

STALEMATE

When Confederate veteran John Singleton Mosby was asked to comment on the trench warfare in Europe, he said that Robert E. Lee or Stonewall Jackson would have found a way around. "As it is, the forces are just killing. The object of war is not to kill. It is to disable the military power."[14] But with all due respect to Mosby, Jackson, and Lee, there was no easy way around.

If you followed the war through American newspapers, you were getting a quick refresher course in the geography of Europe and Asia as generals struggled to find a way to break the deadlock on the Western Front. In 1914, there was the "race to the sea," with both sides attempting to outflank each other in northwestern France and southwestern Belgium. When the belligerents' confronting trenches stretched from the English Channel to Switzerland, there were attempts to turn more distant strategic flanks, as in the Gallipoli Campaign against the Turks in 1915. Of massive battles there was no shortage, but by sticking pins in a map you could see that huge expenditures of men often moved the armies hardly at all, or moved them in ways that seemed marginal to any ultimate victory.

Some fifteen thousand Americans did not content themselves with reading about the war. They volunteered to serve as ambulance drivers (Walt Disney was one; Ernest Hemingway was another) or in the French, British, or Canadian armed forces. Among those serving in the ranks was Alan Seeger, a Harvard-educated poet who found his famous rendezvous with death as a member of the French Foreign Legion on 4 July 1916. He charged across more than two hundred yards of open ground against German machine guns at the village of Belloy-en-Santerre in the Battle of the Somme. Though he did not make it, the legionnaires secured a position in the village and held it for two days, taking 30 percent casualties, until they were relieved.

Seeger had alternated between moods of exaltation ("Every minute here is worth weeks of ordinary experience") to trench depression ("living in holes in the ground and only showing our heads outside to fight and to feed")[15] to admiration for the enemy, saying the Germans were "marvelous"[16] at trench warfare, to blunt realism ("And our rôle, that of troops in reserve, was to live passive in an open field under a shell fire that every hour became more terrific, while aeroplanes and captive balloons, to which we were entirely exposed, regulated the fire").[17] By all accounts he was a brave man, and he was an inspiration for the memorial in Paris dedicated to the American volunteers.

Another American who joined the French Foreign Legion was Kiffin Rockwell, who enlisted with his brother Paul, served with Seeger, and after being seriously wounded hung up his infantryman's rifle and transferred to the French air force. His squadron, later known as the Lafayette Escadrille, was one of two units (the other was the Lafayette Flying Corps) set aside by the French for American pilots. In May 1916, only four weeks into the life of the escadrille,

Rockwell became the first American to shoot down a German plane. His technique in dogfights was to zoom within feet of the enemy before unleashing the lead from his machine guns. In September 1916, he made a diving attack and crashed, threaded with enemy bullets.[18]

Even if one contented oneself with newspaper reports—rather than joining the French Foreign Legion—certain names and battles would have become familiar. There was, for instance, the confusingly named Sir John French who was actually an excessively sociable[19] if hot-tempered Anglo-Irish field marshal who had started life as a midshipman.[20] A veteran of campaigns in the Sudan (1884–1885) and South Africa (1899–1902), he was commander of the British Expeditionary Force (from August 1914 through December 1915) and was neither very fluent in French nor overly keen on cooperating with them. French was a hard charger who thought that if properly supplied with artillery shells and men, he could somehow, somewhere break through on the Western Front.[21] Lord Kitchener, secretary of state for war, doubted such a breakout was possible; and even Kitchener, who expected terrible costs, was appalled at the massive casualty lists from attempted breakouts— these battles seemed more like industrialized murder than war.[22]

French fought the First Battle of Ypres[23] (19 October to 22 November 1914), where each side tried to gain the offensive in southwestern Belgium. The resulting combined casualties were nearly three hundred thousand men. While the Entente Powers blocked German attempts to renew the rightward thrust of the Schlieffen Plan, the battle also marked the end of the British regulars, the "Old Contemptibles." They had fought brilliantly throughout, starting at the Battle of Mons, but were worn to the quick by casualties.

French's last battle with the BEF was the Battle of Loos (25 September to 14 October 1915) in northwestern France. Outnumbering the Germans in front of him, he thought he could blast his way through. The result was fifty thousand British casualties (including Rudyard Kipling's son, John, missing, presumed dead) and half that many German. The British tried using chlorine gas, already employed by the Germans, to overcome the stasis of the trenches.[24] Instead, it blew back over the British, who had to charge through their own poison mist. Lack of artillery support and replacements for exhausted infantry units meant that while the British captured Loos, they could go no farther and were forced to withdraw.

To the relief of the American newspaper reader, French's replacement was the much less confusingly named Field Marshal Sir Douglas Haig. Haig had the additional advantage of confirming American stereotypes that British commanding officers were all bluff, well-turned-out, well-mannered, white-moustached British aristocrats (as indeed many of them were). Haig held command of the British forces through the end of the war, so it was he who would eventually greet General John J. Pershing, commander of the American Expeditionary Forces, in late July 1917, about a month after Pershing arrived in France.

On the French side, American newspaper readers would have been familiar with General Joffre—who actually came to America in April 1917 on a goodwill mission after Congress's declaration of war—because Americans still remembered him as the hero who had saved France at the Battle of the Marne. Joffre, like Sir John French, had believed the Germans could be defeated on the Western Front if the Western Allies applied sufficient artillery and men at the crucial point. Finding that crucial point, however, was proving immensely costly; it was not easily discovered.

Another familiar French general was Joffre's fellow hero of the Marne, Ferdinand Foch. A renowned writer and lecturer on military strategy and allegedly the finest military mind of his generation, he was sixty-two years old in August 1914, and up to that point he had never seen combat.[25] Nor had he served abroad, in the training ground of France's empire. But those disadvantages paled to insignificance compared with his detailed understanding of the German army, which he had always regarded as the main enemy.[26] The key problem for Foch was how to overcome German military superiority in numbers, equipment, and training. He found part of the answer in a patriotic assertion of the French spirit. Foch's own spirit was one of the legends of the Battle of the Marne. Commanding the Ninth Army, his headquarters exposed to the enemy, he famously proclaimed, "My center is giving way, my right is in retreat. Situation excellent. I attack."[27]

Foch and Haig were commanders at the Battle of the Somme, which lasted from July through November 1916. To the newspaper reader, it was doubtless an awful and awe-inspiring event, with more than a million combined casualties between the Germans and the Western Allies. To the soldiers in the trenches, it was a test of fire and endurance that most of them met with incredible but matter-of-fact fortitude, even with "Death grinning at you from all around and hellish 5.9 inch shells shrieking through the air and shrapnel dealing death all round," as one Australian captain wrote to his parents. "I don't know how long I stood it without breaking." He was "very thankful to get my wound as it got me out of the firing line for a rest."[28] Rest, aside from the permanent kind, was hard to come by.

The Battle of the Somme was an Anglo-French offensive to break the German line in northwestern France through a mighty assault; the hope was to force a gap that would allow cavalry (and tanks, which made their first appearance here) to plunge through, starting a war of movement that would end the deadlock of the trenches. The British lost nearly sixty thousand casualties on the first day of the Battle of the Somme trying to make this happen, with an opening artillery barrage so earth-shattering it was heard across the English Channel.[29] But in four and a half months of battle, there never was a major gap to exploit. The Somme was primarily a British battle, and Haig kept thinking that a tenaciously pursued offensive must eventually "overthrow" the enemy. His resolute confidence was not matched by his political minders in London, who wondered how such losses could be justified, even as part of a war of attrition, for such minimal territorial gains. German lines had been pushed back six or seven miles at most.

The Battle of the Somme was preceded and outlasted by another battle equally enormous in cost, the Battle of Verdun, fought between the Germans and the French from February to December 1916. Erich von Falkenhayn, Helmuth von Moltke's successor as chief of the German general staff (since November 1914), recognized that attacks against fortified lines were generally futile, but nevertheless concluded that a decisive blow could be made against Verdun, a heavily fortified French city of the northeast, which projected into a pocket of the German front line. The French, out of pride and because it guarded a path to Paris, could not abandon it, and for that reason Falkenhayn believed he could turn Verdun, ringed on three sides by the Germans, into a killing ground for the French army, a massive battle of attrition fought by artillery. The Germans opened with a barrage that lasted nine hours.

General Philippe Pétain was given command of the citadel of Verdun. He would not relinquish it. Pétain, who believed in superior firepower as the way to win battles, worked hard to keep Verdun well supplied, tried to match German artillery shells with his own, and rotated his men to lessen the nerve-shattering effects of perpetual bombardment. The Germans, commanded in the field by Crown Prince Wilhelm, inflicted enormous numbers of casualties, but ended the battle suffering almost as badly as the French;[30] and because Verdun was held, it was the French who claimed the victory. Frenchmen, and Americans who read about the battle, would remember the order given in June 1916 by Pétain's subordinate, General Robert Nivelle, commanding the French Second Army at Verdun: "They shall not pass"[31]—and the Germans, by battle's end, had not. By the time the Americans arrived in France, Pétain was commander in chief of the French army, and Hindenburg had replaced Falkenhayn as chief of the German general staff.

A WAR ACROSS THE WHOLE WORLD

While the Western Front gained the most American attention—and was the front on which the American Expeditionary Force would later fight—this truly was a world war, having started in the Balkans and spread throughout Eastern and Central Europe, the Ottoman Empire, the Middle East, colonial Africa, and elsewhere (including the islands of the Pacific, where Japan picked off such former German colonies as the Caroline, Mariana, and Marshall Islands).

There was, for instance, the Italian front. The Italians were officially part of the Triple Alliance with Germany and Austria, but diplomatic details allowed Italy to claim neutrality, a relief to Italian generals who feared their own armies were too feeble to fight. In 1915, however, Italy flipped from being a passive member of the Triple Alliance to an active member of the Triple Entente, wooed by British, French, and Russian promises of postwar spoils. Italy declared war on Austria in May 1915, but prudently avoided declaring war on Germany until August 1916.

The realist-pessimist Austrians and Germans were prepared for this, knowing Italians well enough not to trust them; and in the resulting combat between Austrian and Italian forces, it was the Italians who got the worst of it in combat in the frozen Alps. By 1917, the Italians had gained very little territory, and what they had gained would soon be lost in an Austrian counteroffensive. For that, Italy had sacrificed hundreds of thousands of casualties in a front that became as static as the one in the West.

Meanwhile, the Germans' ardent wooing of the Ottoman Empire had been rewarded when the Turks declared war as an ally of the Central Powers in November 1914. The Ottoman army was already well supplied with fez-capped German generals leading goose-stepping Turks, and though the Ottoman Empire was, famously, the sick man of Europe, the Ottoman caliphate did something most belligerents could not: it declared a global holy war against the British, French, and Russians. In the event, the jihad proved of little practical account except perhaps to justify (in Turkish eyes at least) the war against the empire's Christian Armenians, which amounted to mass executions of civilians and selling Armenian women and children into slavery.

The Ottomans' war had several fronts. In Central Asia, the Russians obliterated Turkish offensives, though, fatally for the Czar, the Turks still held the Dardanelles, closing off the Black Sea as a source of resupply for the Russian Empire. Ottoman threats to the Suez Canal were rebuffed by the British, who in, turn, won the support of Sherif Hussein of Mecca for a British-backed Arab revolt against the Ottomans.[32] In Mesopotamia, the Turks forced a humiliating British surrender at the siege of Kut (December 1915 to April 1916), but were in turn driven out of Baghdad in March 1917, losing

Mesopotamia to the British. The one unmistakable Turkish victory was at Gallipoli (April 1915 to January 1916), where the Western Allies had hoped to force the Dardanelles; bring relief to Russia; knock Turkey out of the war; and gain Greek and Bulgarian allies to advance through what would later be called the "soft underbelly of Europe."[33] But the Gallipoli Campaign was a litany of misfortune for the British Empire; an epic, tragic event in the history of the Australian and New Zealand armed forces; and the temporary crusher of political careers, including that of Winston Churchill. Churchill, who had ardently backed the expedition, resigned as First Lord of the Admiralty and took a commission first with the Grenadier Guards and then with the Royal Scots Fusiliers, serving in the trenches at age forty-one.[34]

In the Balkans, everything was a mess as usual. Greece was neutral and politically divided. One parliamentary faction wanted to ally Greece with Britain and France (the Western Allies already occupied Salonika). But King Constantine of Greece was the brother-in-law of Kaiser Wilhelm and had no interest in declaring war against him. Neighboring Bulgaria joined the Central Powers in 1915, invading Serbia just in time to be in at the kill. Romania joined the Allies in 1916 in a bid to strip Transylvania from the Austro-Hungarian Empire. The Romanian army was large—more than 650,000 men—and Romanian casualties by war's end were perhaps equally large. In December 1916, the Romanian government was driven from Bucharest and into exile in Moldova by a German-Austrian-Bulgarian offensive.

Indeed, on the Eastern Front, things were going relatively well for Germany and Austria. In 1915 the Germans and Austrians had pushed east along an eight-hundred-mile front, advancing up to three hundred miles through Russian Lithuania and Poland and regaining most of the Habsburg province of Galicia across the Carpathian

Mountains of northeastern Austria-Hungary. So great was the Austro-German advance that Czar Nicholas felt compelled to dismiss Grand Duke Nicholas, a dashing six-foot-six professional soldier with experience as an engineer and a cavalryman, as commander in chief of the Russian forces and take command himself. It was not a popular move. The imposing Grand Duke was respected by his armies—even in retreat and with losses that amounted to perhaps two and a half million men—while an aura of suspicion hung around the Czar, whose wife, Alexandra, was German.

In June 1916, the Russians launched a massive offensive led by General Aleksei Brusilov (the Brusilov Offensive). Though the Austrians were initially mauled, almost to destruction, losing a million men, four hundred thousand of whom surrendered (and the Germans lost more than three hundred thousand men coming to their rescue), the Russians were halted, the offensive petering out in September. They had moved forward, along a broad Ukrainian front, about sixty miles, which as historian John Keegan noted, "was, on the scale by which success was measured in the foot-by-foot fighting of the First World War, the greatest victory seen on any front since the trench lines had been dug on the Aisne two years before,"[35] or at least since the Germans had lunged across Poland. But it came at a cost of a million Russian casualties. By the end of 1916, it was estimated that another million Russians had deserted; and the Germans still occupied western Russia.

THE IRISH DISTRACTION

In 1916, Britain, seat of a world empire and embattled on a global scale, was obliged to deal with rebellion close to home, in Ireland. The Great War had actually staved off war in Ireland in

1914, when the British Parliament passed a home rule bill. Protestant Ulstermen—and a significant portion of the British army, which was heavily populated with Anglo-Irish officers—were prepared to fight to prevent Ulster's absorption into an Ireland governed by an Irish parliament where Protestants would be doomed to minority status. As First Lord of the Admiralty, Winston Churchill was prepared to use the Royal Navy to fire on rebellious Ulstermen, and any British troops who supported them, in order to enforce home rule.

War in Europe deferred enactment of home rule in Ireland and diverted the fighting Irish of all faiths and none to raise their shillelaghs not against each other, but as members of the British Empire against the Central Powers. There remained, however, a small, secretive group of extreme nationalists who could not wait for the end of the war to achieve home rule. In April 1916, they hatched a squalid little rebellion in Dublin—the Easter Uprising—which, though central to modern Irish myth, was at the time recognized by the vast majority of the Irish as a tawdry thing; after all, nearly a hundred thousand Irish Catholics had signed on to fight in the British army against the Central Powers. The rebels were fewer than a thousand. The British made short work of them. The Royal Navy had intercepted the German arms shipments meant for them, and the rebels, with the resolute approval of the Dubliners themselves, were swiftly put down.

Having quashed the rebellion, the British proved rather less adept at winning the peace. Irish Americans protested against British brutality. Harsh measures in Dublin—courts-martial and firing squads—imposed on the rebels turned them into martyrs. Conscription, which after much debate had become law in Britain, was announced, though never enforced, for Ireland. That unpopular law cost the

British support in Ireland; its non-enforcement meant they gained nothing from it; it was pure political loss.

But Ireland was, perhaps obviously, a noisome sideshow. More important was the fact that the vast might of the British Empire—with troops flocking to the colors from as far away as Canada, South Africa, and Australia—was deployed against the enemy in Western Europe, the Mediterranean, Africa, Arabia, and the Near East, not to mention enforcing a naval blockade on Germany. Still, it was not enough for victory. That would await the arrival of the United States, a scion of the British Empire that had become an empire of its own, stretching from the Eastern Seaboard to the Philippine Islands, brimming with industrial might, but which was as yet a resolute neutral.

CHAPTER THREE

WOODROW'S WAR

Woodrow Wilson was not an obvious war leader. For one thing, he professed not to know what the war was about. He asked the Cincinnati Women's City Club in 1916, "Have you ever heard what started the present war? If you have, I wish you would publish it, because nobody else has, so far as I can gather. Nothing in particular started it, but everything in general."[1]

Wilson entered the White House a foreign policy novice. After winning election as president in 1912,[2] Wilson confided to a friend, "It would be an irony of fate if my administration had to deal with foreign problems, for all my preparation has been in domestic matters."[3] Even after Europe plunged into war, Colonel Edward M.

House,[4] one of Wilson's closest personal advisors,[5] lamented that the president was "singularly lacking in appreciation of the importance of this European crisis. He seems more interested in domestic affairs, and I find it difficult to get his attention centered upon the one big question."[6]

THE WAR COMES CLOSER

If Wilson wasn't "centered upon the one big question," the Army was, even if it seemed unlikely America would enter the war. In September 1915, the United States Army War College issued a report warning that "The safeguard of isolation no longer exists. The oceans, once barriers, are now easy avenues of approach by reason of the number, speed and carrying capacity of ocean-going vessels. The increasing radii of submarine, the aeroplane, and wireless telegraphy, all supplement ocean transport in placing both our Atlantic and Pacific coasts within the sphere of hostile activities of overseas nations." The War College report added, "The great mass of the public does not yet realize the effect of these changed conditions upon our scheme of defense."[7]

To the "great mass of the public" one could perhaps add Woodrow Wilson, though he had scant excuse. Naval guns had sounded in the Western Hemisphere as early as November and December 1914, when British and German ships clashed off the coast of Chile and the Falkland Islands, inflicting casualties of more than 3,500 men. By 1915, the Germans were pursuing a policy of unrestricted submarine warfare, not excepting neutral merchant shipping.

Wilson was nothing if not resolutely neutral. That was his constant refrain. It was endorsed by the majority of Americans, many of whom (especially those of German and Irish heritage) had no desire to join a European war on the side of the British Empire—whatever the Anglophilic sympathies of the educated classes of the South and the East and West Coasts.

In the months before the war, even some of America's European ambassadors felt estranged from a continent apparently febrile for self-destruction. In May 1914, Colonel House wrote from Berlin that the atmosphere in Europe was "militarism run stark mad."[8] The madness was not just in Germany, but in France and Russia, which, he said, wanted only Britain's consent to attack. Walter Hines Page, Wilson's ambassador to Britain, writing as the great powers mobilized for war, saw strange, elemental, barbaric passions consuming Continental Europe: "It's the Slav and the German. Each wants his day, and neither has got beyond the stage of tooth and claw."[9]

In June 1914, House wrote to Secretary of State William Jennings Bryan, "I have never seen the war spirit so nurtured and so glorified as it is [in Germany]. The situation is dangerous in the extreme and I am doing what I can in a quiet way to bring about better conditions."[10] It was not enough.[11]

STUDYING WAR

Former president Theodore Roosevelt, a moralist himself but disdainful of the liberal moralism of Woodrow Wilson and his administration, saw the war at its outset with clear-eyed dispassion: "The melancholy thing about this matter to me is that this conflict really was inevitable and that the several nations engaged in it are, each from its own standpoint, right under the existing conditions of civilization and international relations." Roosevelt recognized Germany's arguments of military necessity even as his sympathies were engaged by the martyrdom of neutral Belgium. America's interests, he thought, were not yet directly at risk; but the country should be ready. He wished the Navy were put "in first-class fighting order" and the army "up to the highest pitch at which it can now be put. No one can tell what this war will bring forth." But of one thing he was certain—President Woodrow Wilson and his secretary of state, William Jennings Bryan, were not the men to see America through the European crisis: "It is not a good thing for a country to have a professional yodeler, a human trombone like Mr. Bryan as secretary of state, nor a college president with an astute and shifty mind, a hypocritical ability to deceive plain people…and no real knowledge or wisdom concerning internal and international affairs as head of the nation."[12]

William Jennings Bryan, if not precisely "a professional yodeler" and "human trombone," was certainly an odd choice as secretary of state. A three-time failed presidential candidate (1896, 1900, and 1908), Bryan was a progressive, a Prohibitionist, a stem-winding (or bloviating, according to taste) orator, and an Evangelical Christian with next to no experience in foreign affairs. During Bryan's second run for the presidency, Roosevelt had urged voters to repudiate Bryan's "populistic and communistic doctrines."[13] To Republicans, Bryan was a demagogic, backwoods, extremist buffoon.

Bryan was something close to a pacifist, distrustful of the military, and suspicious of elitist, imperialist, wine-drinking Europeans. Elitism, militarism, and imperialism were three of his many *bêtes noires*, which made it difficult for him to deal with pinstriped American foreign service officers who actually spoke foreign languages and drank wine, aristocratic foreign ambassadors capable of sophisticated banter, stalwart military officials who believed in power politics, and representatives of the imperial states of Europe who did not think their empires were immoral: he tended to dismiss them all as corrupt. He also refused, as a matter of principle, to offer them alcohol at formal dinners, which had wags smirking at his "grape-juice diplomacy." Bryan's often shambolic appearance—unshaven, untidy, and unkempt—was another source of embarrassment. To his critics, and in reality, he was a blustering yokel. Or as Theodore Roosevelt put it, "a third rate revivalist preacher...and a not wholly sincere revivalist preacher at that."[14]

But Wilson owed Bryan for his vigorous campaigning on Wilson's behalf. Wilson lamented at one point, "If I am elected, what in the world am I going to do with W. J. Bryan."[15] Since Wilson did not care much for foreign affairs, secretary of state seemed as good a place as any to lodge "the great commoner" who, in the event, spent much of his time advancing Wilson's domestic agenda. As far as Wilson had foreign policy prejudices, Bryan often shared them. Both men were liberal moralists. Both repudiated the "financial imperialism" that had American power backing corporate, banking, or European interests around the world. Both, however, also believed in America as a beacon for democracy, even a tutor to those in the less competent and more chaotic parts of the world; and Wilson, at any rate, took an ambiguous position on imperialism per se, appearing at various times to be both in favor and opposed.[16] For all Wilson's praise for meritocracy, he and Bryan both wanted to root out well-educated Republicans from the State Department in favor of Democrat political placemen who were frequently as ignorant of foreign affairs as the secretary of state himself. Bryan almost regarded ignorance as a virtue; it made the State Department more democratic.

Wilson's appointments to the Navy and War Departments were, on the surface, no better. His first choice for secretary of war was a Quaker pacifist, Alexander Mitchell Palmer. When Palmer declined— "As a Quaker Secretary, I should consider myself a living illustration of a horrible incongruity"[17]—angling instead to become attorney general (a position he finally won in 1919), Wilson chose Lindley M. Garrison, a New Jersey lawyer with no military experience. Garrison nevertheless fell out with Wilson over issues of military preparedness. The secretary of war wanted mandatory military training and other reforms that were not popular with Wilson or with Congress. When Garrison resigned in 1916, Wilson replaced him with Newton Baker, a lawyer, former mayor, and suspected pacifist. On the day he was appointed, Baker confessed to reporters, "I am an innocent. I do not know anything about this job."[18] He was a very Bryan-like appointment.

Baker's opposite number, the secretary of the Navy, was Josephus Daniels, a newspaperman rather than a Navy man (though his father had been a shipbuilder), a Democrat Party cheerleader, and a Bryan-like populist. He was also another near-pacifist and a temperance agitator who encouraged sailors to drink coffee (hence "a cup of Joe")[19] rather than rum, and banned alcohol from Navy ships in 1914. An anti–big business populist, he railed against alleged profiteers in private industry and thought the government should have its own steel company to serve the Navy. He also worked, in the democratic style, to reduce officer privileges and improve the lot of the common sailor (aside from denying him a drink).

With Europe engulfed in an all-consuming war, Wilson's cabinet was stocked with men who on the whole would rather have been smashing whiskey barrels than smiting the Hun. At their head, of course, was the liberal, progressive Woodrow Wilson, who had been a college professor, president of Princeton, and governor of New Jersey. Of earnest Presbyterian clerical stock, he was upright, ambitious, determined, and more than a tad self-righteous. He found it hard to see the other chap's point of view and could not easily engage or get on with people who disagreed with him (as president, he used Colonel House as his emissary to tiresome opponents). While Wilson, a Virginian, played the Southern gentleman with women, he was certainly no Southern bravo happiest with horse and gun. He did not pine for the Lost Cause; he thought the South was better off for having lost the war; and he held no reactionary ardor for states' rights—indeed, he believed in a strong central government.

Most of all, Wilson believed in progress; he was in favor of democracy, meritocratic individualism,[20] and government accountability, which he thought was obscured by America's system of constitutional checks and balances. He much preferred a parliamentary system, or at least a more active executive branch. He proclaimed himself a liberal Jeffersonian in his belief in the people, a conservative Burkean in his disdain for ideology, and a democratic friend of the aspiring classes in his support of government intervention to protect small entrepreneurs from being stifled by corporate business power.

If Wilson lacked experience in foreign affairs, he nevertheless had a great capacity for lecturing the world. After the first shots were fired in Europe and declarations of war were flung between belligerent capitals, Wilson was quick off the mark to declare America's moral superiority and neutrality—in no fewer than ten proclamations in 1914. On 3 August 1914, the very day Germany declared war on France and a day before Britain entered the war, Wilson told reporters, "I want to have the pride of feeling that America, if nobody else, has her self-possession and stands ready with calmness of thought and steadiness of purpose to help the rest of the world."[21]

"Self-possession" and "calmness of thought" were so important to Wilson that he reiterated them in January 1915 in his Jackson Day speech to his fellow Democrats, asking, "Do you not think it likely that the world will sometime turn to America and say, 'you were right and we were wrong. You kept your head when we lost ours...now, in your self-possession, in your coolness, in your strength, may we not turn to you for counsel and assistance?'" Whatever the benefits of Wilson's "coolness" and "strength," they did not advance the cause of peace; Europe did not think it needed a marriage counselor.

Wilson was not done, however; in that same speech, he set out an even grander, if still nonbelligerent, role for America. "May we not look forward to the time when we shall be called blessed among the nations, because we succored the nations of the world in their time of distress and dismay? I for one pray God that that solemn hour may come.... I thank God that those who believe in America, who try to serve her people, are likely to be also what America herself from the first hoped and meant to be—the servant of mankind."[22]

This missionary spirit had led Wilson into foreign policy interventions before. Despite his adherence to the anti-imperialist plank of the Democrat Party, Wilson was not opposed to teaching lessons in good government to ignorant, chaotic foreigners. For instance, Wilson was furious when General Victoriana Huerta launched a successful coup in Mexico shortly after Wilson's inauguration. Appalled at Huerta's democratically illegitimate authoritarian rule and suspicious of the business interests that wanted the United States to recognize Huerta, Wilson looked for an excuse to kick the Mexican dictator.

In January 1914, Wilson took the plunge of recognizing Venustiano Carranza's Constitutionalists, who were engaged in an anarchic civil war—among Carranza's commanders were Pancho Villa and Emiliano Zapata—to oust Huerta. In February, Wilson lifted an arms embargo on the Constitutionalists, and in April, after the Huerta regime refused to humble itself after arresting—and then releasing—some American sailors, Wilson ordered the U.S. Navy and Marines to occupy Vera Cruz. His policy, he told British diplomat Sir William Tyrrell, was "to teach the South American republics to elect good men!"[23] Wilson pulled back from going to war in Mexico—indeed, he was shaken that American servicemen had died as part of his tutorial[24]—and eventually the matter was resolved through negotiations mediated by Argentina, Brazil, and Chile, which put a rather humiliating dent in the idea of the United States as tutor to the world. Huerta resigned in July (only to arise again as a would-be conspirator with Germany in 1915),[25] Carranza became president (but was no more friendly to the United States than Huerta), and Wilson's lesson about electing good men seemed not to have advanced the democratic cause very much.

If Mexicans were not apt pupils for Wilson's catechism, the American people were a captive audience: they had made him president. With the Great War now consuming Europe, Wilson cast himself as professor in chief, with a sheaf of lecture notes on the theory and practice of neutrality. On 19 August 1914, three days before the British Expeditionary Force arrived in France, Wilson admonished his fellow citizens that neutrality meant more than the U.S. government not favoring any of the belligerent powers. Neutrality was the responsibility of every American who needed to strive to be "impartial in thought as well as in action." Wilson put special emphasis on "what newspapers and magazines contain, upon what ministers utter in their pulpits, and men proclaim as their opinions on the street." If any doubted that a president of the United States should be dictating what people thought, said, and wrote, Wilson was quick to offer that such uniform neutrality of conscience and deed was necessary to make the United States "truly serviceable for the peace of the world."[26]

In September 1914, Theodore Roosevelt expressed a different view: "President Wilson has been much applauded by all the professional pacifists because he has announced that our desire for peace must make us secure it for ourselves by a neutrality so strict as to forbid our even whispering a protest against wrong-doing, lest such whispers cause disturbance to our ease and well-being. We pay the penalty for this action—or rather, supine inaction—by forfeiting the right to do anything on behalf of peace for the Belgians at present."[27] To Roosevelt, Belgium was the war's "guiltless" victim; Wilson was America's gutless president. "Wilson," Roosevelt concluded, "is almost as much of a prize jackass as Bryan." "The President, unlike Mr. Bryan," Roosevelt noted, "uses good English and does not say things that are on their face ridiculous. Unfortunately his cleverness of style and his entire refusal to face facts apparently make him believe that he really has dismissed and done away with ugly realities whenever he has uttered some pretty phrase about them."[28]

"TOO PROUD TO FIGHT"

Wilson made no protest at German atrocities in Belgium. Through privately pro-British and anti-German, he followed his own advice, trying to be neutral in thought, word, and deed, and to convince himself that the war need not touch America—though of course it did, immediately. In terms of trade and finance, the war was a potential boon to the American economy.

At the war's outset, Britain had imposed a partial blockade of Germany. British foreign minister Sir Edward Grey was solicitous of American opinion and tried to fend off French and Russian calls for a tighter blockade. When cotton, for instance, was added to the list of contraband that could not be shipped to Germany, he had Britain buy American cotton. The partial blockade became a full blockade only after Germany, on 4 February 1915, declared a U-boat war against merchant ships in the waters surrounding Britain and Ireland, a bit of undersea sabre-rattling that even the Wilson administration felt compelled to denounce as an act "unprecedented in naval warfare." The administration warned that if American lives and ships were lost, "the United States would be constrained to hold the Imperial German Government to a strict accountability."[29] If this was a threat of war, the German government discounted it, given Wilson's manifold protestations in favor of peace, neutrality, coolness, and self-possession.

Nevertheless, American foreign policy seemed to be sliding in an almost inevitable pro-Entente direction, despite America's professed neutrality. At first, at Bryan's urging, Wilson agreed to ban loans to the combatant nations of Europe—a policy driven both by the Democrats' suspicion of Wall Street and by Bryan's denunciations of finance as the grease of war. But the ban soon unraveled, and multimillion-dollar loans joined trade in tying America to Britain and France.

German submarine commanders had been secretly advised to avoid striking American-flagged ships; German torpedoes nevertheless exploded through the hulls of American merchantmen carrying oil and grain. In March 1915, the Germans sank a small British passenger ship, killing an American in the bargain. While Wilson believed the American government was obliged to protect its citizens—and dreaded what that might entail—Bryan believed American citizens were obliged not to drag America into war.

This was especially true with regard to the *Lusitania*. In April 1915, Germany informed the United States that the British luxury liner would be carrying not just passengers from New York to Britain, but munitions for the British army and more than sixty Canadian soldiers.[30] The German government took out an advertisement— approved by Bryan—in the New York newspapers warning Americans not to book passage on the ship.[31] Would-be passengers scoffed at the German threat: on the passenger list were such prominent Americans as the millionaire Alfred Vanderbilt. The *Lusitania* was big, fast, and could be outfitted with guns as a precaution (though the guns were never mounted). No one showed fear; no one could imagine that the Germans would, in the event, fire on a luxury passenger ship. But off the coast of Ireland on 7 May 1915, a German U-boat launched a single torpedo that sank the *Lusitania*, killing 1,195 passengers and crew, including 95 children and 124 Americans.

On 10 May, Wilson delivered a speech telling his fellow Americans, "There is such a thing as a man being too proud to fight."[32] Such a man Woodrow Wilson assuredly was—though Bryan worried that the increasingly pro-British Colonel House and others in the administration were leading the president astray. The secretary of state purported not to see any difference between German U-boats sinking ships loaded with civilian passengers and Britain maintaining its naval blockade of Germany. Wilson did. He demanded Germany apologize for sinking the *Lusitania*, pay reparations, and "prevent the recurrence of anything so obviously subversive to the principles of warfare." A month later he added a specific first principle that America would insist upon: "The lives of noncombatants cannot lawfully or rightfully be put in jeopardy by the capture and destruction of an unresisting merchantman."[33] Bryan thought this far too harsh. It would, he warned, goad Germany into war with the United States. Wilson stuck by it, and Bryan resigned, to be replaced by the much more pro-British Robert Lansing. The Germans, less apoplectic than Bryan, agreed to Wilson's demands.

Roosevelt blamed the sinking of the *Lusitania* on the Wilson administration's lack of big-stick diplomacy earlier in the war and its failure to condemn German atrocities. The Rough Rider colonel railed against Wilson's "abject cowardice and weakness" and said that the president "and Bryan are morally responsible for the loss of the lives of those American women and children.... They are both of them abject creatures and they won't go to war unless they are kicked into it."[34] Roosevelt thought America should already be at the side of Britain and France, at least diplomatically, and be prepared for military intervention. German "piracy," which was "on a vaster scale of murder than any old-time pirate every practiced," and "the warfare which destroyed Louvain and Dinant" in Belgium, should end any doubts.[35] Roosevelt wrote his son Archie that "Every soft creature, every coward and weakling, every man who can't look more than six inches ahead, every man whose god is money, or pleasure, or ease, and every man who has not got in him both the sterner virtues and the power of seeking after an ideal, is enthusiastically in favor of Wilson" and his policy of drift, forceless diplomacy, and inaction.[36]

William Jennings Bryan, on the contrary, feared Wilson was far too belligerent. He joined with pacifist congressmen to agitate against military preparedness. He opposed a volunteer officer-training program, paid for by the volunteers, known as the "Plattsburgh Movement" and pushed hard for Congress to prohibit American travel on the merchant ships of combatant powers.

Meanwhile, Americans continued to be killed at sea. In March 1916, a German U-boat sank an unarmed American steamer (the *Sussex*) without warning. Eighty civilians, some of them Americans, went down with the ship. On 1 April 1916, another American steamer (the *Aztec*) was torpedoed, and the Wilson administration and the Kaiser's government replayed their mutual demands and pledges stemming from the sinking of the *Lusitania*.

"HE KEPT US OUT OF WAR"—BUT BUILT A NAVY

But Wilson did something else, too. He recognized that if he was going to continue lecturing the world—which, as a professor, he was fond of doing—and if he was going to adequately defend the United States at a time of world war among the European powers, he needed a Navy that could deliver his message in words that everyone understood. With two vast coasts and commerce that extended across the Pacific and the Atlantic, the United States needed the largest Navy in the world and a greatly enlarged Merchant Marine.

The 1916 Naval Appropriations Act and United States Shipping Board Act proposed to give the United States just that: a Navy bigger than the combined forces of any two other navies and $50 million that would be devoted to building and buying for the Merchant Marine. Though Wilson, trying to be neutral in thought and deed, blamed both "German militarism" and "British navalism" for the calamity of war, he was not a man too proud to indulge in a little navalism himself—and a wee bit of militarism: the 1916 National Defense Act set out an incremental five-year plan to expand the Army to 175,000 men and the National Guard to 400,000.

Wilson campaigned for president in 1916 as "the man who kept us out of war," and he knew the Naval Appropriations Act put him at odds with much of his party. He supported it anyway, out of well-founded prudence—to guard not only, or even primarily, against German U-boats, but against the dominance of Britain's Royal Navy. The United States, rather than Britannia, would rule the waves in the future and ensure the free transport of American goods across the oceans.

Resolute in his neutrality, Wilson dutifully suppressed his naturally Anglophilic sentiments—so much so that Secretary of State Robert Lansing feared the president might actually intervene on the side of the Central Powers. The putative casus belli were British suppression of the Easter Rebellion in Ireland in 1916, British and French interception of American mail, and British blacklisting of American firms that traded with Germany. Lansing's fears were exaggerated, but Wilson was certainly tetchy about these matters in a way that seemed a trifle unbalanced. Wilson came down hard on Britain partly to compensate for his naturally pro-British feelings; partly in response to Democrat constituencies (such as Irish Americans) who were appalled by Britain's undiplomatic acts of self-defense; and partly because he zealously put "America first"—a motto he coined[37]—and was determined that American trade and neutral rights not be constrained by British power. At the outset of the war, Wilson was quick to note parallels with the War of 1812, when clashes on the high seas propelled America into war against Britain. He also noted, rather curiously, that he and James Madison, president during the War of 1812, were the only two Princeton men to have been elected commander in chief.

But whatever the annoyances of British policy, German provocations seemed rather more dangerous to America and her interests. German saboteurs were widely suspected (and much later proved) to have blown up an American ammunition dump on Black Tom Island, New York, on 30 July 1916. The explosion had the force of an earthquake, shattering windows from Manhattan to Brooklyn, sparking fires, damaging the Statue of Liberty, and killing perhaps seven people and injuring hundreds more. This was only the most spectacular incident in a campaign of suspected German sabotage. Between early 1915 and April 1917 there were almost a hundred acts of apparent sabotage against American chemical plants, munitions factories, and merchant shipping,[38] and German agents were suspected of paying union leaders to organize strikes. On more than one occasion in 1916, German U-boats turned up in American harbors and sank ships just off America's coastal waters.

It was, as Wilson predicted, conflict at sea that brought America into the war. Reelected in 1916 on the "he kept us out of war" slogan, Wilson began 1917 by announcing his eagerness to negotiate "peace without victory," a proposal that was inevitably treated with contempt by all sides in the European struggle. On 31 January 1917, Wilson learned that Germany was renewing its policy of unrestricted U-boat warfare. In protest, he severed diplomatic relations with Germany.

The Germans, however, had calculated that they could win the war before the Americans roused themselves to intervene. How could the Kaiser and his generals not sneer when they looked at Wilson: a commander in chief who was too proud to fight, who believed in peace without victory, and who refused to put his Army and Navy on a war footing lest this be thought provocative. Such a man did not impress those who put their trust in "reeking tube and iron shard."[39] The United States was an Atlantic Ocean away. Its Army was pitifully small and ludicrously ill-equipped. Its most recent major military action had been a punitive expedition against Pancho Villa for raiding across the border into the United States. It might very well have seemed in German eyes that all the U.S. Army was good for was chasing Mexican bandits. As General Erich von Ludendorff said, "What can she do? She cannot come here!... I do not give a damn about America."[40]

Wilson now spoke in favor of "armed neutrality," which meant arming American merchant ships. That became rather more pressing after the Germans sank the American merchant vessel the

Algonquin on 12 March 1917. Three more American merchant ships were sunk less than a week later.

Theodore Roosevelt believed that if America had been prepared for war, Germany would not have been so bold. Writing in March 1917, he fumed that Germany's policy of unrestricted submarine warfare against neutral shipping was a manifest act of war against the United States and should have been treated as such. Germany, he wrote, "has sunk our ships, our ports have been put under blockade....If these are not overt acts of war then Lexington and Bunker Hill were not overt acts of war. It is well to remember that during the last two years the Germans have killed as many, or almost as many, Americans as were slain at Lexington and Bunker Hill; and whereas the British in open conflict slew armed American fighting men, the Americans whom the Germans have slain were women and children and unarmed men going peacefully about their lawful business." Instead of recognizing that we were at war with Germany, the Wilson administration was ignobly hiding behind the shelter of Britain's Royal Navy; the slowing pace of U-boat attacks was "due solely to the efficiency of the British navy. We have done nothing to secure our own safety, or to vindicate our honor. We have been content to shelter ourselves behind the fleet of a foreign power."[41]

TO MAKE THE WORLD "SAFE FOR DEMOCRACY"

Then British intelligence handed Wilson the proverbial smoking gun: the transcript of a cable sent on 17 January 1917 from the German foreign secretary Arthur Zimmermann to the German minister in Mexico. Intercepted and deciphered by the British, it read:

On the first of February we intend to begin submarine warfare unrestricted. In spite of this, it is our intention to endeavor to keep neutral the United States of America.

If this attempt is not successful, we propose an alliance on the following basis with Mexico: that we shall make war together and together make peace. We shall give general financial support, and it is understood that Mexico is to reconquer the lost territory in New Mexico, Texas, and Arizona. The details are left to you for settlement.

You are instructed to inform the president of Mexico of the above in the greatest confidence as soon as it is certain that there will be an outbreak of war with the United States and suggest that the president of Mexico, on his own initiative, should communicate with Japan suggesting adherence at once to this plan; at the same time offer to mediate between Germany and Japan.

Please call to the attention of the president of Mexico that the employment of ruthless submarine warfare now promises to compel England to make peace in a few months.[42]

Wilson was informed about the telegram in February and made it public in March—the same month the Czar abdicated the throne, granting Russia a brief interim of liberal (actually, moderate socialist) government. The departure of the Czar made Russia a more palatable potential ally to American liberals, and the sensation of the Zimmermann Telegram made the Allies' cause inescapably America's own.

On 2 April 1917, President Wilson delivered his "War Message" to Congress, affirming that the United States had "no quarrel with the German people," but only with the German autocracy that had forced war upon the United States. "The world," Wilson proclaimed, "must be made safe for democracy." And it would be the doughboys of the American Expeditionary Force who would be charged to do it.

PART II

THE BATTLES

CHAPTER FOUR

THE ROAD TO CANTIGNY

t was one thing for Congress to declare war—which it did on 6 April 1917 against Imperial Germany,[1] adding Austria-Hungary on 7 December. It was quite another for America's armed forces to wage it. Wilson's former strict neutrality—and pacifist politicos who believed preparedness was provocative—had helped ensure that America's war fighters were short of nearly everything but courage. The shortage included men. Though Americans rallied round the flag and damned the Kaiser, relatively few followed that up by marching down to the recruiting sergeant, at least at first.[2] Neither the president nor the Congress had any idea how many men might be needed; some, indeed, thought the United States need only supply aid and perhaps some naval support to the embattled Western allies. Military delegations from Britain and France soon put paid to such minimalism. The war machine in Europe needed men—and America was far wealthier in young men, even if they were not yet uniformed, than it was in military materiel.

The regular Army was 127,000 strong, backed by 67,000 National Guardsmen in federal service and another 100,000 National Guard troops controlled by their respective governors. In terms of numbers, the United States was on par with the military strength of Portugal; in terms of supplies and training for trench warfare, and modern warfare in general, the American Army was hardly prepared at all. It was an army better suited to the wars of the past—fighting Apaches or Filipino insurgents—than the new, modern warfare of artillery and machine guns now being waged by the massive veteran armies of Europe. France and Britain weren't looking for one hundred thousand Americans to join the Western Front—they wanted a million men, at least for starters, and they wanted them fast, before the German armies of Ludendorff and Hindenburg crashed through the Western Front.

BUILDING AN AMERICAN ARMY

Given the task of forming and leading this army was the newly appointed (as of 10 May 1917) commander of the American Expeditionary Force, Major General John J. "Black Jack" Pershing, a veteran of the Indian wars and the Spanish-American War and most recently commander of the campaign against Pancho Villa.[3] Pershing was charged with building a division that could embark for France in June. Wilson and Pershing agreed on another item: American troops would not be fed piecemeal, or "amalgamated," into the

French or British armies—however hungry they were for immediate reinforcements—but remain separate and distinct, under their own officers.[4] This was the military corollary of President Wilson's insistence that the United States had entered the war not as an Allied Power but as an "associated" power. To Wilson, there was still such a thing as a man too proud to be an ally. For Pershing, a different, more readily admirable, martial pride was involved.

Although there was a wave of enlistments in the days immediately after Congress declared war, to put a sufficient number of men in uniform and behind rifles—of which there was inevitably a shortage—the Wilson administration resorted to conscription, the president signing the Selective Service Act into law on 18 May 1917. By the end of the war, the Army had more than 3 million men, more than 2 million of whom had been drafted. Just as the administration resorted to conscription so too did it ditch laissez-faire in favor of a state-directed economy. It created a War Industries Board (founded 28 July 1917), a federal Food Administration (10 August 1917), and a variety of other bureaucratic interventions. Wilson's liberalism thus became statism, as was perhaps inevitable with a professor who wanted to establish a policy curriculum for the country.

Even with a war on, Wilson was not much interested in military affairs. It was still domestic policy that moved him; or, in his increasingly grandiose moments, he focused on shaping the postwar world. But when it came to achieving that world on the battlefield, Wilson was largely disengaged. He met with Pershing only once before Pershing embarked for France, and vaguely envisioned the Army working with the French and the Navy working with the British. The commander in chief delegated military matters to his secretary of war, Newton Baker, the former pacifist whose ignorance of military affairs had been lifelong. Even as a boy, Baker confessed, he had not played with toy soldiers. Now he had an ever-growing number of real ones to uniform, train, and ship—not to a battlefield of the counterpane, but to a real battlefield, a bullet- and artillery-blasted no-man's-land, a Western Front that was contested by armies numbering 6.5 million men.[5]

While Wilson and his bureaucrats felt the great thrill of power and assumed that because they were in command, great things were being done and great decisions were being made, this was not immediately apparent to the man in uniform who might have wondered why he was wearing a British helmet and throwing British grenades. It wasn't until the final months of the war (in July 1918) that General Clarence C. Williams took over as the Army's chief of ordnance and put the bureaucrats in their place, declaring, "If the fighting men want elephants, we get them elephants."[6] Williams was ably supported by Pershing's head of military procurement, Charles Gates Dawes, an enormously successful fifty-two-year-old financier and trust president, who was commissioned as a lieutenant of engineers and given orders to buy whatever the doughboys needed in Europe (thus saving the time, cost, and space of transporting supplies from America). When a congressional committee rapped Dawes's knuckles after the war for allegedly tossing around taxpayer dollars like confetti, he burst out, "Damn it all, the purpose of an army is to win the war, not to quibble about a lot of cheap buying. We would have paid horse prices for sheep if they could pull artillery to the front. It's all right to say now we bought too much vinegar or too many cold chisels, but we saved the civilization of the world.... Hell and Maria, we weren't trying to keep a set of books. We were trying to win a war."[7] Only 3 percent of U.S. Army artillery pieces used in combat during the war had been made in America.[8] For ammunition it was closer to 1 percent. When it came to light machine guns (or "automatic rifles," as the Americans deemed them), the doughboys were handed troublesome, temperamental French Chauchats. In the First World War, it was Britain and France that were the arsenals of democracy. What the United States supplied was masses of raw materials—including, most important, men—and officers who could get things done, like Charles Gates Dawes.

Pershing arranged to have de facto control of the railway lines that supplied his troops in France—an advantage the British didn't have—by importing three hundred American locomotive engines that fit French gauges (and that the French would inherit after the war), along with railway men to do track repairs. The trains were put under the control of Brigadier General William Wallace Atterbury, general manager (and later president) of the Pennsylvania Railroad and a veteran of Pershing's punitive expedition against Pancho Villa. In this creative use of civilian expertise in the rapid construction of ports, hospitals, delousing stations, and supply depots in France, the Americans exhibited the kind of practical can-do spirit captured in the phrase "Yankee ingenuity."

Not all Yanks, however, were created equal. A shocking number of conscripts were deemed unfit for service (about a third). But those who eventually landed in France had an electric effect on the population. The American soldier was big, he was confident, and as he gained experience of the "wind-pipe slitting art," he became sardonic. What he lacked in training he made up for in *élan*, something the French, of all peoples, could well appreciate.

"LAFAYETTE, WE ARE HERE!"

First to arrive were Pershing, his staff officers, and a smattering of sergeants and other ranks, a grand total of 187 men, including

Lieutenant George S. Patton and a former race car driver named Eddie Rickenbacker, now a sergeant and a chauffeur for the general. They disembarked at Liverpool on 5 June 1917—"the first time in history," Pershing noted, "that an American Army contingent was ever officially received in England"[9]—and then on 13 June landed in France at Boulogne-sur-Mer. Two weeks later, the French port of Saint-Nazaire (which the Americans made their own as part of their line of supply) greeted fourteen thousand American troops. On 4 July 1917, Pershing and a battalion of doughboys marched through Paris, the men so garlanded with flowers (not to mention smacked with kisses and sprayed with cologne) by ecstatic Parisians, some of whom marched arm in arm with them, that Pershing thought the column "looked like a moving flower garden."[10]

Standing before the tomb of Lafayette, Pershing, not the speechifying kind, turned to Captain C. E. Stanton to address the crowd. "*Nous voilà, Lafayette!*" the captain declared: "Lafayette, we are here!" Pershing was cajoled into saying something as well, to appease the baying crowd, but it was Stanton's phrase that marked the great comradely handshake between America and France.

Pershing met with General Philippe Pétain, the new commander in chief of the French army who had just averted disaster on the Western Front. In April 1917, his predecessor, General Robert Nivelle, had launched a massive offensive, deploying some 1.2 million soldiers and 7,000 artillery pieces, with which he promised to break the German line within forty-eight hours. More than three weeks later, he had gained 70 square miles at a cost of some 187,000 men. He had achieved no breakout, no rush to victory; instead, it was the long-suffering *poilus* who broke, with mutiny flaming through the French divisions. Nivelle was relieved, and "on the day when France had to choose between ruin and reason," as Charles de Gaulle wrote,

"Pétain was promoted."[11] Pétain was a friend of the common soldier and had been an open critic of Nivelle's plan. He believed in fighting firepower with firepower and in protecting the lives of his men. He made a personal inspection of the front lines, visiting nearly every battalion, reassuring the *poilus* that he would not waste their lives in futile offenses, he would clean up the trenches, he would give them more generous leave; and now he could also promise them that help—in the form of American doughboys—was on the way.

Pétain and Pershing shared a sense of professionalism, duty, and verbal brevity—and they got on splendidly. With Pétain's approval, Pershing targeted a section of northeastern France where he could build up his army and eventually have a place in the Allied fighting line. Pétain told Pershing he only hoped the Americans were not too late.

The situation for the Allies was dire, even beyond the bombed-out muck and mire of France and Belgium. The war at sea, where German U-boats prowled, had the potential of terminating American support for Britain and France before it could effectively begin. In April 1917 Britain's First Sea Lord, Admiral Sir John Jellico, told American Rear Admiral William Sims—former president of the United States Naval War College and Wilson's naval representative in London—that the Germans' unrestricted submarine warfare had so devastated British merchant shipping that Britain was "within measurable distance of strangulation," that measurable distance extending only to 1 November 1917.[12]

The British saw no solution to the U-boats. Sims did. Over the objections of the British Admiralty, he instituted a system of convoys that gathered merchant ships together under the protection of cruisers and destroyers, which together plowed the seas free of U-boats.[13] The German stranglehold was broken. The U-boats went from monstrous menaces to slinking underwater serpents, fearful of American guns, mines, and depth charges. The British had depth charges, too, but it was the Americans who showed how to use them properly (shooting them into the sea with the American-invented Y-gun). The U.S. Navy also made enormous advances in the detection of enemy submarines with an early form of sonar, the "hydrophone," developed by mathematician and future University of Chicago president Max Mason, and in U-boat–exploding mines. The U.S. Navy fought the U-boats wherever they could be found, from the Atlantic coast to the Azores to the Mediterranean.

But if the United States could help the Royal Navy win the battle at sea, it could, for now, contribute little to the Eastern Front, where Russia was convulsed by revolution. The new government of socialist Alexander Kerensky was committed to staying in the war, but the Kerensky Offensive of July 1917 collapsed. The Russian army was rent by massive desertions, the rising menace of Bolshevism, and Kerensky's hostility to the conservative officer corps. In October, the Bolsheviks toppled Kerensky, replacing a democratic socialist regime with a Communist one—and civil war. The Bolshevik government negotiated a truce with the Central Powers on 2 December 1917 and marked Russia's official exit from the war with the Treaty of Brest-Litovsk, which surrendered more than 290,000 square miles of formerly Russian territory, a quarter of the Russian Empire's population, and the vast majority of its coal mines, as well as a good deal of its industry. But in return it freed up the Bolsheviks to concentrate on what they really wanted to do, which was to kill Russian reactionaries. For the British, French, and Americans, it meant that some of Germany's best divisions were going to be moving to the Western Front.

American troops were eager to meet the challenge, though some of the initial arrivals had never even fired their weapons. Pershing would not be rushed; the men must be trained; and he was unimpressed by the British and French instructors available to him; he thought they taught tactical defeatism. American soldiers, he argued, should be riflemen and fight a war of mobility—not hide in trenches, ducking artillery rounds. Through the fall and into the winter—a harsh one for which they were unprepared, reviving historical memories of Valley Forge—they trained for a war of rifle-led firepower.

Men of the 1st Division began moving into a quiet sector of frontline trenches in northeastern France on 21 October 1917. The first American-fired artillery shell was sent crashing into the German lines two days later, though the sector remained relatively quiet. It was a week before an American soldier was wounded (a lieutenant on the twenty-eighth, a private on the twenty-ninth).[14] The first real action was at Artois on 3 November 1917 when a German artillery barrage was followed by a trench raid that captured eleven Americans, killed three, and wounded another five. Small beer by Great War standards, but for the doughboys it marked the beginning of serious engagement with the enemy. The war became real to the folks at home as well. The three American dead were noticed in papers across the country. They became heroes in their hometowns. In the grim toll of the Great War, they were statistics.

At first the Americans' fighting was done under the watchful eyes of French commanders—who could in fact be blamed for the American casualties at Artois. Distrustful of their inexperience, the French general Paul Bordeaux had issued orders that American troops were not to patrol the no-man's-land between the trenches—with the inevitable result that the no-man's-land belonged to the Germans.

That restriction didn't last.[15] Under French instructors, the doughboys learned trench warfare and approached fighting with an ardor long lost by their European colleagues. The 167th Regiment, Alabamans who were part of the 42nd "Rainbow" Division (so named because it was made up of National Guard regiments that spanned the country), became particularly adept at raiding enemy lines. They hung a sign on the German wire as a friendly warning: "Germans, give your soul to God for your ass belongs to Alabam."[16]

THE REAL DEAL

On 21 March 1918, Ludendorff launched an offensive with which he meant to win the war. He knew he had miscalculated the effectiveness of German U-boats to stop the Americans. The Americans had now amassed six divisions in Europe, about 325,000 men, with more on the way. Germany, Ludendorff recognized, must seize immediately on its advantage in defeating Russia; it must fall on the Western Front with a scythe, dividing the British from the French; it must open a gap for a massive and final German invasion leading to French capitulation. Unless the German army could do that, the game was up. Ludendorff thought he had the men—and the new tactics—to make it work. He would not waste time with lengthy artillery barrages; instead they would be relatively short, concentrated, and of unsurpassed ferocity. Allied lines would be penetrated by fearsome storm troops armed with light machine guns, flamethrowers, and other havoc-wreaking weapons. Gains made by the storm troopers would be followed up by masses of infantry, supported from the air. A cousin of Ludendorff's, General Oskar von Hutier, had employed these tactics with immense success on the Eastern Front.

Ludendorff had his Western divisions trained to inflict them on the French and the British.

Ludendorff's offensive, codenamed Michael, was directed at the British along a fifty-mile front stretching south from Arras to La Fère on the Oise River in northeastern France. Under a cloud of poison gas, the Germans hit the Limeys—with General Hutier's Eighteenth Army, on the southern end, making by far the biggest gains, more than nine miles the first day—eventually driving forty miles into France, effectively crippling the British Fifth Army of General Sir Hubert Gough.[17] The French government once again prepared to evacuate itself from Paris, as booming long-range artillery shells came raining toward the capital.

But by 9 April 1918, the Allied lines had stabilized; the crisis seemed to have passed. Ludendorff then launched a second grand offensive, this time on Flanders, farther to the north, on a line extending slightly above Ypres in Belgium, to destroy the British army and isolate the French.[18] British Field Marshal Sir Douglas Haig issued his famous rallying cry to his troops that though their backs were to the wall, they had to fight it out—to the last man if necessary—lest they be driven to the sea and the war be lost.

Pershing had hoped to amass a well-trained million-man army before hurling his doughboys against the enemy, but circumstances had changed. His best-trained troops took up positions in the line. Their first major action took place south of Ludendorff's offensives, in what was supposed to be relatively quiet Lorraine, northeastern France, at the blown-out village of Seicheprey. Two companies from the 26th "Yankee" Division, formed from New England National Guard units, held the town. The division was newly arrived at the sector, having just replaced the American 1st Division, which was moving north, to where the action was hot—though the New Englanders found Seicheprey hot enough. They engaged in small skirmishes with the Germans, the fights growing in size as the Yankees frustrated German attempts to capture prisoners for interrogation (though the Germans got a few), and inflicted embarrassing losses on the Kaiser's troops, who were rightly proud of their professionalism, military intelligence, and ability to infiltrate Allied lines almost at will.

On 20 April, the Germans, hoping to expose American inexperience, walloped Seicheprey with artillery. *Sturmtruppen* then burst among the New Englanders with weapon barrels spewing flame and lead, driving the doughboys out—though only temporarily. The Yankee division counterattacked and retook Seicheprey. But the Germans had scored the propaganda victory they wanted, at least for domestic German consumption: the troops the British were counting on to save their bacon were *schwein* well and truly ready for the slaughter.

The New Englanders of the 26th Division thought differently. They were not shaken by the experience, they were exhilarated by it. They had met the enemy and seen him off—a test of their mettle and a preview of the big show to come. Yes, they had been taken by surprise—but the Germans had crept in under cover of fog, and German artillery had ravaged the American 26th Division's communications. Yes, the 26th had suffered the worst casualties so far for the American Army—more than 650 men, including 136 taken prisoner—but the division had been outnumbered five to one, fought back hard, and recovered its ground in a counterattack. The Germans had hit them with everything they had, and what was the result? Aye yuh, the Yanks were back where they started, still holding the ground at Seicheprey. American newspapers treated the action at Seicheprey as proof of the hard-as-flint New England spirit. Pershing and his generals thought its temporary loss an embarrassment that needed to be expunged, and looked for a chance to strike back—not with the New England troops but with the 1st Division farther north.

At the end of the Flanders offensive, Ludendorff's armies had moved another twenty miles forward, but the British had regrouped, dug in, and were waiting for the next German lunge. Also digging in was the Big Red One, the American Army 1st Division. It was the best-trained division Pershing had to put an American marker against Ludendorff—and it was a division that Ludendorff targeted for special attention by German artillery. The division took the place of two French divisions[19] at Montdidier in northern France and was charged with launching the first American offensive of the war, meant to distract Ludendorff when he made his next major assault on the Allied line. When that assault failed to materialize on the Allied schedule, Pershing and Pétain found an objective for an American attack: Cantigny, a village on high ground that needed to be denied to German artillery spotters who were sending death and destruction into the American lines. The attack would be led by the six-foot-two, 220-pound former West Point football player Colonel Hanson Ely, a man as physically imposing as he was militarily efficient. He would have the 28th Infantry Regiment at his command.

Though he trained his men well and prepared to make up for a lack of numerical superiority with surprise, speed, and massive firepower (including tanks), Ely's operation started badly. On the night of 24–25 May 1918, one of his lieutenants of engineers, carrying maps of the American positions, lost his way in no-man's-land and was captured (and, unknown to Ely, killed) by the Germans.[20] On 27 May, the day before Ely's planned assault, Ludendorff's third great offensive, Operation Blücher-Yorck, came crashing toward the Marne with an apparent objective of Paris, though the actual plan was to draw French armies to the frightened defense of their own capital, and away from the British. As a diversion from that giant feint, the Germans raided the Americans in front of Cantigny.

The Americans repelled the raids against them and went ahead with their own assault. American-manned artillery pieces under the command of General Charles P. Summerall opened up before dawn, and at 6:40 a.m. on 28 May, Ely's units rolled forward led by French tanks.[21] Flame-throwing Frenchmen supporting the Americans burnt the Germans out of their defensive positions, and Cantigny was taken quickly and with relative ease. The doughboys braced themselves for the inevitable counterattack. It started that afternoon with a heavy German bombardment, against which the Americans had little defense because they had scant artillery of their own. The French artillery that was to support them had to be rushed away to meet the new threat on the Marne. By evening, the combination of German shells and machine gun fire had made Ely's position tenuous. But the Americans held nevertheless. They might have been battered to pieces, but they refused to give ground to the German infantry. For three days Ely and his men held on against earth- (not to mention nerve-) shattering bombardment and counterattacks, before it was deemed safe to send in a relief column and pull the 28th Regiment out. It had endured nearly 900 casualties (the division as a whole suffered more than 1,600), but in doing so it had demonstrated to the Germans—and to the French—that the Americans were no callow soldiers, but aggressive in attack and stubborn in defense.

CHAPTER FIVE

BELLEAU WOOD: "RETREAT, HELL. WE JUST GOT HERE!"

Ludendorff chose to redouble the threat to Paris. If he could seize their capital, surely the French would sue for peace, and imperial Germany, greatly enlarged by its annexations in the east, would be victorious. By 3 June 1918, Ludendorff's lunge had left Paris only thirty-five miles from his grasp. The French armies were reeling, and General Pétain needed help. He called on Pershing, and Pershing in turn called his 2nd and 3rd Divisions to Château-Thierry, straddling the Marne River.

The 3rd Division had been in France only since April, but advance elements of it were first on the scene. They discovered that the Germans had occupied the northern half of Château-Thierry, and the best the Yanks could do at the outset was set up machine guns to help extract French troops, Senegalese colonials, caught on the north side of the river. All along the road to Château-Thierry, the Americans had been warned of the German juggernaut by refugees and streams of retreating French troops. But the Americans were unfazed—this was what they had come to do: fight the Germans. Though they were new to combat, the men of the 7th Machine Gun Battalion, an Army unit under the temporary command of a Marine Corps major, did their job beautifully.

"THE BEST BRIGADE IN FRANCE"

The 2nd Division raced to the scene in rattling *camions* driven by exhausted Vietnamese who were prone to swerve off the road and crash, asleep at the wheel. For the Marines attached to the 2nd Division—the 4th Marine Brigade, composed of two regiments, and a machine gun battalion—this was the most dangerous aspect of the war so far. To their frustration, the Marines of the AEF had been delegated as longshoremen and portside military police, a backhanded tribute to their naval heritage. They wanted to get in on the action. They would—in a big way.[1]

The Marines were commanded by James Harbord, an Army brigadier general who had been Pershing's chief of staff. Pershing had originally not wanted Marines in his army. But he told Harbord, "Young man, I'm giving you the best brigade in France—if anything goes wrong, I'll know whom to blame." As Harbord noted later, "They never failed me."[2]

Harbord, recognizing the *esprit de corps* of the Marines,[3] donned Marine Corps insignia (the globe and anchor), and for extra dash wore a close-fitting French helmet rather than the British-inspired broad-brimmed American one, which bore a passing resemblance to an overturned gold prospector's sifting pan. He was proud of his Marines—as well he might be. The 5th and 6th Marine Regiments were the best-trained units in the American Expeditionary Force, aggressive with the bayonet and famously proud marksmen. At the newly built Marine base at Quantico, they had been drilled in muddy trenches to get ready for the Western Front. But even Quantico's famous mud couldn't match the miserable, lice-ridden, dank, dark, waterlogged trenches of France, infested with monstrous rats that feasted on the dead and that Marines bayoneted or shot, treating them like mini-*Boche*.

The 5th Regiment was stocked full of regulars, many of whom had seen action from China to Vera Cruz. Every Marine was a volunteer, and in the great buildup of the American Expeditionary Force, Marine recruiters filled their ranks with only the best. The 6th Marines, officered, for the most part, by Marine veterans and stiffened with a useful smattering of veteran Marine sergeants, was one of the most remarkable regiments in the war. As Marine Corps Brigadier General Albertus Catlin marveled, "If we had time and opportunity to pick our men individually from the whole of the United States I doubt whether we should have done much better. They were as fine a bunch of upstanding American athletes as you would care to meet, and they had brains as well as brawn. Sixty per cent of the entire regiment—mark this—sixty per cent of them were college men. Two-thirds of one entire company came straight from the University of Minnesota." The lieutenants were heavily weighted to college athletes, and according to Catlin, it was American brainpower that won the battle: "when the final showdown comes, when the last ounce of strength and nerve is called for, when mind and hand must act like lightning together, I will take my chances with an educated man, a free-born American with a trained mind."[4]

"A PRICE TO PAY FOR THE LEARNING"

The 2nd Division was ordered to Montreuil-aux-Lions, about nine miles west of Château-Thierry. Cutting through roads clogged with refugees—bedraggled civilians and defeated *poilus* convinced that the war was over and the Germans had won—the division marched to the sound of the guns. One of Pétain's staff officers, Jean de Pierrefeu, noted that "swarms of Americans began to appear on the roads...they passed in interminable columns, closely packed in lorries, with their feet in the air in extraordinary attitudes...almost all bare headed and bare chested, singing American airs at the top of their voices....The spectacle of these magnificent youths from overseas...produced a great effect....Life was coming in floods to reanimate the dying body of France." It wasn't just the French who thought so. Vera Brittain, an English nurse, remembered that the Americans "looked larger than ordinary men; their tall, straight figures were in vivid contrast to the undersized armies of pale recruits to which we had grown accustomed."[5]

The Marines and the French soldiers with whom they had trained—especially the 115th French Chasseurs Alpins, the "Blue Devils"—generally got along well, their friendship lubricated by a shared taste for *vin* and brandy. But the leathernecks were appalled at the demoralized, hollow-eyed, *sauve qui peut* attitude of the French soldiers streaming past them, which led to one of the great exchanges in Marine Corps history. When a French officer told Marine Captain Lloyd "Josh" Williams that the situation was hopeless and he must retreat, Williams replied, "Retreat, hell. We just got here!"[6]

The American 9th Infantry was first into the defensive line backing up the French. French general Jean Degoutte had planned to shuttle American units into the ranks of battered *poilus*, but the Americans insisted on holding a position of their own. When Degoutte asked whether the Americans could really hold against the fearsome *Boche* who had shredded so many Frenchmen, Colonel Preston Brown responded, "General, these are American regulars. In a hundred and fifty years they have never been beaten. They will hold."[7]

The Marines were assigned to the sector of Belleau Wood, and they and the rest of the 2nd Division marched to their assigned places through German shellfire. As men fell to the blasts, Captain Lester S. Wass urged his Marines on, barking, "What do you think this is, a kid's game?"[8] The Americans covered a French retreat, their deadly Marine marksmanship surprising the Germans, and when the French had cleared out—and new French units arrived alongside the Americans—Degoutte and General Omar Bundy, commander of the 2nd Division, decided to go in and take Belleau Wood and the town of Bouresches that lay behind it. The wood, a former hunting preserve, jutted out from the Allied line like an enormous green *croissant*, its total area perhaps half a square mile. The initial attack would be on Hill 142, fronting the northwestern side of the forest. The Marines' maps were inadequate. So were their tactics. Captain John W. Thomason recalled, "Platoons were formed in four waves, the attack formation taught by the French, a formation proved in trench warfare, where there was a short way to go, and you calculated on losing the first three waves and getting the fourth one to the objective. The Marines never used it again. It was a formation unadapted for open warfare, and incredibly vulnerable. It didn't take long to learn better, but there was a price to pay for the learning."[9] The Marines went into action armed with not much more than rifles and bayonets, crossing through fields of wheat and poppies, not knowing that the wood, which they and the French assumed to be lightly held, had over the last few days been planted with German machine guns.

At 3:45 a.m. on 6 June 1918, the Marines plowed through a wheat field against the stinging lead of German machine guns and shrapnel. When someone yelled to First Sergeant Daniel Amos "Pop" Hunter, "Hey Pop, there's a man hit over here!" the thirty-year veteran, directing his troops with a cane, replied, "C'mon, goddamnit! He ain't the last man who's gonna to be hit today."[10] Among those hit was Sergeant Hunter himself: "Hit twice and up twice, hit the third time, he went down for good."[11] Through sheer diligence the Marines kept moving against the confusion and havoc wreaked by expertly fired machine guns, seized Hill 142, and held it against counterattacks. As Marine Captain John Thomason recounted, "The Boche wanted Hill 142; he came, and the rifles broke him, and he came again. All his batteries were in action, and always his machine guns scoured the place, but he could not make head against the rifles. Guns he could understand; he knew all about bombs and auto-rifles and machine-guns and trench-mortars, but aimed, sustained rifle-fire…demoralized him." Thomason took the Marine Corps attitude: "the rifle and bayonet goes anywhere a man can go, and the rifle and the bayonet win battles."[12] Its wisdom was proved at Hill 142.

The price was high, more than a thousand men. For that, the Americans had gained Hill 142, the periphery of Belleau Wood, and the ruins of Bouresches, which had been shelled by both sides and taken, methodically, by Marines using grenade, rifle, and bayonet to root out rubble-guarded machine gun nest after rubble-guarded machine gun nest—the mopping up was not completed until 13 June, when Harbord could report, "There is nothing but U.S. Marines in the town of Bouresches."[13]

INTO THE WOODS

Belleau Wood, meanwhile, remained a devil's den. The German commander, Major Josef Bischoff, a veteran of fighting in West Africa, was as much at home in the forest as in the jungle, and made the tangled woods a nightmarish shooting gallery; his defense of the woods was so gallantly conducted that he was decorated for his efforts, even if they were ultimately unsuccessful. Marine Lieutenant Victor Bleasdale, a former sergeant who had enlisted in 1915, fought in the Caribbean before the Great War, and eventually made colonel, paid the Germans this compliment: they "had some splendid snipers. Those sons-of-bitches seldom missed. They killed a guy I was talking to. I was leaning over, talking to him when the sniper shot him right in the face."[14] But if the Germans were as skilled and tenacious as ever, they found the Marines more ferocious than the accommodating French. One German soldier wrote, "The Americans are savages. They kill everything that moves."[15] From the American perspective, that was the point; they intended to give as good as they got; and the Germans had a reputation for feigning surrender, firing on the wounded, and using Red Cross armbands under false pretenses. The Marines refused to follow Fritz in deceit, but they met him full bore in the brutal business of killing.

There was heroism aplenty, including the advance of the 3rd Battalion, 5th Marines across four hundred yards of open wheat fields. Sergeant Dan Daly, who had already won two Medals of Honor—one during the Boxer Rebellion in China, one in Haiti—roused his men to the charge, shouting, "Come on, you sons of bitches! Do you want to live forever?"[16] Lieutenant Lemuel Shepherd (a graduate of the Virginia Military Institute and a future Marine Corps commandant) was wounded twice in the fighting at Belleau Wood. He remembered the machine guns there as the hardest thing he ever faced—in four decades of service that included two world wars and the Korean War. In his charge through the wheat fields, he was accompanied by his dog, Kiki, who kept him company after Shepherd was shot in the leg and couldn't move. Shepherd wasn't so much worried about his leg—or about getting lost in the wheat, where some casualties bled to death before they were discovered—as he was overjoyed that Kiki hadn't been hit too.

The heroism of the Marines made good press—in part because they were accompanied by Floyd Gibbons of the *Chicago Tribune*, badly wounded and a hero himself, who praised the Marines in red-hot commentary, and in part because Pershing's censors had forbidden reporters to specify any branch or unit of the Army. The Marines, however, weren't part of the Army and could at least be identified as Marines, which meant that when ink was spilled, Marines tended to sop it up. General Degoutte assisted with the Marines' publicity when he declared after the battle that the "Bois de Belleau" should henceforth be named in official papers "Bois de la Brigade des Marines."

To readers at home, early reports from Belleau Wood vindicated their faith in American pluck. German commanders were dismissive, but also insistent on proving that the Americans were no match for the German war machine. So the battle at Belleau Wood became a bloody proving ground. On 9 June, the Marines, now knowing full well the wood was no rural idyll, pounded it with artillery, and the next day they started probing the forest. Parts of it had, indeed, in General Harbord's words, been blown "all to hell."[17] But that did not mean the forest was cleared of the tenacious enemy. In fact, he was still there in force, machine guns rattling in deadly staccato, forcing the Marines to engage in an arboreal version of house-to-house—make it copse-to-copse—combat, a hell of poison gas, explosions, red-hot lead, and bloodied bayonets, where it was all too easy to get lost amid artillery-shorn trees that left no landmarks, and where German machine gun nests were inevitably covered by other machine gun nests, so that it seemed as if the firing would never cease. This went on for two weeks, the Marines joined by the Army's 7th Infantry Regiment, until the Germans were pounded into submission by a second massive artillery barrage on 24 June. After that, it was a matter of mopping up, which makes the fight against the remaining German machine gun nests and trench mortars and infantrymen launching grenades sound easy. It was not, for those involved, though one newly captured Marine bluffed his way into accepting the surrender of eighty-two Germans by warning a German officer that an entire Marine regiment was on its way. The Battle of Belleau Wood cost the Marine Corps more casualties than any battle it had ever fought or would fight until the Battle of Tarawa in 1943. The "Devil Dogs"—a Marine nickname picked up at the Battle of Belleau Wood[18]—suffered casualties of nearly 5,200 men; American casualties as a whole were just under 9,800. But on 26 June 1918, the Marine commander of the 3rd Battalion, Major Maurice E. Shearer, was able to report, "Woods now U.S. Marine Corps entirely."[19]

CHAPTER SIX

CHÂTEAU-THIERRY, "THE ROCK OF THE MARNE," AND SOISSONS

The misshapen croissant of Belleau Wood had been taken, and the American performance there had impressed the Germans. German intelligence noted, "The Second American Division [Army and Marines] must be considered a very good one and may even perhaps be reckoned as a storm troop. The different attacks on Belleau Wood were carried out with bravery and dash. The moral effect of our gunfire cannot seriously impede the advance of the American infantry.... The qualities of the men individually may be described as remarkable.... [T]he words of a prisoner are characteristic—'We kill or we get killed.'"[1]

Still, "Hell Wood," as the Marines took to calling the Bois de Belleau, was only one spinney of concentrated horror in a massive field of battle. Throughout the spring and summer, it was the Germans who had advanced, not the Allies, and where the German army had faltered, it was only because it had outrun Ludendorff's ability to reinforce and supply it. It had also, however, suffered a million casualties and was enduring an epidemic of influenza. Still, Ludendorff was determined to make good his gains and was convinced the Allies were in no condition to strike back. He had one of his best generals, Oskar von Hutier, expand the German salient into France until he was halted by a French counterattack. By the end of the second week of July, the Allied front line appeared to have stabilized. It had stabilized for the Second Battle of the Marne.

"YOU WILL BREAK THIS ASSAULT"

Ludendorff intended, yet again, to separate the British army from the French—to isolate the British Expeditionary Force and annihilate it, while continuing to threaten Paris. On 15 July 1918, the Germans struck through the gap between Château-Thierry and the Argonne Forest. The French knew they were coming; captured German prisoners had divulged all. A week before the German attack, on 7 July, the French general Henri Gouraud rallied his army with a message to rival Haig's "backs to the wall" order of 11 April: "We may be attacked at any moment. You all know that a defensive battle was never fought under more favorable conditions. You will fight on terrain that you have transformed into a redoubtable fortress.... The bombardment will be terrible. You will stand it without weakening. The assault will be fierce.... In your hearts beat the brave and strong hearts of free men. None shall look to the rear; none shall yield a step....Each shall have but one thought, to kill, to kill plenty....Your General says to you, 'You will break this assault and it will be a glorious day.'"[2] The power of these words is intensified if one remembers that the French general, the youngest in the army (forty-six when promoted brigadier, now fifty), was commanding a sector stretching from Verdun to Amiens. He was a dashing veteran of Africa, from which he carried a limp, his right sleeve (the arm sacrificed at Gallipoli) pinned to his uniform, his beard a flaming red, his kepi at a rakish tilt. General Harbord said of him, "His manner, his bearing and address more nearly satisfied my conception of the great soldiers of the First Empire than any other commander I met in France."[3]

When Gouraud referred to the French positions as a "redoubtable fortress," it was not a mere rhetorical sally. He had put into practice General Pétain's doctrine of defense-in-depth: a front line of trenches packed with mines and mustard gas, meant to absorb the terrible German bombardment, and a line of isolated machine gun squads[4] to direct responding artillery fire and alert the stronger subsidiary lines of the coming German assault—though in this case the Allied artillery struck first, on the night of 14–15 July. For weeks, the Germans and Americans had tried small raids across the Marne to capture prisoners until this full-scale collision. Now the Allied shelling was so fierce that some of the assembling German units were decimated and had to be replaced, a blow that more than made up for the risk of revealing the Allied gun placements. Gouraud assumed the enemy would try to force his way down the road to Châlons-sur-Marne. He entrusted the defense of that road to the American 42nd Division. Pershing doubted the 42nd was ready; Gouraud had no such doubts.

When battle came, the French and Americans in this sector bent but didn't break. They fell back no more than four miles, and the

Germans, seeing that their offensive was kaput and under threat of counterattack, gave up trying to dislodge them. A French major who saw the 42nd "Rainbow" Division in action wrote, "The conduct of American troops has been perfect and has been greatly admired by French officers and men. Calm and perfect bearing under artillery fire, endurance of fatigue and privations, tenacity in defense, eagerness in counterattack, willingness to engage in hand-to-hand fighting—such are the qualities reported to me by all the French officers I have seen."[5]

At Château-Thierry, on a line extending northeast along the winding Marne River to Varennes, was the 3rd Division, commanded by General Joseph T. Dickman, a portly sixty-year-old cavalryman and thoroughly professional soldier. A graduate of West Point and honors graduate of Cavalry School, he had also been an instructor at the Army War College and had learned enough of five languages, he said, "that he might get the letter and the spirit of the various writings of European tacticians."[6] In the field he had practiced against the likes of Geronimo in the American Southwest, striking railway men in Chicago, proud Spaniards in Cuba, ungrateful rebels in the Philippines, and perfervid Chinese Boxers. In his position along the Marne, he was not inclined to budge one inch. He placed his units with skill—and against the advice of the French general Degoutte. Degoutte wanted a strong forward line, thinking that to defend the Marne one needed "one foot in the water." Dickman knew this was nonsense; he was already an advocate of defense-in-depth, such as Pétain preached. Dickman said he would welcome ten thousand Germans coming across the river, because if they did, he would "kill every damned one of them."[7] Still, he made a few cosmetic changes to pacify Degoutte— though they were not cosmetic to the men in the forward trenches, who became the first line of defense against the Germans landing in their pontoon boats. When the trenches were overrun, some of the Americans fought their way back in heroic mini-odysseys that seemed more like Indian fighting (though with grenades and automatic rifles) than the over-the-top slaughter of the Western Front.

Aside from such fighting retreats that yielded little to the Germans (Pershing's insistence that the doughboys be taught the tactics of mobile, open warfare paid dividends here), the Allied line was nearly impermeable, even as the fighting was bayonet to bayonet, as could be witnessed by American pilots overhead.

One particular hot spot was held by the anchor of Dickman's right flank, the 38th Infantry, which was positioned along the Marne River, guarding the Paris-Metz road, and straddling the Surmelin Valley, through which the Germans hoped to make a breakthrough. The 38th's fiery colonel was Ulysses Grant McAlexander. He recklessly exposed himself to enemy fire, spent nights in the front lines, and went on sniping expeditions. In one incident, representative of many, a captain asked McAlexander what he was doing in frontline fighting. McAlexander responded, "Well, Captain, I suppose I should be about twenty miles back with a bunch of orderlies around me and a telephone to tell you fellows what to do. But, hell, I want to see what's going on."[8]

The Germans pounded the regiment for two days and charged into the Surmelin Valley—to no avail; in fact, to the near annihilation of some German units, such as the Sixth Grenadiers, who entered the battle with 1,700 men and left it with 150. American rifle fire was deadly accurate, and as at Belleau Wood, the Germans were occasionally dismayed at the Americans' fearsome appetite for battle, an appetite that began with Colonel McAlexander himself, who issued orders stating, "Don't let anything show itself on the other side [of the Marne] and live."[9]

The Germans did breach the Marne and push forward as much as three miles, but their hopes of racing to Paris were thwarted—in large part by McAlexander's stubborn defense of the Surmelin Valley. The Germans' great dash, the *Friedensturm* ("Peace Offensive") to end the war in Paris, was over. The American 3rd Division's valor, and the 38th Infantry's in particular, won it the battle moniker "the Rock of the Marne."

"NO WAY TO TREAT A REGIMENT"

General Ferdinand Foch, the supreme Allied commander, or *generalissimo*, believed Ludendorff had shot his bolt. He ordered a counterattack against the bulge in the German line along the Marne. The Franco-American assault would be a western flank attack through the Retz Forest between Soissons and Château-Thierry. In the front line was the newly organized American IV Corps,[10] incorporating the 1st and 2nd Divisions, under the command of Major General Robert Lee Bullard. Bullard in turn would be serving under the direction of the French general Charles Mangin, commander of the French Tenth Army.

Mangin liked Americans and was the sort of French commander Americans liked—that is, he had a bit of imperial romance about him, from his Senegalese bodyguard and aide; to his reputation for personal courage, recklessly leading from the front; to his experience in colonial wars in Africa and Indochina; to his staff car, a captured German Opel the color of *les pantalons rouges*. No one doubted his tactical and strategic aggression either. Flashy personality aside, he was the Ulysses S. Grant of the French army: derided as a butcher by some, for his willingness to accept heavy casualties; respected for his tenacity by others, for his relentless desire to defeat the enemy.

Mangin acquired nine American divisions—more than three hundred thousand men[11]—to support his offensive, launched on 18 July 1918. It was a tribute to the fighting prowess of the 1st and 2nd Divisions that they were at the far left of the line, pointed to lead the attack at Soissons. Between the Americans was the 1st Moroccan Division, a polyglot array of Senegalese, French Foreign Legionnaires, Arabs, and assorted international riff-raff who wore fezzes and knew how to fight. Behind Belleau Wood were the 26th, 42nd, 4th, and 77th Divisions. At Château-Thierry, marking the center of the German salient that was to be dissolved, were the American 3rd, 28th, and 32nd Divisions.

The American divisions hurried into their lines, hard marched, amid pouring rain, without much in the way of intelligence about the German dispositions before them, or even where they were going, and without much in the way of supplies, lacking ammunition, grenades, mortars, and machine guns; some hadn't slept or eaten for twenty-four or even forty-eight hours. Secrecy and last-minute haste were the watchwords. This was a French show, the battle plan depended on surprise, and the Americans were to be its shock troops, moving behind a rolling artillery barrage rather than a long preparatory bombardment. The big guns sounded off at 4:35 a.m. The Americans advanced, officers to the front, taking heavy casualties, including, before the battle was over, every battalion commander of the 26th Infantry. Junior officers and sergeants filled the breach, and the soldiers did not waver, even as the casualties stacked up to fifty thousand men. The tone was set by the famously hard-charging, demanding Major General Charles P. Summerall, newly elevated commander of the Big Red One. He rebuked a battalion commander who reported his advance had been stopped. "You may have paused for reorganization. If you ever send another message with the word stopped in it, you'll be sent to the rear for reclassification."[12] When stragglers were found, they were shoved back into the action.

One observer of the Americans was Jesuit priest and corporal Pierre Teilhard de Chardin, who was a stretcher-bearer in the 1st Moroccan Division. He wrote, "We had the Americans as neighbors and I had a close-up view of them. Everyone says the same: they're first-rate troops, fighting with intense *individual* passion...and wonderful courage. The only complaint one would make about them is that they don't take sufficient care; they're too apt to get themselves killed. When they're wounded they make their way back holding themselves upright, almost stiff, impassive, and uncomplaining. I don't think I've ever seen such pride and dignity in suffering."[13]

The American advance was swift—they had achieved surprise and struck in greater force than the Germans could have expected—and confused, as units became mixed in the chaos of fiercely contested battle, which included German gas,[14] artillery, and air attacks, over ground the Americans had not, of necessity, scouted beforehand. At least it was no battle of static trenches (though shallow trenches were dug and ducked into) but of open field maneuver, with French tanks in occasional support (they were lightning rods for German artillery); and the doughboys took a perhaps unwise pride in their ability to directly charge and overwhelm German machine gun nests when flanking them might have been less costly. But it was this aggressive spirit that made the doughboys what they were—and that made them think the French were often slow and unreliable. If *élan* had been beaten out of the *poilus*, it was still brimming over in the Americans.

The Germans remained disciplined, resolute opponents. They had given ground the first day of battle, but their fighting retreat stiffened on the second day. By the third, some doughboy units and officers had been pushed to the point of exhaustion. General Summerall met with his regimental commanders to assess their situations and encourage them. Colonel Frank Parker of the 18th Infantry told him, "General, my regiment has lost 60 percent of its officers, nearly all of its non-commissioned officers and most of its men and I don't think that's any way to treat a regiment." According to Parker, Summerall replied, "Colonel, I did not come here to have you criticize my orders or to tell me your losses. I know them as well as you do. I came here to tell you that the Germans recrossed the Marne last night and are in full retreat and you will attack tomorrow morning at 4:30." Parker said he never again questioned Summerall's orders.[15]

"BATTLES ARE WON BY REMNANTS"

The Battle of Soissons—wrapped up, at least in the history books, on 22 July[16]—was the turning point of the war. George Marshall called it exactly that; Pershing compared it to Gettysburg; and German chancellor Georg Hertling offered independent confirmation of how Soissons had changed the war: "At the beginning of July, 1918, I was convinced, I confess it, that before the first of September our adversaries would send us peace proposals....We expected grave events in Paris for the end of July. That was on the 15th. On the 18th even the most optimistic of us knew that all was lost. The history of the world was played out in three days."[17] Ludendorff could not lunge again to destroy the British army. He had used up his reserves extracting his men from across the Marne. The American experience of Soissons was not merely one of victory—but also of what victory cost. To the question what price glory, General Hanson Ely could answer, "Men must be trained that when they have been in battle for days and nights, when perhaps they have been badly handled by the enemy and have had heavy casualties, yet when the signal comes to go they will go again to *the limit of their endurance.*...it is *the last five percent* of the possible exertion that often wins the battle...not the first attack nor the second or the third, but it was that last straggling fourth attack.... battles are won by remnants, remnants of units, remnants of material, remnants of morale, remnants of intellectual effort."[18] The Americans had proved beyond doubt they had the grit to see things through.

CHAPTER SEVEN

SAINT-MIHIEL AND THE MEUSE-ARGONNE OFFENSIVE

The American Expeditionary Force not only had vigor and tenacity, it was building mass and strength, with 1.2 million men under arms in France, joined by more than 60,000 every week. It was the growing power of the AEF that gave Marshal Foch what he wanted—the opportunity to go on the offensive, not merely to halt Ludendorff on the Marne, but to drive the Germans back, perhaps even behind the Rhine. Experience had made Foch cautious, but a spring of near disaster had become a summer of hope for defeating the Hun.

Foch had a special assignment for Pershing's doughboys—to attack the German salient at Saint-Mihiel on the Meuse River, south of Verdun. The Americans would go into action led by Pershing in a newly configured United States First Army.[1] Pershing, if not Foch, had his eye on a bigger prize than reducing the salient; he wanted to liberate Metz, a French city on the Moselle, a little more than forty miles due east. That would be a battle honor worthy of his new First Army and would put it in a position to threaten the industrial Saarland of Germany.

Planning for the offensive was handed to Lieutenant Colonel George C. Marshall, tapped to join Pershing's staff as an assistant operations officer. Marshall was known as a master at organizing, supplying, and preparing men for combat, though this was easily the biggest assignment of his career. He and Pershing's staff had similar ideas about how to crack the German nut, but on 30 August 1918 Foch told Pershing to scrap his planned assault. Instead, Foch wanted a massive coordinated attack along the length of the Allied line north of Verdun, all the way to Belgium. The American Army was to be parceled up as needed to assist the British and the French. Pershing, having just organized his United States First Army, was not about to see it piecemealed into a supporting role; nor was he prepared to fold up his battle maps and forget his planned attack at Saint-Mihiel. He refused to accept Foch's plan. The American Army, he assured the generalissimo, would fight wherever Foch wanted it to fight—*but only as an independent army*. That was Pershing's right and duty, given him by President Wilson.

Pershing finally won the argument with a compromise. Foch agreed to let Pershing assault the German salient at Saint-Mihiel; and Pershing agreed to launch, only two weeks after his planned attack at Saint-Mihiel, an offensive in the Meuse-Argonne sector sixty miles to the north. The Americans would be the right flank of Foch's big push. Even on paper, let alone in action, with the inevitable friction of war, the plan for the American Army looked audacious. It would be one huge attack followed immediately by another, more than six hundred thousand troops pivoting from Saint-Mihiel to engage the enemy in some of the toughest terrain in one of the most fortified sectors of the Western Front. There could be no greater test for the doughboys. Pershing was eager to set them to it.

THE TRAINING GROUND OF SAINT-MIHIEL

If Foch had begrudged Pershing his attack on Saint-Mihiel, the French nevertheless were generous in supplying the Americans with artillery, tanks (more than four hundred organized into two battalions, with the crews trained by Lieutenant Colonel George S. Patton), and air support. Never before, in fact, had so many artillery pieces, more than 3,000, including 5 American naval guns mounted on railway tracks,[2] and so many planes, nearly 1,500, been available to a British or French commander directing a battle. The planes were commanded by Colonel Billy Mitchell, Pershing's talented and aggressive air officer, who intended to use his aircraft as other commanders might use artillery, hitting the enemy's rear areas, suppressing the enemy's own air power, and, when the infantry could supply him with adequate coordinates, striking against German machine gun emplacements. Once the army started rolling up the German line, Mitchell's planes would take on the role of cavalry, harassing the German retreat. When the battle was over, Mitchell's pilots claimed to have downed more than fifty German planes.

The Americans also tried their hand at counterintelligence, setting up a fake headquarters—even the faux headquarters' commanding officer, Major General Omar Bundy, didn't know it was a fake—to convince the Germans that the Americans would attack about 125 miles farther south, in an area that the general dutifully scouted, that Pershing visited, and where an intelligence officer intentionally left behind a carbon copy of fake orders, which were duly intercepted by German agents. The Germans prepared to meet this immaterial challenge, but they were not surprised when the real attack came at Saint-Mihiel.

The French assumed Pershing's attack would be an easy, morale-boosting American victory; and they were right. Unknown to the Americans, Ludendorff had ordered a withdrawal from the more lightly defended front line (the Wilhelm Line) to the stiffer defenses of the secondary line (the Michel Line), which meant that Pershing's attack was directed, initially, at a phantom.

The salient, in relation to the German line, looked a bit like the base of the number 2, with Saint-Mihiel at the forward point of the base. The Americans intended to flank the base and leave the actual liberation of Saint-Mihiel to the French II Colonial Corps, almost fifty thousand men, who were incorporated into the United States First Army. The greatest risk to the Americans' initial assault was expected from German artillery on the high ground at Montsec, which the Americans hoped to simply skirt by launching their attacks farther east. The American line, left to right, along the base of the 2, led with the 1st Division, moving out from Seicheprey, followed by the 42nd and the 89th from IV Corps, and from I Corps the 2nd, the 5th, the 90th, and the 82nd, which was as far east as the Moselle River. Striking down from the north would be the 26th Division of V Corps. It intended to meet the 1st Division at the approximate midpoint of the salient, the town of Vigneulles. In the process, the salient would be crushed.

The attack began at 1:00 a.m., 12 September 1918, with an artillery barrage, which it was hoped would clear German obstructions (chiefly barbed wire). This it did with extraordinary success because the wire was rusty, old, and brittle and burst apart when struck. At 5:00 a.m., the infantry moved out under cover of fog and made rapid progress. By noon the Big Red One was halfway to Vigneulles. The German units on the withdrawing Wilhelm Line were not the best, and some of them were close to utter demoralization. A lone American lieutenant on horseback, riding ahead to find a quicker route to bring ammunition and supplies to the forward infantry, came upon a detachment of twenty-six German soldiers. Rather than blasting him off his saddle or taking him prisoner, the Germans surrendered and demanded the lieutenant escort them back to the American lines; they didn't want to be mistaken for active soldiers and get shot. In another incident an American sergeant with an empty pistol (though the Germans didn't know that) rousted more than three hundred German soldiers out of a dugout and into captivity.

Coming from the north, the 26th Division had to cut through forests, but found these amazingly lightly defended, and by 2:00 a.m., 13 September, the division had reached Vigneulles. By the end of 13 September, the job was essentially done. The Germans were fully withdrawn behind the Michel Line, and Pershing was content to leave them there and move his troops on to the Meuse-Argonne. It sounds easy on paper, and relatively speaking it was, but the Americans still suffered 7,000 casualties (the Germans, about 22,500: 15,000 surrendered, 7,500 killed or wounded). Pershing was bullish, and the reduction of the Saint-Mihiel salient was considered an American success. It was the largest American battle since the War Between the States, and the troops had executed their assignments admirably. If the German units were not the best, if they were in the process of withdrawing anyway, it was equally true that the Germans had held this line for four years; that in that time the Germans had repelled two French attempts to drive them out; and that the German high command considered Saint-Mihiel a terrible defeat. Hindenburg was appalled at how quickly the salient had been overrun; Ludendorff was depressed to the point of a nervous breakdown. Two hundred square miles of French territory had been liberated, and the Americans had badly dented the Germans' sense of military superiority. But in retrospect, for the Americans the battle of Saint-Mihiel was in many ways a meticulously well-planned, enormous live-fire training exercise. The Meuse-Argonne Offensive would be something else entirely.

NO EASY DAY

Colonel George C. Marshall, operations officer of the First Army, had a fortnight to get nearly a million tons of supplies and four thousand guns, not to mention more than six hundred thousand men, to their new positions above Verdun for the Meuse-Argonne Offensive. It was, as one historian has written, "the biggest logistical undertaking in the history of the U.S. Army, before or since."[3] Units were regrouped after the battle of Saint-Mihiel and rushed onto inadequate roads that were bogged with mud, jammed with masses of men, machines, and horses, clogged by accidents, and patrolled by military police who tried desperately to keep the traffic moving and douse the hot tempers of frustrated drivers. If there was to be any hope of secrecy, all movement had to be at night. Artillery took priority. Units that had been held in reserve at Saint-Mihiel were next in line, for they were moving to the front; and then the combat units that had crushed the salient. The Americans succeeded (with the help of the French) in moving this giant anaconda of men, machines, and supplies into position. But even Marshall was left wondering "how in the world the concentration was ever put through in the face of so many complications."[4]

The doughboys arrived to confront what First Army chief of staff Colonel Hugh Drum called "the most ideal defensive terrain I have ever seen or read about. Nature had provided for flank and crossfire to the utmost in addition to concealment [for the German defenders]...."[5] Major General Hunter Liggett, commander of I Corps, on the left side of the American line, facing the Argonne Forest, was put in mind of one of the most famous battlefields of the American Civil War:

> The region was a natural forest besides which the Virginia Wilderness in which Grant and Lee fought was a park. It was masked and tortuous before the enemy strung up his first wire and dug his first trench.... The underbrush had grown up through the German barbed and rabbit wire, interlacing it and concealing it, and machine guns lurked like copperheads in the ambush of shell-fallen trees. Other machine guns were strewn in concrete pill boxes and in defiles. On the offense tanks could not follow, nor artillery see where it was shooting, while the enemy guns, on the defense, could fire by map.... Patently it would be suicidal to attack such a labyrinth directly; it must be pinched out by attacks on either side.[6]

Liggett had only one consolation: the Germans considered their defenses in the Argonne so formidable that they garrisoned them with second-class troops.

Pershing's goal was a drive north to Sedan, a distance of about forty miles. Throughout this sector, bordered by the Argonne Forest to the west and the Meuse River to the east, the doughboys would be fighting over ground that the Germans had held and fortified since 1914. The German defenses centered on three east-west ridge-lines, as well as defensive positions on the Heights of the Meuse, which was partially forested high ground running north-south behind the Meuse River, where the Germans stationed most of their heavy artillery. The Americans' one advantage was that Ludendorff expected an attack at Metz—the attack Pershing had wanted to make, following up on the American victory at Saint-Mihiel, rather than the one Foch compelled him to make at the Meuse-Argonne. But whatever hope Pershing drew from the Germans having only an estimated five divisions in the sector was tempered by the fact that the Germans could rapidly reinforce the area. They had even built rail lines that could rush troops and supplies to the front. Pershing's staff estimated that within three days those five German divisions could become twenty, with four of them arriving in the first twenty-four hours; and there were many more divisions in reserve that could be called into the battle, so that the twenty could be nearly doubled. Pétain thought Pershing would be lucky if he reached Montfaucon, about five miles north from the Americans' starting position, in three months. A French liaison officer told Major General Robert Alexander, commander of the 77th Division of I Corps, which would have to fight through the Argonne Forest, "Sir, I have no doubt that your men are brave and that you have made every preparation that will give them a chance for victory tomorrow, but permit me to say that, in my opinion, the [German] line in your front *will not move*. It has been in place for four years, is solidly established, well wired in, and the Boche is a good soldier. I fear that you will not be able to make the advance you hope for." Alexander replied, "The line *will* move."[7]

Pershing's audacious plan was to blast ahead faster than the Germans (and Pétain and the French liaison officer) thought possible; he would sacrifice numbers in the interest of speed, choosing nine divisions for the initial assault. He gave his commanders a first-day objective of the *Kriemhilde Stellung*, a heavily defended ridgeline that was part of the Hindenburg (or as the Germans called it, the Siegfried) Line, which was meant to be impassable.[8] It was ten miles to the north, five miles deeper than Montfaucon, the fortified Mount of the Falcon that Pétain thought Pershing might need three months to reach. Pershing planned simply to storm it on his way to the strongest part of the German defenses, the *Kriemhilde Stellung*. He trusted to determined commanders like Alexander—and that his doughboys would make up in spirit what they lacked in experience.

At 11:00 p.m., 25 September 1918, the American artillery erupted (among the artillery commanders was a creatively swearing Captain Harry S. Truman). The doughboy infantry had been given no warning—in order to maintain secrecy—and sleepers got rude awakenings. Some troops cheered the astonishing flash of lights and the explosions that marked shells hitting home on German ammunition dumps. Others quavered under the thunderous roar—or were torn to pieces by German artillery firing in response. Under the lightning of the guns, the men were hustled into their positions, past withdrawing French troops—220,000 of them in total from the French Second Army—who had held the trenches awaiting the Americans' arrival.

The Americans leapt into the Meuse-Argonne Valley at 5:30 a.m., 26 September, piercing a thick fog made thicker by a covering smoke barrage. Commanders were under orders to press the advance and bypass German pillboxes and machine gun nests that could not be reduced immediately. The first objective had to be Montfaucon. It blocked the center of the American advance and was the high point of the Meuse-Argonne Valley. The French had failed to wrest it from the Germans in 1914 and 1915, but Pershing and his staff believed it could be taken swiftly, counting on surprise, artillery and air support (tanks were on hand too, if they could handle the terrain), and American fighting prowess. Pershing was so confident of the superiority of his American troops that "he devised an attack timetable fit for an army of supermen," in the words of one historian.[9] The supermen were organized into three corps, with Liggett's I Corps having orders to sweep the Argonne Forest on the American left; V Corps under Major General George Cameron was given the task of taking Montfaucon; and, on the right, III Corps, commanded by Major General Robert Bullard, would advance along the west side of the Meuse River and protect V Corps' flank.

The American commanders thrust forward Pershing's trident. On the left, I Corps had to battle through the treacherous terrain of the Ardennes, but did reasonably well. On the right, III Corps made good progress, not much stymied by German resistance. The crucial point, however, was the center of the line, and here Montfaucon did not fall as easily as was hoped. Cameron's two-pronged attack on the objective began well, but as the morning fog lifted, German machine guns and artillery pinned down both sides of the assault, which was entrusted to the 79th Division, a majority of whose men had been in the Army for less than four months. Hard-charging American troops briefly occupied the town but could not dislodge the Germans from the Butte of Montfaucon. With that, Pershing's hope for a bold start was squelched. The German commander of the Meuse-Argonne sector, General Max von Gallwitz, noted that the attack appeared uncoordinated and led by inexperienced troops. He was confident he could turn them aside and remained suspicious that the attack was really a feint.

Inexperienced many of the doughboys might have been, but they made good for their commanders by noon, 27 September, taking the Butte of Montfaucon—even if they were then cut off and had to survive three days without supplies. Indeed, all along the American advance, even where it had gone well, the friction of war had sown confusion. Troopers and generals got lost. Traffic jams of artillery and men (including evacuated wounded) clogged the miserable, muddy roads. The delay to Pershing's plan was costly. German reinforcements rapidly stiffened the defenses the doughboys had to breach, and the Americans found it impossible to break through the *Kriemhilde Stellung*. On 29 September, Pershing had to concede that his great lunge had failed. He called a halt until he could bring up veteran reinforcements.

THE BIG PUSH

Pershing was fighting the biggest and costliest battle in American history. By battle's end, which was the end of the war, 11 November 1918, 1.2 million American troops had been involved, one-tenth of them were casualties, and more than 26,000 of those were dead. Pershing had a gargantuan task in front of him: doing his not inconsiderable part to roll back the Germans from France and win the war.

New divisions brought up, units reorganized, orders issued, Pershing's army went back into action on the morning of 4 October—and found the Germans waiting with reinforced positions and showers of artillery shells raining down from the Heights of the Meuse. Against this storm of steel and lead, the doughboys set their helmet straps and trudged forward, but bullets and artillery shells can slow an advance even more effectively than rain and mud, so Pershing ordered the French XVII Corps (which included an American division) to suppress the German guns on the Heights of the Meuse with a direct assault.

In the west, in the Argonne Forest, the 77th Division had a similar task—to find and suppress the big German guns—but it had to fight amid the large, dense, tangled forest that effectively cut regiments into their component parts and that was spiked with German machine gun nests, snipers, and blockhouses. It left some troopers feeling, not for the first time, as if they were reliving their ancestors' experiences of Indian fighting, though the Indians in this case had higher-powered weapons and better discipline.

The landscape itself was sobering. If Belleau Wood was "Hell Wood," it was but a small corner of hell compared to the Argonne, which, as one American officer charged with its conquest wrote, "was a bleak, cruel country of white clay and rock and blasted skeletons of trees, gashed into innumerable trenches and seared with rusted acres of wire, rising steeply into claw-like ridges and descending into haunted ravines, white as leprosy in the midst of that green forest, a country that had died long ago, in pain."[10]

Some of that pain was assuaged, at least for the troopers, when they found abandoned blockhouses laden with almost unimaginable luxuries, including the odd piano, a wine cellar, and other signs of how well-supplied these long-standing German positions had been. The doughboys liberated a few bottles into the security of their packs, but they had to be careful—some abandoned German dugouts were booby-trapped—and their orders were to continually press forward the attack.

THE LOST BATTALION

Those orders—and the intrepid spirit of the doughboys—led Major Charles W. Whittlesey into an action that earned him a Medal of Honor. Whittlesey, thirty-four years old, a battalion commander of the 308th Infantry, was in civilian life a New York lawyer and graduate of Harvard Law School notable for his round spectacles and gentlemanly demeanor.

Pressing ahead in the Argonne Forest, he was twice cut off by the enemy. The first time his men were without supplies or reinforcement for three days. On 2 October, he was on point leading another advance into the Argonne. Whittlesey had a reputation for coolness under fire and a steely aggression that sometimes showed itself in sardonic humor, yet he was no gung-ho enthusiast. He thought the attack he had been ordered to make was suicidal. But after delivering a formal protest, he did his best to execute his orders. Galloping Charlie, a nickname he had earned for his quick march, stayed true to his moniker. His was the only successful attack that day in the Argonne.

His "battalion" was a cobbled-together unit made up of six companies of the 308th Infantry, one from the 307th Infantry, and two from the 306th Machine Gun Battalion—all from the motley 77th Division, the "melting pot" division from New York, with replacements coming from western states. His objective was the Charlevaux Mill road. When he reached it, his men dug in on a slope facing the road and formed a defensive perimeter. He sent word to his regimental commander that they had taken their position. Whittlesey had advanced well beyond any units covering his flanks, but this was in keeping with Pershing's order that units of the 77th Division should push ahead "without regard of losses and without regard to the exposed conditions of the flanks."[11] Pershing refused to slow his timetable either to accommodate the lack of progress by the French, who were supposed to assist in the attack, or in deference to the difficulty of communicating with units in the Argonne. The best course was to press ahead.

The success of Whittlesey's advance, however, was more notable at division headquarters than it was on the patch of land occupied by his men. They were short on rations, short of ammunition, short of medical supplies (indeed these were rapidly used up as casualties mounted), ring-fenced by enemy mortars, and apparently surrounded by German troops. Two companies of men were missing, and attempts to find them only led to more casualties.

Division commander Major General Robert Alexander,[12] sensing Whittlesey had made an advance that should be exploited, dispatched an infantry battalion to reinforce him. Only one company of that battalion made it, and it confirmed for Whittlesey not only that he was surrounded, but that the Germans were tightening the noose, stringing new wire and planting new machine gun nests.

Whittlesey's second-in-command, Captain George McMurtry, a former Rough Rider and a fellow Harvard man and Wall Street lawyer, wrote an order for Whittlesey's approval and then delivered it to the company commanders: "Our mission is to hold this position at all costs. No falling back. Have this understood by every man in your command." It was of a piece with an order that General Alexander had issued on 28 September at the beginning of the campaign: "Ground once captured must under no circumstances be given up in absence of direct, positive and formal orders to do so emanating from these headquarters."[13] Whittlesey had no such orders. He would hold his position. He had 550 men.

Whittlesey communicated with headquarters via carrier pigeon. General Alexander knew where Whittlesey was, knew of his dire straits (at least as far as scraps of paper tied to a carrier pigeon's leg could describe them), but trusted that a Franco-American attack announced for the next day, to hit the Germans at the 77th's front from either side of the Argonne, might bring relief. The attack, however, failed; and a subsequent artillery barrage on 4 October, instead of scattering the Germans, landed on Whittlesey's own men. Whittlesey released his last pigeon, named Cher Ami, with the message, "Our own artillery is dropping a barrage directly on us. For heaven's sake, stop it."[14] The pigeon landed on a tree and had to be driven away by a trooper climbing up and shaking the branch. Whether through the pigeon's courageous flight or the artillery's schedule, the firing ceased. Aerial attempts to resupply the battalion dropped food, water, medicine, and ammunition to the enemy—and two planes and their crews were lost. Despite this, Whittlesey, McMurtry, and Captain Nelson Holderman, whose Company K had been the battalion's sole reinforcement, were exemplary in keeping the men steady. Whittlesey was intelligent and cool under fire; McMurtry was tough enough to ignore serious wounds and gregarious enough to roam the lines offering words of encouragement despite an injured knee; Holderman, a California National Guardsman with experience along the Mexican border, was wounded (as they all were), but maintained the command presence of a natural-born officer and doughty fighter.

The German attacks continued with mortars, flamethrowers, grenades, rifles, and machine guns—and still there was no relief, no food, no water (drinking from a nearby stream was perilous because the path to it was raked by German fire; the Americans relied on rainwater in shell holes), and no clean bandages for the wounded. But on 7 October, units of the 82nd Division were sent on an attack to pry the German grip off Whittlesey's trapped battalion. This attack succeeded, the Germans fell back, and the survivors of "the lost battalion," as the press had dubbed them, emerged from their position in the Argonne where they had been trapped for five days; there were only 194 of them who staggered out.[15] Whittlesey was promoted to lieutenant colonel, and he and McMurtry and Holderman were awarded the Medal of Honor, as were four others. Cher Ami, wounded in action, won a Croix de Guerre among other awards, and was later stuffed and put on exhibit at the Smithsonian, the most famous pigeon of the war. Whittlesey, celebrated as a war hero, went aboard a ship bound for Cuba in November 1921 and was lost at sea, a presumed suicide. McMurtry became a millionaire Wall Street lawyer. Holderman, regarded as a soldier's soldier by his men, retired a colonel in the California National Guard and served as commandant of the Yountville Soldier's Home.

TO THE END

On 8 October, the day Whittlesey's men were rescued, President Woodrow Wilson responded to a note from Prince Maximilian von Baden, Germany's new chancellor, seeking an armistice on the grounds of Wilson's Fourteen Points, which put forward a liberal program of open diplomacy, freedom of the seas, free trade, freedom for Belgium and France (and Alsace-Lorraine) from German occupation, disarmament, borders drawn on the basis of nation-states rather than multinational empires, and the establishment of a League of Nations. Prince Max, as he was known, did not agree with everything in the Fourteen Points, but offered to accept them as the basis for negotiations. A democratically inclined aristocrat, he had clipped some of the powers of the Kaiser, brought Social Democrats into the government, and removed Generals Hindenburg and Ludendorff as the de facto leaders of Imperial Germany. Hindenburg and Ludendorff had towered over the civilian government, but they now conceded that the war was lost and that Germany must seek terms. Their goal was an orderly retreat to Germany's western borders in exchange for Britain, the United States, Italy, and France accepting Germany's territorial gains in the east.

Wilson took four days to respond to Prince Max—and then it was through Secretary of State Robert Lansing. Lansing sought assurances that the prince did in fact speak for the German government and stated flatly that no negotiations could begin while the Germans occupied Belgium and France. Nothing came of the overture, and the war continued.

West of the Argonne, the American 2nd and 36th Divisions—the former a collection of Marines and soldiers, the latter made up of cowboys and Indians from the Texas and Oklahoma National Guard—took over a position from the French and on 4 October seized the Blanc Mont Ridge in tough fighting. The Americans then led the French in driving the Germans to the Aisne River, so that by 27 October the French Fourth Army could finally take its place alongside the American First Army.

The First Army, meanwhile, had continued to slog its way through the Meuse-Argonne. As Laurence Stallings, a Marine veteran of Belleau Wood, put it in his own history of the war, "From now until the end...it was to be five weeks of unremitting pressure all along the front, and for the Doughboys in the line, of 'one damn machine gun after another.'"[16] In front of them lay the still unbroken *Kriemhilde Stellung*, reinforced by the Germans, who now had forty divisions in the Meuse-Argonne. Organized both by terrain and by its grid of trenches into interlocking fields of defensive fire, the *Kriemhilde Stellung* allowed the Germans to move from one strong point to another, which meant the Americans' only strategy could be tenaciously repeated assaults. It was now the French who were demanding that the Americans move more quickly. The Germans were everywhere falling back, while in the Meuse-Argonne the Yanks were clawing their way forward against stiff resistance. But they were making progress. By mid-October, the Argonne Forest had been cleared, which put the American main thrust between the River Aire on the left, just east of the Argonne, and the River Meuse on the right. The chief objective was the area surrounding Romagne, about five miles north from Montfaucon, bracketed by the Côte de Châtillon and the Côte Dame Marie on the one side and Cunel on the other. The Côte Dame Marie was considered the key to unlocking the *Kriemhilde Stellung*. On 14 October, the Americans seized it and Romagne, but they could advance no farther until they reduced the Côte de Châtillon, with its newly rewired trenches and perhaps two hundred machine guns. It had to be taken, and in the undaunted assault, as General Douglas MacArthur remembered, "Officers fell and sergeants leaped to the command. Companies dwindled to platoons and corporals took over. At the end Major [Lloyd] Ross [leading one of the attacking battalions] had only 300 men and six officers left out of 1,450 men and 25 officers. That is the way the Côte-de-Châtillon fell...."[17]

The United States was now fielding two armies. The Second Army, with more than 175,000 men under General Robert Lee Bullard, was east of the Meuse River, covering the American right flank. The First Army, more than a million strong, under the capable General Hunter Liggett, held the center. Having cracked the Hindenburg Line, Liggett paused to reorganize his exhausted troops, and then paused again waiting for the French to catch up to him. Allied war planners had assumed that they could drive to victory in 1919. But now it seemed possible that if they were aggressive enough, they could pummel Germany into a far more rapid defeat. Pershing was bullish, and Colonel George C. Marshall reckoned that in ten days, if the American advance could be maintained, "about a million German soldiers in front and to the west of us would either have to surrender or disperse as individuals."[18]

The attack timetable Pershing had originally drawn up for his army of supermen at the beginning of the Meuse-Argonne Campaign took on a new realism in this great charge of the First Army. Again, the Americans lined up three corps, left to right, I Corps, V Corps, and III Corps, with V Corps taking the lead. The goal was to press ever harder, expanding each day's gains as the Germans lost their artillery and were forced into an ever more debilitating retreat—and that was what happened. The attack commenced on 1 November. By 5 November, the Americans had cleared a broad swath of territory to the River Meuse; the Meuse-Argonne sector was theirs. But Pershing pressed on—first making a move to capture Sedan in the French sector to the North (until French protests had him rescind the order) and then crossing the Meuse against German artillery bombardments. An armistice was arranged to take place at 11:00 a.m., 11 November, but Pershing kept his men fighting to the end—and regretted that he had not been given a few more days to drive the American Expeditionary Force into Germany, not for glory, but to put a formal mark on Germany's defeat. As it was, the forty-seven day battle of the Meuse-Argonne marked the end of the First World War.

PART III

THE GENERALS

CHAPTER EIGHT

JOHN J. PERSHING
(1860–1948)

The General of the Armies, John J. Pershing was born in Missouri a year before the War Between the States. One of his earliest memories was of his proudly Unionist, anti-slavery father barricading the house and holding off pro-slavery raiders (when Pershing was four).

His father, whose family had emigrated from Germany in 1749, was a successful businessman. Starting as a railway track foreman, he had married a Southern girl and turned shopkeeper and farmer—until the depression of the 1870s, when he became a traveling salesman. As a boy, Pershing ploughed his father's fields with singular dedication—he spent hours ensuring that every furrow was straight—

and ploughed through the family library of classics, while also enter-taining himself with dime novels. He loved adventure stories and in due course became as strapping a young man as any dime novel hero. As a schoolboy he was a scrapper, a gamecock in schoolyard fights; and he liked to hang around the town's army supply depot, where a kindly sergeant would give him a chunk of hardtack. Proud, young Pershing considered it his daily ration.

At the end of his teenage years, he became a school teacher, and showed a facility for facing down young toughs, and occasionally their parents—at least in the case of one rawboned farmer who came riding to the school swearing murder, packing a gun, and looking for vengeance against the teacher who had dared whip his son for kicking a dog. The stalwart Pershing presented himself to the farmer and convinced him to settle the matter mano-a-mano; Pershing, eighteen years old, took the farmer apart, and in the rough-and-ready fashion of the time, farmer and son came to see things Pershing's way.

When not laying down the law in the classroom, he was attending classes himself at a small local college, where he scraped together enough credits to be awarded a bachelor's degree in something called "scientific didactics." When the chance presented itself to take the qualifying examination for West Point, he seized it, not because he wanted to be a soldier—he had his eye on practicing law—but because he considered it a free ticket to a quality education. He passed the preliminary qualifying examination and then crammed his way through the even more exacting entrance test into the Academy.

A NATURAL LEADER

Older than most of his fellow cadets—in fact at twenty-two Persh-ing was just under the age limit for entering the Academy—he took naturally to command; and for someone often regarded as austere, unsentimental, and a bit of a martinet, he was surprisingly prominent at dances and popular with girls. Some looked askance at this, but among his fellows he was a soldier's soldier, and his interest in presenting an immaculate appearance was as military as it was social. His one unmartial characteristic—unexpected in one so self-disciplined—was that he was perpetually late. A middling student, he was nevertheless class president and captain of the cadet corps. He graduated and was commissioned a second lieutenant in 1886. Given a choice of branches, he selected the cavalry, hoping to get a shot at some Indian fighting.

His wish was granted on his very first assignment, when he was sent to New Mexico and skirmished against marauding Apaches. He later saw action against the Sioux in South Dakota. Throughout his years as an Indian fighter, Pershing distinguished himself as a tough, talented, and dedicated officer. He taught himself Indian languages; led a company of Sioux scouts; became an expert marksman with revolver and rifle; looked after his men to an unusual degree, ensuring they were properly provided with clothing, supplies, and equipment (especially during the winter campaigning in South Dakota); and almost invariably retired with a book in his hand. For him, soldiering was not tedium punctuated by hard drinking, poker, and occasional action. He did not mind the odd drink or card game, but he took his profession seriously, even if he still hankered after the idea of becoming a lawyer, and indeed he earned a law degree from the University of Nebraska in 1893 while posted there as commandant of the school's cadets. He taught mathematics, military science, and drill—and attended school dances, a rather dashing older man in uniform who was gracious with the girls and an admirably hard taskmaster with the cadets. His stiff discipline instilled an *esprit de corps* in what had formerly been a rather dispirited unit, admired by neither the students nor the administration. Indeed, seeing the transformation of the school's previously lackluster cadets, the university president noted Pershing as a remarkable man, "the most energetic, active and industrious, competent and successful [commandant] I have ever known...thorough in everything he undertakes, a gentleman by instinct and breeding, clean, straightforward, with an unusually bright mind; and peculiarly just and true in his dealings."[1] That was Pershing at age thirty-four.

Before he took up instructing duties at West Point in 1897, he commanded a unit of "Buffalo Soldiers," black cavalrymen, in Montana. His mission was to catch and return renegade Cree Indians to Canada. He had already caught the eye of veteran Indian fighter General Nelson Miles, who made Pershing his aide-de-camp and then recommended him as an instructor to the Military Academy.

He was less successful with the cadets at West Point than he had been with the cadets in Nebraska. The West Pointers found him too strict by half. Behind his back they called him "Nigger Jack," from his experience with the buffalo soldiers. What started as an insult became his *nomme de guerre*, for nothing better described Pershing's tough, hard personality than "Black Jack"—the sort one cracks over another's skull.

When the Spanish-American War erupted in 1898, West Point instructors were charged with staying at their posts and training new officers. Pershing naturally wanted to see action. He pleaded his case, succeeded, and rejoined his Buffalo Soldiers, this time as a quartermaster of the 10th Cavalry Regiment. It wasn't the job he wanted, but amid the chaos of preparing for the invasion of Cuba, he ensured that his men were as well provisioned as possible. In Cuba, his conduct under hostile fire was exemplary. His commanding officer,

Colonel Theodore Baldwin, was so impressed he wrote Pershing a letter stating flatly, "I have been in many fights and through the Civil War, but on my word 'You were the coolest and bravest man I ever saw under fire in my life.'"[2] Pershing charged up San Juan Hill, battled through malaria (which cut a swath through the Americans), and added to his duties that of regimental adjutant and commander of three troops of cavalry. Even with a fever, he relished his additional responsibilities.

MORO-TAMER

With the war in Cuba won, Pershing was sent to Washington to work in the War Department, where Secretary of War Elihu Root recognized him as a plain-talking, can-do officer who wasn't afraid of making a decision and who, like Root, had a law degree—useful in the War Department now that it was charged with governing the territories acquired in the Spanish-American War. There was still fighting to be had in the Philippines, however, and Pershing wanted part of it; Root granted Pershing's request to return to the field in 1899.

He was sent to Mindanao, where the challenge came not from Filipino insurrectionists, but from ever-restive Moro tribesmen who killed or enslaved Christian Filipinos who wandered into their territory. Pershing, as he had with the American Indians, made a study of the Moros, and decided that a Moro was made up of one part savage, one part Malay, and one part Mohammedan. He concluded, "The almost infinite combination of superstitions, prejudices, and suspicions blended into his character make him a difficult person to handle until fully understood."[3] He noted that "The pride of the Moro" is his fighting blade, and "much as the Moro appreciates the

value of money, he will not part with his cherished weapons...."[4]
He liked using them, too. Many Moros took an oath to become
blade-wielding assassins of infidels. They drugged themselves and
wrapped themselves so tightly with binding cloths that they could
charge right through rounds fired from an Army issue .38 caliber
revolver. The Army responded by issuing .45 caliber pistols, which
packed enough punch to stop a Moro, permanently.

Captain Pershing was an educated soldier. He studied Spanish
and the Moro dialects, and as a budding Moro expert he was given
the job of figuring out how to keep the peace with these island jihadists. The goal of the military was, if at all possible, to befriend the
Moros, a task made more difficult because the Moros, a violent
people, found the idea of friendship with strangers difficult to grasp.
Pershing did not try to change the Moros; he did not campaign
against polygamy or slavery or any other aspect of their culture;
indeed, as his friendship with the Moros grew, he turned their culture
to his advantage, asking them to deliver malefactors' heads, which
they happily did. He also employed Moros to help build schools and
level roads and bought Moro goods at the local market. Simultaneously, he drilled the troops under his command into a far higher
order of discipline, both for their own sake and to impress the
natives.

But while Pershing's success with the Moro tribes spread, not
every chief was won over. His critics—among the Moros and his
fellow officers—thought him too forbearing to be effective. He
proved them wrong. Realizing he had to crush a tribe of taunting
Moro rebels *pour encourager les autres*, he did just that, cutting a
road through the jungle, using massive firepower to intimidate most
of the tribe into flight, cutting down the recalcitrant chief, and burning his fortified encampment. Pershing succeeded as the Spanish

never had, and that deeply impressed the Moros; they even made
him a Moro chief. It was not his last campaign against rebellious
Moros, but it laid the groundwork for the success of his other campaigns, including a more-than-sixty-mile fighting march around Lake
Lanao that helped make Pershing something of a legend on the island
of Mindanao and a celebrity in the United States.

Pershing returned stateside in the summer of 1903 and swiftly
met the girl of his dreams. She was Helen Frances Warren, twenty
years his junior, the wealthy daughter of a U.S. senator. They were
married in January 1905. After his honeymoon, he was sent to Japan
to observe the Russo-Japanese War. President Theodore Roosevelt
promoted Pershing to brigadier general in 1906, leaping him over
more than 860 senior officers. Pershing, in succession, commanded
Fort McKinley in the Philippines, just south of Manila; toured
Europe (including Germany, which impressed him with its military
prowess); and spent a brief period stateside before returning to the
Philippines in 1909 as civil governor and military commander over
the Moros, who were again proving restive. He settled one dispute
with a baseball game. The Moros were surprised they lost; they had,
Pershing noted, been practicing. He settled others by embedding
soldiers throughout the Moro province to act as peacekeepers. He
formed columns of bandit hunters, buried slain jihadists with pigs
so that they faced the prospect of going straight to hell (according
to their Mohammedan beliefs) and as a warning to other would-be
jihadists that a paradise of virgins might not be theirs, and instituted
a legal system of local Moro (rather than Filipino) courts. Pershing
also took up the white man's burden of building schools, medical
clinics, roads, and trading posts and stringing telephone lines. Most
Moros regarded the Americans as a useful buffer between them and
the hated Filipinos. Taking advantage of that, Pershing tried to turn

Moro swords and knives into ploughshares, seeking to convert the Moros to a life of farming and demanding, most audaciously, that they disarm. It is a tribute to his stature that the vast majority did. The others—the jihadists and hardened bandits—he then campaigned to destroy, always with the goal of losing as few of his own men and killing as few of the enemy as possible (in all his Moro campaigns, he was careful to leave open an escape route for women, children, and Moros disinclined to fight to the death; he measured victory in terms of conciliation, not body counts). The fighting was hard but crowned with victory. Pershing proved himself a clever and successful military commander and a top-notch colonial administrator.

In January 1914, he returned to the United States to take command at the Presidio in San Francisco, though by that spring he was on the Mexican border at El Paso, guarding against raids from Pancho Villa. He hoped to have his family join him at Fort Bliss, but his wife and his three daughters (aged six, seven, and eight) died of smoke inhalation when their house at the Presidio burned down; the lone survivor was his five-year-old son, Warren. Pershing's family life had been tremendously happy; now the hard man became inevitably harder; he remained in a state of suppressed mourning for the rest of his life.[5]

FROM THE BORDER TO THE MARNE

On 9 March 1916, Mexican rebel leader Pancho Villa, angry at American support for his nemesis Mexican president Venustiano Carranza and hungry for supplies, raided Columbus, New Mexico, killing eighteen Americans and leaving more than two hundred of his own banditos behind as casualties. Pershing's mission was to track him down (with the help of Apache scouts), punish him, and avoid provoking the Mexican government, which was itself at war with Villa but did not welcome gringos across the border. Pershing's column traversed hundreds of miles into Mexican territory. While Villa avoided capture, Pershing's troopers bloodied Villa's banditti (and Villa himself) and effectively ended the guerrilla threat to America's southern border. It was, de facto, a tremendous training exercise. Pershing had under his command the largest American army in the field since the War Between the States. The fact that Pershing's men had skirmishes with Mexican troops, which fell short of escalating into war, only added to the vigor of the exercise—useful experience when, just two months later, the United States was officially at war with Germany.

Secretary of War Newton Baker narrowed the competition for command of the American Expeditionary Force to two candidates—Leonard Wood and Pershing. Wood, though the senior of the two, had the disadvantage of being highly political, a friend of Theodore Roosevelt, and a possible Republican presidential candidate. All that leapt Pershing to the top of the list—and Baker stayed resolutely loyal to his chosen commander. Pershing needed loyalty because his task was formidable. He had to create, from the barest of essentials already in existence, a massive new army that could join the fighting line in Europe. He would, at least, have very little interference from the White House. The president disdained military matters, and his one instruction to Pershing was entirely to the general's liking. Pershing's first—and near constant—battle was to prevent America's infantry from being parceled up into replacement units for the French and the British. This Anglo-French tack had behind it the logic of speed—it would get American combat troops to the front faster. From the Western Allies' point of view, it had the additional advantage of expediting American casualties, which they assumed would heat up the blood of the American people for jumping into the fray.

Pershing was insistent that the American Expeditionary Force remain an independent American command, entire and whole, and not be amalgamated piecemeal into the British and French armies. President Wilson's orders to Pershing, via Newton Baker, stated,

> In military operations against the Imperial German Government you are directed to cooperate with the forces of other countries employed against that enemy; but in doing so the underlying idea must be kept in view that the forces of the United States are a separate and distinct component of the combined forces, the identity of which must be preserved. This fundamental rule is subject to such minor exceptions in particular circumstances as your judgment may approve.... You will exercise full discretion in determining the manner of cooperation.[6]

Just as Field Marshal Haig and Marshal Joffre seemed to epitomize their respective nationalities, Pershing fit the British and French image of what an American officer should be: a fit, confident, firm-jawed, no-nonsense man of military business. Even if his opponents had been heretofore limited to Indians and banditos, Moros and Spaniards, behind him lay the immense promise of America's manpower—if only it could be mobilized, trained, and brought to bear on the Western Front in time.

Pershing was confident, but a realist too. France's armies were demoralized and, as General Pétain warned him, incapable of mounting large offensives. With France now at the breaking point, the

Italians stymied in the South, the British pinned down everywhere from the Middle East to the Western Front, and Russia in chaos since the abdication of the Czar, the doughboys became the repository of the Allies' hopes.

Pershing was convinced that if his troops were to achieve what was expected of them, they needed to be trained in more than the essentials of trench warfare (which he thought defeatist). He wanted emphasis put on marksmanship and bayonet drill, open warfare, a war of maneuver such as British and French commanders might find hopelessly naïve, given the machine guns, artillery, and entrenchments that kept a deadly watch over the Western Front. But Pershing would be vindicated by the spirit that Americans brought to battle, where units cut up and separated in the Ardennes or Belleau Wood relied on rifle power backed with grenades and artillery. He also wanted his men to be trained behind the lines, not in the field of battle. Pershing was jealous of his soldiers' lives and determined, just as he had been in the Philippines, not to waste them.

Aside from trench raids and scuffles, it was more than a year from Pershing's appointment as commander of the American Expeditionary Force to its first major battle, at Cantigny. But once committed, Pershing expected his men to show their tenacity. At Cantigny they did, taking and holding their position at the cost of more than a thousand casualties. A small theater of war, perhaps, but big enough for those who were in it, and big enough for Pershing to prove that the Americans could hold a position that the French had not. In June 1918, the Americans proved their mettle again—this time at Belleau Wood. It was a small patch of hell that cost the Marines five thousand casualties, but once again the Americans showed an offensive spirit that had long abandoned the French and that impressed the Germans. Pershing, visiting a hospital after the battle, received an apology from a wounded

Marine for not saluting. His right arm was gone. Pershing replied, "It is I who should salute you."[7] In July, Pershing's men turned back the German assault at Château-Thierry, with the 3rd Division earning its distinction as "the Rock of the Marne."

ON TO VICTORY

With Ludendorff's offensives spent, Pershing was for going on the attack. The American Expeditionary Force could now bring, in rough terms, as many fighting men to the Western Front as the British or the French. They were much less experienced, but their *esprit de corps* was unmatched; indeed, their only real match were the elite units of the German army. Despite the machinations of Marshal Foch, who wanted to subordinate the AEF to the French, Pershing stubbornly insisted on—and with the help of General Pétain succeeded in—keeping his army intact to reduce Saint-Mihiel, which the Americans did before rapidly swinging into action for the final great push in the Meuse-Argonne Campaign. If there was any doubt about the AEF's fighting prowess, about its crucial role in ensuring an Allied victory, it was answered here.[8] As Pershing later wrote of his audacious plan to defeat the Germans at Saint-Mihiel and then pivot into the giant Meuse-Argonne Offensive, "When viewed as a whole, it is believed that history gives no parallel of such an undertaking with so large an army....It was only my absolute faith in the energy and resourcefulness of our officers of both staff and line and the resolute and aggressive courage of our soldiers that permitted me to accept such a prodigious" task.[9] It was Pershing who kept them pressing forward.

It was Pershing too who pressed for an armistice on the basis of unconditional surrender—until he was told by Colonel House that peace terms were a political matter. In Pershing's own view, the

Germans had to be convinced they were utterly beaten. He foresaw that anything short of unconditional surrender would leave the impression among some in Germany that they had not lost the war, only the peace; and revanchist sentiment, like that which had waxed in France after the Franco-Prussian War, would wax in Germany. He might have been right about that—circumstances are hard to judge in retrospect—but when he was told to keep his nose out of the political settlement, he did. In the meantime, he helped win the war.

Pershing did, however, have a flicker of political ambition; on his return stateside he let it be known that he might consider a presidential run in 1920. When it became clear that this was a quixotic hope, he swiftly withdrew. Congress, meanwhile, rewarded him with the highest rank ever given to a military officer, General of the Armies. The only other American general to hold that rank is George Washington, who achieved the distinction posthumously in 1976. In 1921, Pershing took up his last post, as the Army's chief of staff. He tried—and largely failed—to save the Army from Congress's swingeing budget cuts. But he also tried—and largely succeeded—in maintaining the morale of the officer corps, improving their training and education, and creating a general staff ready for any military challenge. He retired in 1924.

Pershing's days as chief of staff, dismantling the Army he had created, had been unhappy. His nights were no happier; he disliked Washington social life. In retirement, he turned to writing his memoirs (another noisome task, though they won a Pulitzer Prize); leading the American Battle Monuments Commission[10] (less bothersome, in part because he was aided by a highly efficient major named Dwight David Eisenhower); and making the argument for military preparedness. The Second World War did not surprise him. He had no direct role in the war (at that point he was living in the Walter Reed Army Hospital) but played an indirect role through the generals he had helped train, especially George Marshall (whom he admired), George S. Patton (whom he liked), and Douglas MacArthur (whom he tolerated)—and the Moros, who still remembered him and killed Japanese on his behalf. He died in 1948. Of few generals can it be said that they never lost a battle. It can be said of Pershing.

CHAPTER NINE

PEYTON C. MARCH
(1864–1955)

I f not exactly a child prodigy, Peyton C. March, who became chief of staff of the Army during the Great War, passed the entrance examination into Lafayette College when he was not quite sixteen. A lanky scholar-athlete, tall, thin, and studious, his youth didn't stop him from becoming class president, captain of the baseball team, a starter on the football team, a record-setting member of the track team (scoring the school's best time in the half mile), and graduating with honors in classics. His father was a distinguished, easygoing, well-liked professor at the school. Peyton was impressed by his father, but did not follow in his footsteps. While many Lafayette graduates went on to advanced degrees, Peyton wanted to be a soldier. His

father approved, and in due course Peyton entered the Military
Academy at West Point. Lafayette had provided Peyton March with
a fine education, but West Point was even more rigorous. March,
dedicated to his studies, finished tenth in his class—fewer than half
of whom made it to graduation. Two years ahead of him was cadet
president of the class of 1886, John J. Pershing.

March's first posting after graduation was with the 3rd Artillery
Regiment in Washington, DC. The 3rd Artillery's name was perhaps
a slight misnomer. The unit's duties involved very little artillery practice—they were ceremonial troops in the nation's capital—and to fill
the time March studied French and other topics suitable for an
officer and a gentleman. Like Pershing, he had little interest in booz-
ing or card playing; but unlike Pershing he married while still in his
twenties (age twenty-six), to a captain's daughter.

In 1894 he was sent to the 5th Artillery Regiment in San Francisco, where, as usual, he was judged "zealous, capable, and efficient
in the discharge of duty."[1] Not quite two years later, he was sent on
a nearly two-year course at the Artillery School at Fort Monroe,
where the curriculum covered everything from ballistics to photog-
raphy. If nothing else, American officers were kept broadly educated,
because truth be told, with Indians no longer on the warpath, there
was not that much for them to do.

"WARLIKE SKILL AND GOOD JUDGMENT"

That changed in April 1898 when Spain declared war on the
United States—and for March it changed in dramatic style. He was
given twenty-four hours to decide whether he would accept command of a volunteer light artillery unit donated—that is, underwrit-
ten—by John Jacob Astor. March replied, "I don't want twenty-four

seconds…I accept the detail at once."[2] It was up to March to assemble the unit from scratch. He bought uniforms from a private firm in New York, imported guns from France, and recruited a strong contingent of collegians admixed with mule drivers, policemen, a couple of West Pointers, and adventurers who had soldiered in the British Empire. He gave them a crash course in artillery work, transported them to San Francisco, and then embarked with them for the Philippines. The battery saw action at the invasion of Manila, where General Arthur MacArthur asked for a volunteer to lead a charge against the Spanish. March sprang up, pistol in hand, shouting out, "Come on, men!" and sprinted directly into Spanish rifle fire, which finally forced March and his men to take cover. He nevertheless reported on the Spanish dispositions to MacArthur, rolled his artillery into position to blast the enemy, and then volunteered to lead a reconnaissance to judge the effect—which was that the Spanish had fled. MacArthur wrote, "The brilliant manner in which Lieutenant March accepted and discharged the responsible and dangerous duties of the day…was an exceptional display of warlike skill and good judgment, indicating the existence of many of the best qualifications for high command in battle."[3] He recommended March for a Medal of Honor, but it was denied. In fact, on 12 August, the day before the Astor artillery went into combat, President McKinley had ordered an end to the fighting, though the word had not reached the Philippines. When it did, the Astor artillery took part in four months' worth of occupation duties before returning home in December.

In February, a new war broke out between the United States and the Filipino rebels. MacArthur offered March a job as a staff officer. The War Department approved, and by May 1899 March was back in the Philippines doing a bit of everything MacArthur needed done, including leading men in combat. In July, he was assigned to the 33rd

Volunteer Infantry Regiment. He led it into action against Filipino *insurrectos* and captured rebel commander Emilio Aguinaldo's chief of staff. Before he left the Philippines in 1901, March had, in addition, served as military governor of two provinces and, in Manila, overseen the treatment of captured *insurrectos*. His colonial experience was thus usefully varied—from staff officer to judge advocate to combat officer to military governor—and he earned high marks from General MacArthur as one of the outstanding officers of the war.

March returned to take command of an artillery battery at Fort Riley, Kansas. In 1903, he was selected to join the new General Staff Corps created by Secretary of War Elihu Root, an appointment that marked him as an officer of special promise. In 1904, he served as a military observer of the Russo-Japanese War—an experience he relished, but that was marked with tragedy. During the assignment he received news that his wife had died. She had borne him six children, whom he now raised with the help of a cousin and later his sister.

Returning home, he briefed President Theodore Roosevelt on the war. March had seen that while Japanese government officials maintained the diplomatic niceties, in the field Japanese soldiers had watched him beady-eyed and even chanted, "Down with the Americans!" March was convinced, as he told students at the Army War College, that "if Japan wins this war, nothing less than predominance in the Pacific will satisfy her. The slightest study of the strategic weakness of our situation in the Philippines should show us that possibly the time may come when we shall have to play a hand ourselves."[4]

He resumed his duties at the War Department until 1907, when, as per his wishes, he returned to Fort Riley as commander of a battalion of field artillery. Though he was a terrific administrator and paper pusher, March enjoyed service in the field, and he stayed at Fort Riley until April 1911, after which he was recalled to administrative duties. In 1913, he was assigned to the office of the adjutant general in Washington, DC, where he supervised Army recruiting.

By October 1916 he was again at Fort Bliss, a full colonel now in command of an artillery regiment. Sharply martial in appearance, March was regarded as brilliant, direct, laconic, decisive, fair, and reserved. He trained his men very much with a mind that war was imminent—and it was not the ongoing skirmish in Mexico that dominated his thinking; it was the war in Europe. After the United States declared war on imperial Germany in April 1917, March expected to see summer in France. He did, as commander of a brigade of artillery.

"THE RIGHT MAN IN THE RIGHT PLACE"

By September he was a major general and chief of artillery for the American Expeditionary Force. Even so, he insisted on joining the gunners on the artillery range. But his days in the field were numbered. In February 1918, Secretary of War Newton Baker announced he had chosen March to become Army chief of staff.[5] Baker had long admired March as an efficient man of military business—just the sort he needed to expedite the training, deployment, and supply of the rapidly expanding AEF. Indeed, March believed that "entirely too much time was spent on the training considered necessary by General Pershing."[6] He wanted men in the field now.

He also wanted Army administrators working with the same dedication as field officers in combat. When March arrived, he found that the general staff worked normal business hours. That changed. There was a war to be won, and the general staff would work round the clock until it was. His sense of duty was stringent. His eldest son, an Army aviator, had died in February after a plane crash.[7] As with his wife's death, March was stoical; he became even more dedicated to his work.

It was clear Baker had chosen the right man—even if March himself deeply regretted being trapped behind a desk in Washington. When Baker asked him if he had received his promotion as chief of staff with "mixed emotions," March replied, "No, Mr. Secretary, it made me sick at my stomach."[8] Still, Baker was well satisfied that in March he had a man who was a remarkably quick study, astute, and effective as an administrator. Indeed, within a matter of weeks March had doubled the monthly totals of doughboys crossing the Atlantic—and then doubled them again. If the price Baker had to pay for March's efficiency was the bruised feelings of others—including Pershing, senior to March in rank, but in March's view a mere leader of the American Expeditionary Force under the Army chief of staff—it was a small price to pay for the results achieved.[9]

March's dedication to victory could not be doubted. He was going to provide the American Expeditionary Force with every bit of manpower he could muster—no matter the cost. "We are going to win this war if it takes every man in the United States."[10] And he was not one for compromises. He wanted everything done well and fast. He wanted his briefings to the point. His questions were terse and penetrating. He wasted no time in micromanagement either, assuming that every man knew his job and should do it unhindered. Inefficiency was the enemy he slew—and kept slaying—in the War Department. Few liked him, most respected him, some hated him—though he counted the haters as a badge of honor: it meant he had crunched the toes of useless bureaucrats beneath his boots.[11] March gave shape to the general staff and to the wartime U.S. Army, successfully merging the Army and the National Guard and creating new branches of the service covering the Air Corps, Transport Corps, Tank Corps, and Chemical Warfare Corps. Financier and presidential advisor Bernard Baruch told March's biographer that March was "the right man in the right place."[12] It is hard to gainsay that.

THE DEMOBILIZATION AND THE NEXT WAR

Having built the Army up, in victory he had to take it down—and while March was advised by progressives and economists to demobilize according to the needs of industry, he decided that the best and fairest way to demobilize was in terms of military units, with the easiest (those still stateside) disbanding first, though a few exceptions were made for men in vital industries (such as coal miners). Within ten months, more than three and a quarter million men had been mustered out of the service. To March, it was a point of pride that it had all gone so smoothly. To many of those in uniform, however, ten months was ten months too long. March made more enemies by taking responsibility for demoting generals, of whom there was an inevitable surplus. He made even more enemies when he ordered a reform of the West Point curriculum—he wanted the education it offered to be simultaneously broadened and tightened into a three-year course—and appointed a young general, Douglas MacArthur, to carry it out.[13]

March initially hoped to retain a five-hundred-thousand-man Army after the war, but Congress was of no such mind. His proposal for three months of military training for all nineteen-year-old men was also a nonstarter. March believed, "You cannot run a war on tact,"[14] but his brusque ways had not only made him enemies, they had put him at odds with a postwar Congress disinclined to take orders from the Army chief of staff. Congressional feeling was on display when the House gave a standing ovation to President Wilson's recommendation that General Pershing be elevated to four-star rank and then sat and grumbled when the president recommended four stars for General March. In the end, Congress slashed appropriations for the Army, agreeing to a standing Army of nearly three hundred thousand men but providing funding for an Army of no more than two hundred thousand, and threatened in subsequent years to cut the Army even further. March was no politician, and his plans were opposed not just by pacific congressmen but by a great many officers, including General Pershing.

In 1920, Warren G. Harding was elected president. His new secretary of war, John W. Weeks—a Naval Academy graduate and former congressman and U.S. senator from Massachusetts—initially rejected March's offer to resign. In June 1921, however, March became expendable after Weeks reorganized the War Department and made Pershing chief of staff. Though Weeks wanted to keep March employed in Washington in some capacity, the general decided to retire. He spent the next five years traveling in Europe. What started as a presumed unofficial fact-finding mission—including a cordial interview with Hindenburg—became an extended European dalliance (along with trips to Turkey and North Africa) and honeymoon, as he remarried. He returned from his travels worried about the rise of dictators and the apparent animosity of debt-ridden Europe to its creditor, the United States.

Provoked by Pershing's memoirs of the war and other accounts that he thought were factually incorrect, he waded in with his own book, *The Nation at War*, in 1932, which irritated Pershing and his camp as much Pershing's book had irritated March and his. The two generals resented what they regarded as the other's presumptions of omniscience, but March was far more openly polemical than Pershing had been. Pershing had annoyed March by saying little; March annoyed Pershing by saying much.

In the 1930s, March foresaw the coming world war and knew the United States would have to fight Japan. He was an ardent supporter of Franklin Delano Roosevelt because he liked him personally, and March associated Republicans with military cuts (though the Democrats had been no better) and with his nemesis Pershing. During the Second World War, March thought air power overrated (he had always had this opinion). He believed in not messing about in North Africa, but driving directly across the English Channel into France (just as in the Great War he had argued vehemently against messing about in revolutionary Russia and for focusing all resources on the Western Front). He opposed the policy of unconditional surrender. And he was an advocate, as he had been in the First World War, of giving the American public as much information about the war as possible. He believed in exposing difficulties and in open criticism of military failures.

March was always fit, liked to play tennis and walk, and was an ardent baseball and football fan who retained his ramrod posture and good health until roughly the last two years of his life. He eventually took up residence at Walter Reed—ironically in the same rooms that had been Pershing's. He died aged ninety, remembered as a brilliant military administrator, though he would no doubt have relished Douglas MacArthur's reminder that he was also a combat soldier: "The sights and smells of a battlefield which are repugnant to many were exhilarating to him. He always wanted to go to the front."[15] It was March's fate, however, that the front for him was most often the political battles of Washington.

CHAPTER TEN

DOUGLAS MacARTHUR (1880–1964)

O n 25 November 1863, Lieutenant Arthur MacArthur, seizing the colors of the 24th Wisconsin from the hands of a fallen corporal, stormed Missionary Ridge, leading his men with the shout, "On Wisconsin!" and earning himself a Medal of Honor. By the end of the war, he was nineteen and a colonel, the youngest in the Army. In 1875, he proved his audacity and gallantry again when he won the hand of Mary Pinkney "Pinky" Hardy, a Southern belle of old Virginia heritage whose brothers were graduates of the Virginia Military Institute and had fought for the Confederacy. He met her in New Orleans—perhaps that helped—and they were blessed with three sons: Arthur MacArthur III, Malcolm MacArthur (who died of measles as a young boy), and the youngest, Douglas MacArthur.

Douglas MacArthur said his earliest memories were of Army bugles and a three-hundred-mile march from Fort Wingate, New Mexico, to Fort Selden, Texas, where his father and his men were to guard the crossings of the Rio Grande against Apache raiders. MacArthur was then four years old. The frontier army that director John Ford later portrayed in his cavalry films was the army experienced by young Douglas MacArthur—or so his memory told him. When it came to movies, he always liked Westerns.[1]

DUTY AND DESTINY

There was never much doubt about Douglas MacArthur's career; he was a precocious soldier. He grew up in the saddle, rifle in hand, the son of a war hero. He spent his boyhood listening to old soldiers spin their yarns. His mother venerated Robert E. Lee and military service and instilled in her sons a sense of aristocratic honor, a catechism of duty and destiny.

After stops in Fort Leavenworth, Kansas, and Washington, DC, the family returned to Texas, and Douglas, at age thirteen, was enrolled at the West Texas Military Academy. His father had tagged his youngest son as a likely soldier (the eldest son, Arthur III, had entered the Naval Academy), and Douglas took to the military school regimen with *élan*. A previously indifferent student, he excelled at the academy. Like Winston Churchill's at Sandhurst, MacArthur's marks soared when education had a martial cast: "Abstruse mathematics began to appear as a challenge to analysis, dull Latin and Greek seemed a gateway to the moving words of the leaders of the past, laborious historical data led to the nerve-tingling battlefields of the great captains, Biblical lessons began to open the spiritual portals of growing faith, literature lay bare the souls of men."[2] In addition, if he did not quite excel at sports, he wanted to, and he was a gamer: a scrappy shortstop, a tough quarterback, and a somewhat awkward but school-champion-caliber tennis player. At military drill he was an acknowledged leader, and he graduated as class valedictorian.

His appointment to West Point would have seemed inevitable, but despite—or perhaps because of—the political connections of his grandfather (a judge) and his father (both Republicans), he was passed over twice for an at-large appointment (made by the president, in the first case the Democrat Grover Cleveland) and once flunked the physical (for having mild scoliosis). A friendly congressman came to the rescue, inviting MacArthur to sit the West Point entrance exam as a grandson, if not son, of Wisconsin. Douglas moved to Milwaukee with his mother and spent a year establishing residency while attending school to cram for the examination and seeing a doctor who prescribed a regimen of exercise to strengthen his back. The work paid off: MacArthur's score was far and away the best, and in due course, in 1899, he received his appointment to West Point.[3] Mom went too, staying four years at a hotel near the Military Academy where she could remain his confidant while he was a cadet.

MacArthur immediately impressed his fellows as tall and dashingly handsome, with an arresting command presence, a lightning-fast brain, and a determination to excel. None of this spared him the brutal hazing that plebes then had to get through—so brutal that it killed one—and MacArthur exerted every sinew to endure it (stifling cries of pain and attempting to hide the fact that one of the ordeals had given him convulsions). When called to testify to Congress about what had happened to him and other plebes, MacArthur conceded little about the regime's cruelty, which made him a hero to the cadets, though the system was necessarily reformed.

MacArthur graduated not only top of his class, but one of the highest-scoring cadets in the Military Academy's history, just below his mother's hero, Robert E. Lee. He was cadet captain, like Pershing, and for three of his four years at West Point played baseball—a weak-hitting but canny and determined right fielder. On graduation, he wanted a posting in the cavalry, but the Army made him an engineer. Brains like his weren't to be wasted on a horse.

After a layover in San Francisco, MacArthur was off to the Philippines, where his father had been military governor (until relieved by the new civilian governor, William Howard Taft). He had his baptism of fire—his hat took a bullet; he shot down his two would-be killers—as well as his baptism of malaria, and earned promotion to first lieutenant. After a brief return stateside, he was named aide-de-camp to his father, assisting him in an Asian *tour d'horizon* of the Far East and the Pacific, from Japan to Java, from Bangkok to the northwest frontier of the British Raj, from Singapore to Saigon and Shanghai. His father had already been a military observer of the Russo-Japanese War in Manchuria, and the younger MacArthur was one of the notable few who saw America's future in the Pacific rather than in Europe or in isolation.

Returning to America, he was sent to engineering school, served as an aide to President Theodore Roosevelt, and eventually moved back with his parents to Milwaukee, where he had engineering duties. But engineering bored MacArthur. He was slack in his studies and more interested in talking with his father about Asia and the Pacific than he was in working on projects in the upper Midwest—and both shortfalls were noted in his military record. Rejuvenation came when he was assigned to Fort Leavenworth and command of a company of engineers. Drilling men was more his style. The twenty-eight-year-old lieutenant shook off his anomie, relished taking Company K from the lowest ranked on the post to the highest, and again seemed an officer of remarkable activity and distinction. In 1911 he was made captain and sent on tours of duty that included Panama and Texas. In 1913, his father died and his mother became a grief-stricken invalid, at least temporarily. With his brother's long absences at sea, it was left to MacArthur to look after her—something he found hard to do at Fort Leavenworth. But Army chief of staff Major General Leonard Wood helped finagle MacArthur a job with the general staff in Washington, which settled Mrs. MacArthur nicely.

MacArthur got a chance for action, too, sailing to Vera Cruz in 1914 as an intelligence officer. His mission into the Mexican interior, a reconnaissance that might be useful in case of war, was so top secret that the American commander in Vera Cruz didn't know about it. MacArthur operated on his own with initiative and bravery and proved himself a dab hand at gunfights, of which he had several, leaving many of his would-be assailants dead and his own uniform perforated by bullets. He was recommended for a Medal of Honor, and when that was denied lest it encourage other officers—without MacArthur's War Department orders—to go secretly into Mexico, he protested. Self-regard was an unfortunate component of his merit—and there were those who held it against him.

THE "RAINBOW" DIVISION

In 1916, MacArthur became military assistant to Secretary of War Newton Baker and took on the duty of press officer for the Army. The press liked him—and so did Baker. The two of them shared a belief that National Guard units should be melded into the American Expeditionary Force, and won the president to their side; MacArthur, in fact, played a formative role in the 42nd "Rainbow" Division (MacArthur called it that because it was assembled from National Guard units that spanned the country). Baker rewarded him with a promotion to colonel (at MacArthur's request, a colonel of infantry, not engineers) and chief of staff to the brigadier general commanding the division. It was, MacArthur knew, his ticket to battle and command.

By November 1917, MacArthur was in France with advance elements of the Rainbow Division, soon to be commanded by Major General Charles Menoher, a favorite of Pershing's. MacArthur, in turn, became a favorite of Menoher's—and of the men of the 42nd. MacArthur was openly proud of the division's men, praising them and defending them at every opportunity, and impressing them with his dash. He removed the wire innards of his hat to give it a more swashbuckling look and patrolled into no-man's-land armed with a cigarette holder, a long knitted scarf, a West Point letterman's sweater, and a riding crop, earning himself the nickname "the d'Artagnan of the A.E.F."[4] While diligent in drafting his plans and pushing paperwork, he was also deliberately not a micromanager. He did not want to make himself indispensable behind a desk. He wanted to be in the field with his men. When an officer reminded MacArthur that a chief of staff's duties did not normally include raiding enemy trenches, MacArthur replied nonchalantly, "It's all in the game."[5] For one raid he was awarded a Silver Star, for another the Distinguished Service Cross for "coolness and conspicuous courage."[6]

He seemed invulnerable. Indeed, he once said, "All of Germany cannot fabricate the shell that will kill me."[7] His men wore helmets.

He wore his soft cap. He ordered them to wear gas masks but did not stoop to such precautions himself—and twice paid the price during German gas attacks, and once had to be hospitalized. But he believed such shows were important to inspire his men. "There are times," he said, "when even general officers have to be expendable."[8] French officers admired MacArthur's *élan*; Pershing was less impressed. Seeing MacArthur's men just out of the fighting line in Lorraine, he rebuked MacArthur for what he took to be their slovenly appearance—and it was telling that he berated MacArthur rather than Menoher. Within the American Expeditionary Force, it was well known that the 42nd Division took its tone from its chief of staff. If an officer personified the Rainbow Division, it was MacArthur, and MacArthur's attitude to dress and conduct was obviously not regulation or parade ground; it came perhaps from his mother's tales of Confederate valor, of *beau geste* officers like J. E. B. Stuart and loyal fighting men in the ranks dressed in any old combination of butternut and grey. In June 1918, MacArthur became a brigadier general—the youngest in the Army. Unknown to him, he had not been on Pershing's list for promotions. Army chief of staff Peyton C. March had put him on the list and deleted five of Pershing's staff officers.

MacArthur won his second Silver Star defending the road to Châlons against Ludendorff's pressing legions in July 1918. Menoher said, "MacArthur is the bloodiest fighting man in this army. I'm afraid we're going to lose him sometime, for there's no risk of battle that any soldier is called upon to take that he is not liable to look up and see MacArthur at his side."[9] MacArthur took his greatest pride—and pleasure—in the fact that when he advanced against the enemy, he need have no doubt that the men of the 42nd would be swarming ahead with him.

At Château-Thierry, MacArthur led his men with "tactics I had seen so often in the Indian wars of my frontier days. Crawling forward in twos and threes against each stubborn nest of enemy guns, we closed in with the bayonet and the hand grenade. It was savage and there was no quarter asked or given."[10] It was successful too, and MacArthur earned his third Silver Star.

Menoher then gave him command of the division's 84th Brigade to put some fire in its belly, turning him loose from his responsibilities as chief of staff.[11] MacArthur was immediately at the front, pressing the attack on the enemy. In one eerie reconnaissance through the dead and dying in no-man's-land, a flare suddenly burst overhead, illuminating a three-man German machine gun crew; MacArthur hit the dirt. After a tense few moments, he realized they were dead: "the lieutenant with shrapnel through his heart, the sergeant with his belly blown into his back, the corporal with his spine where his head should have been."[12] He also established the Germans had withdrawn. He personally reported the news to Menoher and Major General Hunter Liggett, commander of I Corps, and then promptly collapsed with fatigue. He had not slept for four days. He had just earned his fourth Silver Star.

He earned his fifth leading his men in the reduction of the enemy salient at Saint-Mihiel. He also deeply impressed Lieutenant Colonel George S. Patton, who called MacArthur "the bravest man I ever met." At one point the two officers were standing on a little hill, when a German barrage began beating its way toward them. Patton flinched slightly when a shell burst nearby, sending up a shower of dirt. MacArthur remarked coolly, "Don't worry, Colonel, you never hear the one that gets you."[13]

At the outset of the Meuse-Argonne Campaign, MacArthur earned yet another Silver Star for two successfully conducted raids. But there was a bigger battle to come. MacArthur was drawing up plans to attack the Côte de Châtillon, a key point in the German line, when Major General Charles Summerall, commander of V Corps, told him, "Give me Châtillon, MacArthur. Give me Châtillon, or a list of five thousand casualties." MacArthur, who was still suffering from gas poisoning, replied, "If this brigade does not capture Châtillon you can publish a casualty list of the entire Brigade with the Brigade Commander's name at the top."[14] After two days of fierce fighting, MacArthur delivered Châtillon. Reflecting on the cost, MacArthur later said of Summerall, "I have hated him ever since."[15]

In the final push to victory, MacArthur was awarded his seventh Silver Star and was briefly given command of the division (Menoher had taken command of VI Corps). He then led the 84th Brigade for its triumphal march into Germany and occupation duties. In April 1919, he and the Rainbow Division came home.

PEACETIME TASKS

MacArthur wasn't left unemployed long. Peyton March tapped him to reform and revitalize West Point as superintendent of the Academy. Not surprisingly, perhaps, MacArthur suppressed hazing, formalized the honor code, broadened the curriculum (though not nearly so much as he wanted, because the faculty opposed him), posted maps of Asia (remember the Philippines) around the campus, and ramped up the Academy's athletic program. MacArthur even provided the motto for Army athletics—"Upon the fields of friendly strife / Are sown the seeds / That, upon other fields on other days / Will bear the fruits of victory"—and had it carved in stone over the school gymnasium.

Most superintendents served four-year terms. Pershing, who disliked MacArthur's reforms, had him transferred to the Philippines in 1922, but not before MacArthur had married a rich, flapper-like divorcée with whom he shared nothing but a profound physical attraction that had him proposing at their first meeting. Her name was Louise Cromwell Brooks, and she brought to their union two children (on whom MacArthur doted) from her previous marriage.

In the Philippines, the MacArthur name was already legend (from his father, Arthur MacArthur), and like his father, MacArthur established a sincere rapport with the Filipinos. His title was commander of the military district of Manila. Among his official responsibilities was leading a surveying team in Bataan. Among his unofficial responsibilities, he spent a great deal of time building relationships with prominent Filipino political figures, most especially Manuel Quezon, president of the Philippine Senate. MacArthur loved the Philippines. His wife, predictably, hated it; she wanted MacArthur to become a stockbroker.[16]

Promotion to major general (the youngest in the Army) brought MacArthur and his bride stateside with an assignment first in Atlanta (command of the IV Corps Area) and then in Baltimore (command of the III Corps Area)—dull for him, heaven for her, as it put her back on the social circuit. In 1925, he was detailed to serve on the court-martial of Billy Mitchell, which MacArthur called "one of the most distasteful orders I ever received." MacArthur defended Mitchell—"It is part of my military philosophy that a senior officer should not be silenced for being at variance with his superiors in rank and with accepted doctrine"—but could not prevent the airman from being convicted.[17]

In 1927, MacArthur was named president of the U.S. Olympic Committee. After the 1928 Olympic games, he was assigned as commander of the Philippine Department, a prospect that delighted him and prompted his wife (from whom he was already de facto separated) to file for divorce.[18] In 1930, he became Army chief of staff. If not a meteoric rise, it was certainly an impressive one, and MacArthur was a formidable man, striking in manner, quick in decision, neither bound by precedent nor contemptuous of eternal verities, disdaining regulation uniform and useless traditions if he found more dashing or practical alternatives, while holding firmly (and famously) to duty, honor, country, and to the corps, the corps, the corps.

He was an accomplished man—and one who continued to prepare himself for great things. To that end, he kept up a regular exercise regimen. He paced constantly when at work.[19] His demeanor was that of a gentleman, his tone usually level, and though prone to dramatic pronouncements and monologues of such flamboyant color that listeners marveled at him, it was part of his self-image and mystique that he kept his temper in check and similarly kept his appearance immaculate even in the tropics. Comprehensive in his views, he expressed them clearly, delegated authority, and did not micromanage his subordinates. He spent most of his evenings reading military history. His mind was powerfully stocked with knowledge and swift in judgment. Dwight Eisenhower, who was his aide for seven years, remarked, "He did have a hell of an intellect! My God, but he was smart. He had a *brain*."[20] At the same time, MacArthur's egotism and eccentricities as chief of staff were also marked. He was notably devoted to his mother—indeed, they now lived and lunched together at Fort Myer.[21] He began referring to himself in the third person (as MacArthur). As a confirmed orientalist, he wore a kimono at his desk.[22]

It was not a pleasant time to be chief of staff. MacArthur wanted a larger Army. But in the Great Depression, and with budget-minded Republicans in office and Herbert Hoover (whom MacArthur liked)[23] as president, he had to find creative ways to protect what was most essential in the Army budget. To MacArthur, the priority was not guns and trucks and planes[24]—which could be manufactured by industry in due course—but an educated officer corps, without which an Army was nothing. MacArthur always believed that it was the human element, the moral element, that was vital in war. He was, at bottom, a romantic.[25]

It was that quality, too, which helped him in what he called the "most poignant episode during my role as Chief of Staff": dispersing the "Bonus March" on Washington. In 1932, thousands of unemployed veterans (or purported veterans; Hoover and MacArthur thought most of them were frauds) camped out in Washington demanding relief. For weeks, the authorities treated them gently and encouraged them to go home (and offered to pay their way). Still, perhaps ten thousand remained, and as incidents of crime increased, as well as intimations of Communist influence among the marchers, the police were ordered to move them out. The police were met with violence, and the president ordered MacArthur in with the Army. MacArthur succeeded in pushing the marchers out of Washington, and under the circumstances, it was extraordinary that the marchers—or at least the Communists among them looking for a fight—were evicted so easily. Nevertheless, the image of American troops, a zealous MacArthur at their head, shoving unemployed men, whether veterans or not, out of Washington made many liberals view MacArthur with suspicion. MacArthur had no doubts and felt vindicated by later testimony about Communist activists behind the marchers. But to liberals, MacArthur seemed too much an American Caesar, a man who might, someday, reach for the purple.[26]

Franklin Roosevelt, elected president in 1932, shared this suspicion, though not to the point of accepting MacArthur's resignation when it was offered during a heated budget discussion. He kept MacArthur on for an extra year past the end of the chief of staff's traditional four-year term. Besides saving the Army from budget cuts that might have utterly eviscerated it, MacArthur won Roosevelt's favor with the Army's work in operating the Civilian Conservation Corps.

In 1935, MacArthur became that unlikely thing for an American general—a field marshal, albeit a field marshal of the Philippine army, a rank that went along with his role as military advisor to the Philippines, which was on a congressionally mandated track to become independent in 1946. He had been invited by Manuel Quezon, who had won election as president of the Philippine Commonwealth in September 1935. MacArthur's job was to ensure that the Philippines could defend itself when it became independent, something American military planners thought was impossible. While most American strategists considered the Philippines peripheral or a liability to America's security interests, MacArthur saw the Philippines as the keystone of America's influence in Asia and the Pacific. It was here, not in Europe, that the future would be made. In the event of a Japanese invasion of the Philippines, Army and Navy war planners envisioned a speedy American withdrawal. To MacArthur, this was heresy and defeatism. The Philippines, he thought, had to be and could be defended. MacArthur's plan was for a small, professional army, with a well-trained, Swiss-style ready-reserve to be called up in time of war, supplemented by a fleet of swift PT boats navigating between the islands. This combined stinging force could make attacking the Philippines too painful for any potential aggressor to contemplate. It also offered Quezon the possibility of defending the 7,100-island archipelago on the relative cheap and in time for independence (though Quezon hoped the American military would stay). Opposition to

MacArthur's plan from Frank Murphy (the American high commissioner to the Philippines and soon to be governor of Michigan), as well as from other isolationist and pacifist-leaning liberals in the administration and in Congress, convinced MacArthur to resign from the U.S. Army at the end of 1937. He returned to the Philippines as a civilian military advisor—fully expecting to be recalled to the colors in case of war.

While MacArthur's plans were meant to be economical, political realities made them unaffordable. MacArthur's annual budget amounted to less than a third of the $25 million his staff said was necessary to defend the islands (and fell to as little as $1 million in 1940). Support MacArthur expected from the United States was either denied or else doled out with congressional parsimony, his plan was opposed by Quezon, and Filipino recruit training was often more a matter of advancing rudimentary education than passing on military instruction and drill. It seemed to Quezon that the Japanese were the more virile force in the Pacific, and that perhaps it might be wiser to seek an accommodation with the Rising Sun than to rely on MacArthur and the Americans.

But for all these frustrations, MacArthur was happy in his role in the Philippines—because he was perfectly cast for it by birth and by temperament, and because on his passage to Manila he had met the perfect field marshal's lady, Jean Marie Faircloth, a poised, attractive, vivacious, wealthy, never-married thirty-seven-year-old Southerner and Daughter of the Confederacy who became the second Mrs. MacArthur. They were married in 1937, had a son the following year, and were utterly devoted to each other. Like his mother, she held sacred the flame of Robert E. Lee; and unlike MacArthur's first wife, she was a duty, honor, country gal, not a flapper; she venerated soldiers, patriotism, and the domestic virtues.

Theirs was, for a while, a colonial idyll, even against a backdrop of looming war. In 1941, after the Japanese invasion of French Indo-China, MacArthur was made commander of the U.S. Army Forces in the Far East, and American supplies suddenly flowed to the Philippines. The brigadier general of the Great War was now, in rapid succession, major general and then lieutenant general in an even bigger war, with a theater of operations that covered the entire Pacific.[27]

"I SHALL RETURN"

The attack on Pearl Harbor, Hawaii, on 7 December 1941, however, had caught him by surprise; and he was not prepared for the Japanese attack on the Philippines the next day. His air force was pinned to the ground, and much of it was destroyed. After its main base at Cavite Bay was bombed by the Japanese, the U.S. Asiatic Fleet, save for PT boats and a contingent of sailors and Marines (numbering about 4,300 men), evacuated (the fleet would make its last gallant stand on the Java Sea and Sunda Strait in early 1942). With the Japanese invasion, the years of neglect of the Philippine army reaped their reward. On 23 December, MacArthur scrapped any aggressive plans he had and ordered a fighting retreat to Bataan on the island of Corregidor. Ever mindful—this was a constant in his career—to shield civilians as much as he could, he declared Manila an open city. The Japanese would prove not as considerate as MacArthur.

The defense of Bataan was heroic. MacArthur, as in the First World War, was supremely indifferent to enemy shelling. But because he spent so much time in his underground headquarters at the fortress of Corregidor, he gained, to his dismay, the moniker of "Dugout

Doug" from the "battling bastards" of Bataan (as they were dubbed by a war correspondent). What finally defeated the battling bastards was not so much the Japanese as a lack of food, ammunition, and supplies of all kinds, not to mention malaria and every other jungle plague that struck the vast majority of the troops.[28] President Franklin Roosevelt ordered MacArthur to evacuate to Australia. On 12 March 1942, he, his family, and some members of his staff boarded four submarine-dodging PT boats (three of them made it), and MacArthur was successfully spirited to Del Monte Airfield on Mindanao, whence he was flown to Batchelor Field in Australia in a B-17. It was here that he told reporters, "The President of the United States ordered me to break through the Japanese lines and proceed from Corregidor to Australia for the purpose, as I understand it, of organizing the American offensive against Japan, a primary object of which is the relief of the Philippines. I came through and I shall return."[29]

It was not just the Filipinos he needed to inspire but Australians who thought they were next on the conquest list of Dai Nippon. The fact that MacArthur was awarded the Medal of Honor helped, as did Roosevelt's decision to send two divisions to Australia (MacArthur was shocked that there were only twenty-five thousand American troops there). MacArthur, who was deeply shaken by his defeat in the Philippines, kept up a brave face, and as he assembled his American-Australian force and took the battle to the enemy, starting in New Guinea, his sense of destiny returned—and so too did his sartorial command presence: the field marshal's cap, the aviator's leather jacket (he had become an evangelist for air power), the sunglasses, the corn cob pipe (he was a dedicated smoker). His troops notched up victories in slogging campaigns in New Guinea, expelling the Japanese from some of the most hostile terrain on the planet. As they marched their way north toward the Philippines, MacArthur went with them, exposing himself to enemy fire to dispel the "Dugout Doug" calumny.

As the Allies advanced in the Pacific, Admiral Ernest King, chief of naval operations and commander in chief of the United States Fleet, proposed bypassing the Philippines. For MacArthur it was a matter of national, and personal, honor that this not happen. Complicating the situation was that some members of the Republican Party wanted to tap an already existing populist movement and run MacArthur for president in 1944. MacArthur let this romantic, and extremely unlikely, possibility play out until it became a threat to his continuing command of the southwest Pacific, from which President Roosevelt could dismiss him. Desperate not to lose his chance to liberate the Philippines and force the surrender of imperial Japan, he belatedly repudiated any political ambitions in April 1944.

In Hawaii in July he met directly with President Roosevelt and Admiral Chester Nimitz, commander in chief of the Pacific Fleet, to press his case for the liberation of the Philippines. He won the argument. On 20 October 1944, he waded ashore at "Red Beach" (Palo Beach), at Leyte Island. MacArthur chose to make his appearance here because it was where the fighting was reportedly the hardest. With Japanese snipers still only yards away from where he stood on the beach, he proclaimed, "People of the Philippines: I have returned."[30] From Leyte it was on to Luzon and the liberation of Manila in February 1945, where again MacArthur did everything he could to minimize civilian casualties. The Japanese commander, however, Rear Admiral Sanji Iwabuchi, did the reverse, murdering civilians and leaving the city a smoldering ruin.

While fighting continued in the Philippines, MacArthur (who had become a five-star "General of the Army" in December 1944)[31] directed the liberation of Borneo, again at the front, nearly oblivious to the gunfire around him (even as it killed a photographer trying to get his picture). He was named commander in chief of the U.S. Army Forces of the Pacific. After the dropping of the atomic bombs on Hiroshima (6 August) and Nagasaki (9 August), the Japanese Empire was finished. MacArthur formally accepted Japan's surrender aboard the USS *Missouri* in Tokyo Bay on 2 September 1945. But that was not the end for MacArthur. As supreme commander of the Allied Powers, he became the shogun who would rebuild shattered Japan, giving it a new democratic constitution (still reserving a place for the emperor), demilitarizing Japanese society, punishing war criminals (a distasteful but necessary duty to him), keeping the Soviets out of the occupation, encouraging the spread of Christianity,[32] instituting a free press, promoting major land reform, creating a free-enterprise economy, encouraging the formation of independent trade unions that could not coerce workers to join (an important principle to MacArthur), and acting in essence as a kindly, beneficent dictator until handing over power to the newly elected Japanese government in 1949.

THE KOREAN WAR

MacArthur was seventy years old and still in Japan as supreme commander of the Allied Powers when North Korea invaded South Korea in 1950. The Truman administration had taken little interest in South Korea. American occupation troops, stationed there at the end of the Second World War, had been rapidly withdrawn, and Secretary of State Dean Acheson had publicly, in a speech, left it outside the arc of American interests in Asia and the Pacific. But to Japan, a Korea united under an aggressive Communist regime was a major threat. The Truman administration did not immediately understand that, but once it did—or once Truman grew incensed enough at Communist North Korea's invasion of South Korea—the president and many of his advisors, who loathed MacArthur and had wanted to remove him from his position in Japan, realized they needed MacArthur to rescue a desperate situation. Once again, MacArthur became a battlefield commander, adding to his titles commander in chief of the United Nations Command.

It was in Korea that MacArthur unleashed the most brilliant stroke of his career—the landing at Inchon, which caught the North Koreans in a double envelopment: the anvil provided by the American and Allied forces at the Pusan Perimeter (the UN defensive positions around the port of Pusan at South Korea's southeastern tip); the hammer coming from the Marines and other units landing at Inchon on 15 September 1950, near the North Korean border. Seoul was liberated, the North Korean army was driven back across the border with heavy losses, and the UN forces moved north, with the possibility of a united non-Communist Korea apparently in the offing.

MacArthur's great gamble had come up trumps. What came next, however, was a turnabout that ended his career: a massive Red Chinese intervention that he did not expect. Nor, when he realized its magnitude, could he crush it, as he had hoped, with air power. Instead, victory appeared to turn to disaster as the North Koreans recaptured Seoul in January 1951 and MacArthur pleaded for massive reinforcements, without which, he said, the war was lost. It was General Matthew Ridgway, appointed by MacArthur to take command of the U.S. Eighth Army in late December 1950, who turned the tide against the North Koreans and Communist Chinese, driving them out of Seoul and back across the border in

March 1951. Ridgway's success and MacArthur's criticisms of Truman administration policy made MacArthur dispensable to an administration that had wanted to sack him ever since it had come to power. He was relieved of his command—and because the news had leaked and the administration wanted to make an official announcement before it hit the presses, he discovered the fact from news reports of a 1:00 a.m. press conference announcing it. In MacArthur's words, "No office boy, no charwoman, no servant of any sort would have been dismissed with such callous disregard for the ordinary decencies"[33] as he had been dismissed by President Truman. Nevertheless, he returned a war hero, addressed a joint session of Congress (MacArthur was a far more popular man than the president), and became a political hero to Republicans, who took his comment that "there can be no substitute for victory"[34] as incisive wisdom ignored by Truman and his administration.

In that same speech, MacArthur reminded his listeners of a line from an old barrack room ballad, "Old soldiers never die, they just fade away." That did, indeed, seem to be his choice, as his first love in retirement was watching sports—boxing, baseball, and football. He kept himself busy, though: he served as chairman of the board of Sperry Rand and impressed President Kennedy, among others, with his still-sharp intellect and grasp of world affairs.[35]

In 1962, two years before he died, MacArthur spoke at West Point, where he told the cadets, "The shadows are lengthening for me. The twilight is here. . . . But in the evening of my memory, always I come back to West Point. Always there echoes and re-echoes: duty, honor, country. Today marks my final roll call with you, but I want you to know that when I cross the river my last conscious thoughts will be of the corps, and the corps, and the corps."[36] MacArthur's loyalty, like his brilliance, was never in doubt. What is sometimes forgotten is how one of the greatest generals in American history was formed in the Great War, a war that is itself fading from America's memory.

CHAPTER ELEVEN

BILLY MITCHELL
(1879–1936)

L ike many rebels, Billy Mitchell came from a prominent, wealthy
family—in his case, one shot through with Scotch belligerency as
well. His grandfather, direct from Scotland, had made the family
fortune; his father largely spent it; and Mitchell tried to maintain a
precarious aristocratic lifestyle on an Army salary that needed to be
supplemented by other means (chiefly his wife's fortune and his
mother's remaining savings). His parents had a taste for the cosmopolitan life, which accounts for his birth in France. The family
returned to Wisconsin three years later, where young Billy (or Willie,
as his mother called him) swiftly developed a love for mischief and,
eventually, fast horses and loud guns. He attended an Episcopal

school and after his father was elected to the United States Senate transferred to a private school in Washington, DC, and enrolled at Columbian College.[1]

The Spanish-American War displaced all thoughts of study, and he enlisted, but his father intervened and won the eighteen-year-old a second lieutenant's commission, making him the youngest officer in the Army. Mitchell was a natural soldier. He arrived in Cuba too late to see action but volunteered for the Philippines, where there was still fighting to be had in 1899. In the Senate his father, a liberal Democrat, railed against American imperialism.[2] Billy, meanwhile, gloried in it. For Christmas, he asked his parents to send him a "Mauser automatic or any other *good* automatic pistol with 500 rounds of ammunition for same."[3]

LOOKING FOR ADVENTURE

After convalescing from malaria, predicting (in a letter to his mother) a future war with Germany, and returning home on a round-about path (through the Middle East and Europe) Mitchell accepted an extended assignment with the Signal Corps[4] in Alaska, where he worked as a surveyor and helped construct an Alaskan telegraph system. He did good work and at twenty-three was promoted cap-tain—the youngest in the Army. He also got married, to Caroline Stoddard, a graduate of Vassar, and in due course was assigned to Fort Leavenworth, Kansas, where he taught at the Signal School, commanded a company, got to dabble in the latest signal technology, and even gave an early aeronautics lecture (on the potential use of balloons or dirigibles in military operations). His military education proceeded apace; he attended the School of the Line in 1907 and the Staff College in 1909. Having earned his sheepskin as a Signals officer, Mitchell tried to transfer into the cavalry (where he had always wanted to be), but his request was denied.

If he was looking for adventure, he found it anyway. The Army sent him to the Philippines—where he investigated Japanese ambitions—and on a tour of Asia that allowed him to observe the Chinese, Japanese, and Russian armies. His conclusion: Japan was America's enemy in the Pacific; there would be a war; and likely it would be in the Philippines.[5]

In 1913, he joined the general staff in Washington, where, ironically given later developments, he downplayed the prospects for air power, advocated keeping airmen under the authority of the Signal Corps (on the theory that aircraft were machines best used for reconnaissance), and actually helped draft the rules governing the Aviation Section of the Signal Corps (which included the requirement that pilots be under thirty and single; Mitchell, of course, was neither).

The war in Europe led to a radical reconsideration of and an enormous congressional funding boost for air power. The age restriction on pilots was dropped, and Mitchell's superiors recognized in the frustrated cavalry officer a potential airman. Mitchell, a top-flight athlete in tennis and polo, was a man far better fitted for field duty than the confines of staff work, which was taking a toll on his health (he suffered from rheumatism). He was an outdoorsman wilting behind a desk, weighed down by piles of paper, his vitality leeched by artificial light. In 1916, he was assigned to the Aviation Section (which promised plenty of outdoor work), was promoted to major, took off-duty flying lessons (which he paid for himself), and was sent to the Western Front in March 1917 as a military observer.

By the time Mitchell arrived in Paris in April, the United States had declared war on Germany. If the Yanks were coming, Mitchell was already there, and he took advantage of the interval to train with experienced pilots. If there was going to be action in the air, he was going to be a part of it—and what he saw of French air power amazed him: fast bombers and even speedier fighters, far more technologically advanced than the planes in America's sparse inventory. "I had been able to flounder around with the animated kites that we call airplanes in the United States, but when I laid my hand to the greyhounds of the air they had in Europe, which went twice as fast as ours, it was an entirely different matter."[6]

Flying over the Western Front, Mitchell noted, "One flight gave me a much clearer impression of how the armies were laid out than any amount of traveling around on the ground. A very significant thing to me was that we could cross the lines of these contending armies in a few minutes in our airplane, whereas the armies had been locked in the struggle, immovable, powerless to advance, for three years....This whole area over which the Germans and the French battled was no more than sixty miles across....It looked as though the war would keep up indefinitely until either the airplanes brought an end to the war or the contending nations dropped from sheer exhaustion."[7]

Fluent in French since his childhood, Mitchell was the perfect liaison officer and perfectly suited to gain a quick appreciation of what the United States could learn from the French and British experience—especially the British, for despite his father's Continental tastes, Billy Mitchell was an Anglophile. He was particularly impressed by his interview with the gruff but visionary Major General Hugh Trenchard, commander of the Royal Flying Corps in France and advocate of relentless aerial offensives.

Though he was promoted to lieutenant colonel in May 1917 and the first American officer to see action on the Western Front (winning a Croix de Guerre from the French), Mitchell's reports gained little attention in Washington. That didn't matter after General John J. Pershing arrived in June. He made Mitchell his aviation officer, separated the Air Service from the Signal Corps, and in September 1917 promoted Mitchell to colonel.

Pershing pegged Mitchell as his aerial combat commander—he was certainly combative enough with his superiors—and it was in that role that Mitchell directed air operations at Saint-Mihiel (after which he was promoted to brigadier general) and during the Meuse-Argonne Campaign. At Saint-Mihiel, Mitchell scouted the German lines from the air and insisted, when others argued for delay because of rain, that the attack go ahead as planned. Mitchell's pilots flew and fought regardless of conditions.

APOSTLE FOR AIR POWER

He returned from the war not as a well-known hero—except among his fellow airmen—but as an aspiring prophet of the future of air power.[8] He was named chief of Air Service training and operations, serving in Washington under Major General Charles C. Menoher, an infantry officer now commanding the Air Service, who gave Mitchell free rein. Budget-slashing congressmen ensured that Mitchell could not roam far. Indeed, his and Menoher's greatest task was to keep the Air Service from extinction.

Mitchell made the case that air power was essential to the defense of the United States. U-boats and long-range bombers (flying from ships or offshore bases) meant America's coasts were no longer immune from enemy attack. The United States needed command of the air; and it would certainly need a vastly improved Air Service for any future war—because the next war, Mitchell had no doubt, would be decided in the air.

Mitchell was a whirling dervish of activity: inundating Menoher with proposals for guns, shells, dirigibles, air transports (he had already envisioned paratroopers), and even aircraft carriers (which might have been thought the Navy's concern). He spoke incessantly about the wars of the future, giving speeches and testimony. He fueled his imagination by flying, meeting with aircraft designers, studying, and nightly parties with his staff—Mitchell was waging a private war against Prohibition—where ideas were bounced around freely. Mitchell's vision was not popular. The Army concluded that air power had not been decisive in the Great War and would be no more decisive in the next; aircraft were essentially tools of reconnaissance. While these objections were annoying, Mitchell thought his greatest enemies were in the Navy, which seemed to take an even dimmer view of air power, though Mitchell believed that controlling land or sea was dependent on controlling the air. Mitchell knew that there were political difficulties as well: bomber aircraft that could fly beyond the battlefield and hit industrial targets in civilian areas could be regarded as immoral; he regarded such "total war" as inevitable but couched his arguments carefully. He was keen to illustrate the practical—and dramatic and inspiring—applications of air power, with cross-country flights that were expensive in pilots (because of fatal crashes), but which laid the routes for air mail and challenged aircraft companies to improve their designs and technology. Mitchell thought the stakes could not be higher: "There can no longer be any doubt that complete control of the air by any nation means military control of the world."[9]

Actually, there was some doubt about that—and the question burst into the public imagination in a terrific spectacle, a challenge: Mitchell said an aerial bomber could sink any vessel afloat. His view won enough support in Congress that the Navy was obliged to test his claims. Mitchell, at the time, had no trained bomber pilots.

Undaunted, he set up a pilot training program, had ordnance men design and build new bombs big enough to sink a battleship, slapped together a team of aerial cameramen to record the big event, and fought a relentless campaign for funds to keep his preparations going. The terms of the challenge were set by the Navy. The targets, captured German war ships, were put at the end of the bombers' range, the amount and type of ordnance they could drop was limited, and there would be pauses between bombing runs so that the vessels could be inspected. Navy pilots, who had a stake in the challenge, and Army pilots would fly on alternate runs. The first target was a U-boat, scheduled to be attacked by Navy planes on 21 June 1921. The naval airmen made short work of it. On 13 July, Mitchell's boys tore apart a German destroyer; and on 18 July the Navy, Marines, and Army took turns on a German light cruiser, which held up under the lighter bombing of the Navy but was sent below by Mitchell's big bombs.

The prize target was the presumed unsinkable German battleship *Ostfriesland*, which was attacked on 20 and 21 July. Her survival of the first day's attacks seemed to justify the Navy's confidence; Mitchell's unexpected sinking of her the next day stunned the Navy and convinced the admirals (and their supporting congressmen), as nothing else could, of the priority of building aircraft carriers. Mitchell was right. To control the seas, you had to control the air.

Still, many purported to be unconvinced. The Navy argued that if the *Ostfriesland* had had a crew, it could have patched the damage. A joint Army-Navy board, led by General Pershing, tried to take a balanced position, arguing on the one hand that battleships still ruled the waves and on the other hand that it was only prudent to invest in aircraft carriers and the rapid development of Army and Navy air power.

Mitchell had won a major victory for air power in the eyes of the public, but his enemies—the Navy, which he had antagonized, and the Army establishment, which distrusted opinionated, headline-seeking officers, especially for a service so unproven (in their opinion)—regarded him with eyes more gimlet than admiring. Mitchell politicked to be named Charles T. Menoher's successor as chief of the Air Service. It was a sign of his lack of clout in the Army that while he had the overwhelming support of his fellow airmen, he was nevertheless passed over for General Pershing's favorite, Major General Mason Patrick, who was promoted and given command on 5 October 1921. Patrick was regarded as a troubleshooter; Mitchell was regarded as the source of much of the trouble. Mitchell knew what to expect, as Pershing had appointed Patrick to ride herd on Mitchell during the war. Mitchell tried to reorganize the Air Service so that more power would be concentrated in his hands. Patrick rejected the proposal. Mitchell threatened to resign. Patrick called him on it and marched him over to General James Harbord, deputy chief of staff. Mitchell retracted his proposed resignation.

Patrick had his man pegged: Mitchell, he wrote, is "very likeable and has ability; his ego is highly developed and he has an undoubted love for the limelight; a desire to be in the public eye. He is forceful, aggressive, spectacular. He had a better knowledge of the tactics of air fighting than any man in this country....I think I understood quite well his characteristics, the good in him—and there was much of it—and his faults."[10]

Lieutenant Jimmy Doolittle—of later Doolittle Raid fame—remembered this about the deputy air chief: "I was Mitchell's aide for one day, and on that day, I've never moved as fast or covered as much country before or since. He was a veritable dynamo of energy. Everything he did, he did just as hard as he could."[11] Mitchell was no desk jockey: he flew, a skilled and daring pilot; he pressed constantly for improvements in every aspect of aircraft design—for bombing, for flying in bad weather—and knew engines like a doctor knows the human body; he inspected planes and ground crews frequently (sometimes passing out five-dollar bills for good work); he kept tabs on foreign air services; he read constantly (he had three pairs of reading glasses so that he was never without one); and he kept a rapid stream of recommendations flowing to General Patrick.

In December 1921, he embarked on a European tour. He found the French terrified of a resurgent Germany. Italy was full of technical geniuses but unlikely to build a significant air force. The Germans were disarmed but as militarist as ever, openly chafing under Allied restrictions on their military development. They remained a powerful, dynamic people, almost certain to absorb Austria and be a force in the center of Europe. When it came to aeronautics, Mitchell thought German engineers were the best in the world. He was also impressed by the airplane manufacturer Anthony Fokker of the Netherlands, who, during the war, had sold thousands of planes to the Germans after the Allies declined to buy them. In Britain, Mitchell renewed his friendship with Sir Hugh Trenchard. Mitchell rated British airmen among the best but thought the British were too conservative in aircraft design.

Mitchell's wife disliked his incessant working, flying, traveling, and alleged erratic behavior (linked in her mind to overwork and drinking), and when he returned from Europe the couple divorced; Mitchell bought a fast car that he drove at speed; and Mitchell's mother and his sister Harriet came to live with him until his mother's death in December 1922. He deferred to his mother (far more readily than he deferred to senior officers), and his sister enjoyed his parties, was impressed by his aura of celebrity, and despite the emotional toll of the divorce on him[12] thought he was tremendous fun to be around.

Mitchell was pessimistic about government support for the Air Service, especially after President Warren Harding's death in August 1923. That meant the elevation of Vice President Calvin Coolidge, whose campaign for government economy specifically targeted Billy Mitchell and military aviation. Mitchell angered the Navy again with more bombing tests—and pleased himself by taking a new bride, Betty Miller, a woman who shared his love of horses. They were married in October 1923.[13] Their honeymoon was combined with intelligence duty, taking them from San Francisco through Hawaii (whose defenses he thought outdated, an opinion that won him the lasting enmity of the Army's commander of the Hawaiian Department, General Charles P. Summerall), Guam,[14] the Philippines, Java, Singapore, India, Siam, China, Japan, and Korea.

COURT-MARTIAL

Mitchell's 1924 report of his findings is famous for its detailed prediction of a Japanese attack on Pearl Harbor and the Philippines. He thought that war between Japan and the United States, the two great powers of the Pacific, was inevitable. It would be an epic clash, a war not just of nations but of civilizations, with enormous consequences for the region's future.[15] Mitchell's prophetic report was dismissed by the Army as nothing more than propaganda for the Air Service. Indeed, for all his many talents, Mitchell was increasingly regarded by his superiors as erratic, flamboyant, impulsive, and opinionated, a difficult subordinate and a martinet to his men (though his junior officers were terrifically loyal to him). At the same time, because he was ever the star witness at congressional hearings on air power, and gave speeches and wrote articles on the topic, he was rarely out of the public eye. He continued to goad the Navy and annoy the Army by asserting that voices like his own were being silenced. Proving Mitchell's contention, Secretary of War John Weeks refused to reappoint Mitchell as assistant chief of the Air Service despite a recommendation from Air Service chief Mason Patrick. Losing the position meant a demotion in rank, to colonel; Mitchell was also denied his preferred posting (Chicago) and instead sent to Fort Sam Houston, Texas, where he took up his new duties in June 1925, after turning down an offer to run for Congress from Wisconsin. An article he wrote that summer ran with the headline, "Exploding Disarmament Bunk: Why Have Treaties about Battleships When Airplanes Can Destroy Them?" He would not go quietly into the Texas desert.

After two naval air disasters in September—a failed attempt to make the first flight from California to Hawaii, with one plane unable to take off, another crashing, and the third lost at sea (its crew was later rescued); and the crash of the Navy dirigible *Shenandoah* on an unnecessary overland flight in bad weather—Mitchell was besieged by the press demanding a statement. He gave them one, precise and deadly: "My opinion is as follows: These incidents are the direct result of the incompetency, criminal negligence and almost treasonable administration of the national defense by the Navy and War Departments."[16] That was the short of it. His full statement was a six-thousand-word elaboration of his summary indictment. It was also more than the War Department was prepared to tolerate.

Mitchell hoped it would be. He relished the chance for a hearing, even a court-martial, which would be the biggest platform yet for him to promote the future of air power. He got all that. He was called to testify to a presidential commission (dubbed "the Morrow Board" after its chairman, Dwight Morrow) investigating the state of American aviation—and read to its members at length from one of his books. A Navy court of inquiry into the crash of the *Shenandoah* requested his appearance. Most important, the Army announced it was going to put him before a court-martial in Washington.

The court-martial of Billy Mitchell was one of the most spectacular news events of the 1920s. Just as the War Department did everything it could to keep the court-martial from becoming a media circus, Mitchell's goal was to put his message on the front pages of the newspapers every day. He succeeded better than the War Department did.[17]

Not one of his judges was an airman, though a few (like Douglas MacArthur) were good friends, and three, including General Summerall, were dismissed after the defense argued they were prejudiced against Mitchell. The trial lasted seven weeks. Mitchell's defense centered initially on his First Amendment rights and then on the accuracy of his criticisms, which were supported by a litany of his fellow airmen, including "Hap" Arnold, future five-star General of the Air Force. Mitchell himself seemed glamorous, boyishly upbeat and enthusiastic, and certain he was getting a great national airing of his ideas and would emerge victorious. He was inundated with the cards and letters of supporters, the backing of veterans' groups, and editorials in support of his case by many (though certainly not all) newspapers. He was, however, inevitably found guilty of insubordination and sentenced to a five-year unpaid suspension from duty. The conviction was approved by President Coolidge on 26 January 1926, the sentence mitigated to reduce but not eliminate his pay. Mitchell's response was to resign, effective 1 February; his resignation was accepted by the president; and so ended the court-martial and Army career of Billy Mitchell.

Far from allowing his conviction to silence him, he immediately embarked on a speaking tour to highlight the need for America to pursue a rapid development of air power for its national defense. He was urged to run as a Republican for a senate seat from Wisconsin but didn't think much of his chances and declined. He wrote articles. To supplement his speaking and writing fees, he bred horses at his retreat in Middleburg, Virginia. After a flurry of activity, however, interest in his speeches, articles, and books waned, and he dedicated himself to his rural equestrian pursuits. His health, unfortunately, declined swiftly. Heart disease was the cause, and a bad case of the flu finished him off on 19 February 1936. Ten years later, on 8 August 1946, he was awarded a posthumous Congressional Gold Medal. Mitchell, who was proud of his medals, would probably have laughed.

CHAPTER TWELVE

JOHN A. LEJEUNE
(1867–1942)

John Archer Lejeune was born in Louisiana, the son of a planter whose prosperity and land were gone with the wind after the War Between the States. Nevertheless, Ovide Lejeune, whose family had emigrated from Canada to Louisiana in the eighteenth century, and his wife, the former Laura Archer Turpin, a descendant of Huguenot immigrants, made their son's education a priority. At the age of fourteen, John Lejeune was sent as a military cadet to Louisiana State University, which ran a college preparatory program. His curriculum was classical (this was Lejeune's choice; the other options were agricultural or mechanical curricula), and he was enrolled for three years, which was all his family could afford.

Lejeune needed a free education, and that meant one of the service academies. His first choice was West Point, but the only slot open was at the Naval Academy. He won a recommendation for an appointment from his senator, crammed for the difficult entrance exams, and entered the Naval Academy in the summer of 1884. Lejeune did well academically, though he had to work hard, particularly at mathematics. He did far less well when it came to small infractions of discipline, such as smoking outside of allowed times and places. He was, indeed, a great ignorer of regulations, but was proud of the rigors of the school. On the other hand, he was not at all impressed by the moral tone of his fellow naval cadets. Perhaps he needn't have worried about them, as year by year the chaff—in the form of fellow students who failed academically or amassed even more demerits than Lejeune—was winnowed out. Of the ninety cadets of his class, only thirty-two made it through all four years. Lejeune graduated second in his class academically, thirteenth overall.

Next came two years as a midshipman.[1] Lejeune was reluctant about his looming naval career, but his father encouraged him, and in 1889 Lejeune gained a brief taste of adventure as he was assigned to a sloop sent to Samoa as part of a show of force to keep the Germans from annexing the islands. There was no fighting, but his ship was wrecked in a storm.

THE MARINES

Lejeune was regarded as no better than a middling midshipman, but when he returned to Annapolis for his final examinations, he placed sixth, high enough to earn him a recommendation to the naval engineers. Lejeune, however, had a different career path in mind. He wanted to be a Marine. He protested his assignment all the way to

Washington, DC, where a naval officer told him, "Frankly, Mister Lejeune, you have altogether too many brains to be lost in the Marine Corps."[2] Lejeune repeated this comment to the commandant of the Marine Corps, who then specifically requested that Lejeune be commissioned in the Marines; and so it was that one Marine Corps commandant, Charles G. McCawley, ensured the career path of a future Marine Corps commandant.

The *Army-Navy Journal* took a typically dismissive attitude toward the Marine Corps of the time, saying of it, in 1886, "The Marine Corps is the oldest, the smallest, the best uniformed and equipped and most artistically drilled branch of the fighting wing of the government."[3] Its officers were regarded as overpaid, underworked rejects from the Army and the Navy. Indeed, critics claimed the Marines' initials, USMC, stood for "Useless Sons Made Comfortable." The Marines, it was said, had antiquated duties (guarding ships) and a body of enlisted men scraped together from seafaring immigrant toughs with nothing better to do. This was changing, though, under pressure from Commandant McCawley, the Navy, and Congress, including a provision in the August 1882 Navy appropriations bill that Marine officers be Naval Academy graduates.[4]

Assigned to duty in Portsmouth, Virginia, Lejeune met a judge's daughter, Ellie Harrison Murdaugh, and after a prolonged courtship married her in 1895. The courtship was prolonged because Ellie was popular with young men and because Lejeune's pursuit of her was interrupted by sea duty. He found sea duty dull and was marked down as an indifferent officer, and while marriage and family spurred him to improve his standing in the Corps, he was melancholy during his long separations from home.

In the Spanish-American War, he saw slight action in Cuba and Puerto Rico. Rather more exciting for him was landing in Colombia in November 1903, de facto on the side of the Panamanian rebels, but with the official purpose of guarding American transit rights across the isthmus. Lejeune's detachment sailed home in December 1904, and Lejeune was made commander of the Marine Barracks in Washington, DC. He served there for a year and a half before leading a battalion back to Panama, where he contracted malaria. In 1907, he was off to the Philippines. Unlike every other Marine officer at Cavite, Lejeune brought his family—his wife and three young daughters—with him. Family life, morality, and religion (he was an Episcopalian) were central to his character, and he was determined to be as little separated from his wife and children as his career would allow; indeed, he regarded them as more important; his career was a mere irksome necessity, though he did become the Marines' brigade commander in the Philippines.

He was ordered home in 1909, promoted to lieutenant colonel, and given the opportunity to attend the Army War College, where he excelled, catching the eye of future senior Army officers. In November 1910 he took command of the Marine Barracks in Brooklyn, New York; in 1912 he led a Marine peacekeeping force ashore in Cuba; and in 1914 he commanded the Marines occupying Vera Cruz. Colonel Lejeune returned home to become assistant to the commandant of the Marine Corps, Major General George Barnett, and in 1916 was promoted to brigadier general.

The Marine Corps had been slowly expanding even before World War I to meet the need for small expeditionary forces that could be deployed around the globe, but especially on extended constabulary deployments in the Caribbean and Latin America. With the declaration of war on Germany in April 1917, the Marines were eager to be in on the action—one of their recruiting slogans during the war was "First to Fight"—and through deft political maneuvering the 5th Marine

Regiment sailed off with the American Expeditionary Force in June. Lejeune was not with them, but he was pressing for a command. In September 1917, he became commander at Quantico, supervising Marines training for combat service.

"THE DIVINE SPARK IN MEN"

In May 1918 he finally got his orders for France, arriving in-country a month later. His goal was to create a Marine division, though this was opposed by General Pershing, who wrote to Secretary of War Newton Baker, "While the Marines are splendid troops, their use as a separate division is inadvisable."[5] The Marines got wonderful press, which irked the Army, and if Pershing had his druthers, the Marines would be kept guarding ports and acting as auxiliary military police. If Pershing was worried about uniformity of training, formations, and equipment, there was every reason to form a Marine fighting division, but even Lejeune had to concede, in due course, that "Headquarters could scarcely provide [Marine] infantry replacements for the Fourth Brigade—impossible for an entire division."[6]

In July, Pershing appointed Lejeune commander of the Marine 4th Brigade. Lejeune was ecstatic; it was the 4th that had won such renown at Belleau Wood. No sooner had he been made brigade commander than a shakeup of assignments put Lejeune in command of the 2nd Division of the American Expeditionary Force, which included the Marine 4th Brigade as half its infantry strength. Promoted to major general, he was the first Marine officer to command a division.[7] Lejeune's division fought at Saint-Mihiel and with heavy casualties seized the heights of Mont Blanc. Though he chafed under the bellicose leadership of his corps commander during the final push of the war— General Charles Summerall, commander of V Corps—Lejeune was proud of the fighting spirit of the 2nd Division, which simply would not be stopped, advancing by day and by night, as it battled against the retreating Germans. The war ended with Lejeune's 2nd Division having just crossed the Meuse.

The Marines as a whole took more than 50 percent casualties in the war. Lejeune, totting up his losses but proud of his division's victories, wrote, "While war is terribly destructive, monstrously cruel, and horrible beyond expression, it nevertheless causes the divine spark in men to glow, to kindle, and to burst into living flame, and enables them to attain heights of devotion to duty, sheer heroism, and sublime unselfishness that in all probability they would never have reached in the prosecution of peaceful pursuits."[8]

Lejeune's Army superiors were of mixed opinions about him. They could not deny the success of the 2nd Division—it gained more ground than any other—but some found him too independent-minded and too ready to question orders, and held suspect Lejeune's style of leading men rather than driving them. Still, Pershing kept him on. The 2nd Division was not pulled out of the line and sent home; instead, it was assigned to occupation duty in Germany until late summer 1919.

In October, Lejeune took command at Quantico. He had three immediate objectives: to rebuild the base, which had taken a beating during the rush to train Marines for the war; to provide vocational training for the enlisted men so that service in the Marines was not a dead end; and to turn Quantico into a center for advancing the education of Marine officers.

COMMANDANT

He wasn't at Quantico long. Secretary of the Navy Josephus Daniels had long had his eye on Lejeune as a future commandant of the

Marine Corps, and in 1920 Daniels ousted the sitting commandant, General George Barnett, and put Lejeune in his place. Like the leaders of the other services, Lejeune had to find a way to stave off draconian congressional budget cuts. Marines were still quick-fix troops whenever there was trouble overseas, from Nicaragua to China, but to keep the Corps in the public eye, Lejeune pitted Marine athletic squads against college teams and put Marines in the forefront of Civil War reenactments. He renewed the traditional Marine training emphasis on marksmanship, and his publicity campaign received a boost when President Harding asked the secretary of the Navy to assign Marines to guard railway mail cars. These had suffered a spate of robberies, and the Navy secretary's order to the Marines could only bolster their public image: "If attacked, shoot, and shoot to kill. The mail must be delivered or there must be a Marine dead at the post of duty."[9]

Lejeune proved himself a deft administrator, doing much with the small budget Congress allotted him, including keeping Marine Corps aviation alive and laying the intellectual groundwork for the Marine Corps of the future—as an amphibious assault force. Stark reductions in manpower, which left the Marines barely able to fulfill their current duties (two-thirds of them were at sea or on overseas assignments), made planning for amphibious warfare, on a far larger scale than Marine Corps police actions, seem visionary.

With Marine Corps strength slipping beneath twenty thousand men, Lejeune economized by closing recruiting stations, raising recruiting standards (with few slots open, the Marines could be choosy), and extending enlistments to keep trained men a year longer. In 1925, Lejeune was reappointed as commandant for a second four-year term, and he likely could have been reappointed to a third term had he not tendered his resignation, effective the day after Herbert Hoover was inaugurated president in March 1929.

LEADERSHIP AS A MORAL CALLING

Though Lejeune had not planned it this way, he was offered the perfect position for a general so dedicated to improving the education of his officers and enlisted men. The superintendent of the Virginia Military Institute was retiring. The VMI Board of Visitors presented the job to Lejeune, who accepted it gratefully. Using his connections in Washington, Lejeune embarked on a major refurbishment and expansion of the school, which received a massive influx of dollars from Washington in the 1930s. President Franklin Roosevelt, a former assistant secretary of the Navy, was a friend, and construction projects were part of the administration's recovery program from the Depression. VMI, under Lejeune's leadership, was a beneficiary.

Lejeune's devotion to the school, however, nearly killed him. Inspecting a newly built water tower in September 1932, he fell, cracked his skull, broke an arm, and was unconscious for days. Before the accident he had been an inspiring speaker. After, he could speak only from prepared remarks, which he read ploddingly. He nevertheless recovered well enough to continue to lead the school until October 1937.

The former commandant and superintendent retired to Norfolk, Virginia. When Hitler and Stalin parceled Poland between them in 1939, Lejeune sensed war was near and offered to come out of retirement to lead Marines. The commandant of the Marine Corps, General Thomas Holcomb, politely declined his offer, though in 1942 Lejeune received a post-retirement promotion to lieutenant general. The only other Marine to hold that rank at that time was Holcomb himself, promoted by Roosevelt slightly earlier in 1942.

Lejeune died in November 1942, from prostate cancer. His doctors had long advised him to have his prostate removed, and he had long denied them the honor, trusting that horseback riding and, later, golfing would keep him healthy. Before he died, he had the pleasure of seeing a grandson, a Naval Academy graduate, class of 1939, commissioned into the Marine Corps.

Though he looked like an old boot—naturally, perhaps, for a general of leathernecks—it might strike some as ironic that one of the most famous commandants of the Corps was a teetotal, highly religious Episcopalian whose idea of a good time was Sunday dinner with his family. But it shouldn't. Lejeune—the general whose name is remembered on halls at the Naval Academy, VMI, LSU, and the Marine base at Quantico, not to mention Camp Lejeune in North Carolina—believed that leadership was a moral calling. He believed in leading by example. He wanted the example he set to be a good one—and as evidenced by the honor of Marines ever since, and the continued affection and esteem of his fellow Devil Dogs, it was.

PART IV

THE YOUNG LIONS

CHAPTER THIRTEEN

GEORGE S. PATTON (1885–1945)

Patton's paternal line was Virginian—Confederate, martial, gentlemanly. His father, a VMI graduate (as was his grandfather), was a lawyer and occasional district attorney in Los Angeles, where his family had moved after the War Between the States. His mother was from Southern California—well-to-do and well educated, a Western aristocrat with a pioneer father, a family ranch, and the conservative politics that typified much of Southern California for the next hundred years. Patton and his younger sister grew up at his mother's family ranch, fishing, shooting, riding, and playing soldier.

Patton had doting parents and a happy childhood, and he did some of his schooling at home because he was dyslexic. Though reading was consequently difficult for him, memorizing poetry was not—and Patton committed to memory swathes of the Bible, Shakespeare, and Kipling. He relished tales of heroism (usually read to him), be they Norse legends or the chivalric novels of Sir Walter Scott, or better yet, familial stories about the Pattons (seven Patton brothers had served as Confederate officers, and both bloodlines, originally from Scotland, counted patriot veterans of the Revolutionary War).

THE CADET

The young Patton regarded himself as part of a noble class for whom character, including courage, was everything. He could not let his ancestors down. He was already determined to be an officer; his most avid reading at school was in military history, learning lessons he intended to apply in his own life.

The first goal was West Point, but he didn't go directly; he enrolled at the Patton family alma mater, VMI, spending a year there as preparation. At VMI, Patton took the same uniform size as his father and grandfather, and the handsome, blond, blue-eyed, consciously stern-visaged young man applied himself rigorously to his duties. He made a near-perfect cadet and thrived at VMI. But the goal was still West Point. Patton's father had lobbied Thomas Bard, U.S. senator from California, for an appointment. The Republican lawmaker invited Patton to return to Los Angeles and sit an examination with other candidates. Three passed, and Patton was the one selected.

He found the cadets at West Point, on the whole, socially inferior to the cadets at VMI—not all of them were Southerners, after all. Still, his dyslexia meant he had to study harder than most; he was no languid aristocrat but a striver, fearful of failure, eager to be a master of his profession. He needed steely self-discipline to get through his books, exams, and written presentations that meant standing before a class and writing on a blackboard, trying desperately not to misspell words. Dyslexia was not a recognized diagnosis in those days, and Patton felt it only as a great vulnerability: he thought he was smarter than many of his classmates but had to wonder if he was somehow stupid given how much more effort it took him to succeed. He had to repeat his first academic year at the Point.

He took to keeping a notebook. Its first entry: "Do your damdest [sic] always." He wrote that he was determined to be a great man, a great soldier: "I am different from other men my age. All they want to do is to live happily and die old. I would be willing to live in torture, die tomorrow if for one day I could be realy [sic] great."[1] There was no failure, he thought, in dying in battle—but the battle must be won. Every attack—and a commanding officer should always be on the attack—must be all in, because "the world has no use for a defeated soldier."[2]

He made lists of books—military histories—that he thought he needed for his professional education, and he read them.

> In order for a man to become a great soldier...it is necessary for him to be so thoroughly conversant with all sorts of military possibilities that when ever an occasion arises he has at hand with out effort on his part a parallel. To attain this end...it is necessary...to read military history in its earliest and hence crudest form and to follow it down in natural sequence permitting his mind to grow with his subject until he can grasp with out effort the most abstruce

[*sic*] question of the science of war, because he is already permiated [*sic*] with all its elements.[3]

For all his academic struggles, he was an educated soldier, a lifelong student of military history.

When not reading or studying or performing the other duties of a cadet, he was training his body through athletics. He played football, but an injury cost him his spot on the team. He ran track (setting an Academy record in the hurdles), fenced, rode horses, and was a marksman with pistol and rifle. He tested himself in other ways too. Once, he stood up in the pits where cadets raised and lowered targets for rifle practice. He wanted to see what it was like to get shot at, to reassure himself of his courage. He was lucky the cadets were on-target.

THE CAVALRY

Patton benefited from having six years of formal military education. He graduated at twenty-four, accepting a commission in the cavalry and duty at Fort Sheridan, Illinois. He liked the men, considered his commanding officer a true gentleman, but had doubts about some of the other officers, especially those who had come up from the ranks. In 1910, he was married to Beatrice Ayer, a family friend he had long courted. She, though Patton paid scant attention to this, came from a wealthy family. It wasn't money that mattered to him, but the fact that she was poised, pretty, and polished (she had been educated in Europe, spoke French, as did he, and played the piano). He credited her strength of character with strengthening his own. She also helped his spelling, as he now took to writing articles on military subjects (as well as riding to hounds, playing polo, and other recreational endeavors appropriate for an officer and a gentleman). She bore him two daughters and a son.

At the end of 1911, he was transferred to Fort Myer, Virginia, where many senior officers lived, making it a prime duty post for an ambitious cavalryman. But aside from his ardor for his duties and his active social life with the right sort of people, Patton was starting to make his mark as an athlete—indeed, in 1912 he represented the United States at the Olympics, competing in the modern pentathlon, which tested a competitor's equestrian skills with a steeplechase, marksmanship with a pistol, fencing, swimming three hundred yards, and running cross country two and a half miles. The event reflected the actions that might be required of an officer delivering military dispatches. He came in fifth.

Back home, he wrote an article that led to the 1913 redesign of the U.S. Cavalry saber. In the fall of 1913, he was sent to the Cavalry School at Fort Riley, Kansas, where he was to be both student and instructor, serving as "Master of the Sword." At his own expense, he went to France to hone his swordsmanship before taking up his new post. When war erupted in France in 1914, Patton wanted to take up the sword in earnest, fighting in the French army. He wrote to General Leonard Wood asking for his advice and assistance. Wood replied, "We don't want to waste youngsters of your sort in the service of foreign nations....I know how you feel, but there is nothing to be done."[4] Patton, like a young Napoleon, had ambitiously hoped to be a brigadier general by twenty-seven. At twenty-nine, he was not yet a first lieutenant.

Ambitions thwarted, his thirst for action still would not be denied. In 1915, he was sent to Fort Bliss, Texas, where the cavalry troops were all turned out in "Patton swords": "It was a fine sight all with sabers drawn and all my sabers. It gives you a thrill and my eyes filled with tears...it is the call of ones [sic] ancestors and the glory of combat. It seems to me that at the head of a regiment of cavalry any thing would be possible."[5] What seemed immediately possible, or so Patton hoped, was war in Mexico that would involve the United States. When, in 1916, General Pershing was ordered to lead a punitive expedition into Mexico, Patton's regiment—and Patton—were to stay behind in Texas. But Patton would have none of this. He convinced General Pershing that he should serve him as his aide. He was zealous in his duties and got the action he sought. Leading an expedition of three cars and ten men whose mission was to buy corn for the soldiers in camp, he organized an impromptu raid that netted him one of Pancho Villa's officers and two banditos shot down in a gunfight—Patton armed with revolver and rifle. Patton and his men returned to camp with the corpses of the Villaists strapped over the hoods of their cars. He was promoted to first lieutenant.

He came away from his experience in Mexico full of admiration for—and a desire to emulate—Pershing. Under Pershing's command, "Every horse and man was fit; weaklings had gone; baggage was still at the minimum, and discipline was perfect....By constant study General Pershing knew to the minutest detail each of the subjects in which he demanded practice, and by physical presence and personal example and explanation, insured himself that they were correctly carried out."[6]

Patton followed Pershing to France as his aide. It was in this capacity that Patton met Field Marshal Haig. Haig, who didn't think much of most American officers, liked Patton, calling him "a fire-eater" who "longs for the fray." Patton, in turn, liked Haig, a fellow cavalryman, thinking him a proper polo-playing gentleman and even "more of a charger than I am."[7]

THE TANK CORPS

Patton wanted combat and knew he couldn't find it as a staff officer to Pershing; to see action he had to either lead infantry or train to become a tank officer. He chose the latter, thinking it the quickest way to combat and further promotion. He wrote to Pershing, reminding him that he was "the only American who has ever made an attack in a motor vehicle"[8] (he was referring to the motorized ambush he had led in Mexico), that his fluency in French meant he could read French tank manuals and converse with and take instruction from French tank officers, that he was good with engines, and that as tanks were the new cavalry it was an appropriate branch for a cavalry officer like himself. Privately, he noted to his father, "There will be hundred[s] of Majors of Infantry but only one of Light T[anks]." He had his progress mapped out: "1st. I will run the school. 2. then they will organize a battalion and I will command it. 3. Then if I make good and the T. do and the war lasts I will get the first regiment. 4. With the same 'IF' as before they will make a brigade and I will get the star"[9] (of a brigadier general).

It worked out more or less that way, with Patton the first officer—or soldier of any rank in the United States Army—assigned to the Tank Corps, where he was charged with establishing the First Army Tank School. Before he did that, Patton gave himself a crash course in French tanks, which included test-driving them, firing their guns, and even walking the assembly line to see how they were made. He used that experience to write a masterly summary of everything one needed to know about tanks.

His new commander in the Tank Corps, as of December 1917, would be Colonel Samuel D. Rockenbach, a VMI graduate with an aristocratic wife, a taskmasterly way with subordinates, and the massive responsibility of creating the Tank Corps from scratch, including acquiring tanks from the French and the British. When it came to men, Patton intended that the Tanks Corps' standards of discipline and deportment would exceed those of other American units, and he made a special point of looking after his men, ensuring they were given the best food and billets he could muster.

Patton's efficiency as a tank commander won him promotion to lieutenant colonel, but he worried the war would end before he had a chance to lead his tankers in combat. That chance came at Saint-Mihiel on 12 September 1918. Unsurprisingly, he didn't stay at his command post but roamed the field under fire, directing attacks; his tankers did well and showed plenty of fighting spirit.

He had been chastised for leaving his command post during the battle at Saint-Mihiel, but he did the same during the Meuse-Argonne Offensive. He followed his tanks into combat, even helping to dig a path for them through two trenches (and whacking a recalcitrant soldier over the head with a shovel). While attempting to lead a unit of pinned-down infantry against the Germans,[10] he was shot through the leg but continued to direct the attack. He wrote to his wife from his hospital bed on 12 October 1918, saying, "Peace looks possible, but I rather hope not for I would like to have a few more fights. They are awfully thrilling like steeple chasing only more so."[11] He was promoted to colonel. The Armistice came on his thirty-third birthday. All in all, Patton had had a quite satisfactory war.

Peace was another matter. There was no glory in it and no chance for him to achieve the greatness he sought. Polo was his substitute.[12] He studied military history, as well as the last war and current developments. He formulated his own views in articles, including his conclusion that "Tanks are not motorized cavalry; *they are tanks, a new auxiliary arm* whose purpose is ever and always to facilitate the advance of the master arm, the Infantry, on the field of battle."[13]

Before the next great war he amended that view, recognizing that tanks could be an offensive force of their own.

On 1 October 1919, Patton gave a speech to the Tank Corps on "The Obligation of Being an Officer." It touched on Patton's grand view of the profession of arms: "Does it not occur to you gentlemen that we...are also the modern representatives of the demigods and heroes of antiquity?...In the days of chivalry, the golden age of our profession, knights (officers) were noted as well for courtesy and being gentle benefactors of the weak and oppressed....Let us be gentle. That is courteous and considerate for the rights of others. Let us be men. That is fearless and untiring in doing our duty as we see it."[14] Patton concluded with a list of recommendations for good behavior and decorum, essentially acting as Colonel Manners. Patton could, famously and frequently, swear up a storm.[15] But he was nevertheless punctilious about gentlemanly conduct.

When the Tank Corps was assigned to the infantry, Patton rejoined the cavalry. His wartime rank of colonel was reduced to captain, though he was swiftly promoted to major, and he was assigned to Fort Myer. In 1923, he was sent to the cavalry field officers course at Fort Riley, Kansas, and then on to the Command and Staff College at Fort Leavenworth. His previous studies helped him excel here and earned him staff officer posts in Boston, Hawaii, and Washington, DC; enrollment at the Army War College; and his eventual return to Fort Myer in 1932, where he had the "most distasteful" service of dispersing the bonus marchers.[16]

In 1935, now a lieutenant colonel, he sailed his yacht from California across the Pacific to take up a new post as director of intelligence for the Hawaiian Department. He returned stateside in 1937, and while on leave suffered a serious horseback-riding accident, breaking a leg, and leaving him bedridden for months with complications; it was even feared it might end his active service in the Army. He became an instructor at Fort Riley and worked diligently to regain full use of his leg; when he did, in 1938, he was sent to Fort Clark, Texas, to command the 1st Cavalry Division as a colonel.

But just as he was thrilled to be training a division for combat, he was recalled to Fort Myer, which required officers of means, like Patton, who could afford to keep up the social obligations of the post. The posting had the compensation of reuniting Patton with his fellow veteran of the Great War George Marshall. In 1940 Marshall, as Army chief of staff, recommended him for promotion to brigadier general and assignment to the 2nd Armored Division. Patton was back in tanks and began earnestly preparing for the next great war.

"AMERICANS DO NOT SURRENDER"

He relished training troops because he believed it was men—not weapons—that were decisive in war and that the crucial factor in making a good soldier was providing him with good leadership. Patton was certain he could do that. He was an active, encouraging officer and imparted his knowledge of war with morale-raising gusto. In 1941, he became a major general. After Pearl Harbor he was made commander of the I Armored Corps, and in February 1942 was ordered to the California desert to train for fighting in North Africa against German General (later Field Marshal) Erwin Rommel.

As good as he was at training men, Patton inevitably wanted to lead them into action. ("All my life I have wanted to lead a lot of men in a desperate battle,"[17] he later wrote his brother-in-law.) When President Roosevelt gave orders for Operation Torch, the

American invasion of French North Africa, Patton was given his chance. In early November, as the transport ships neared Morocco, Patton issued an order to his troops to "remember your training, and remember above all that speed and vigor of attack are the sure roads to success and you must succeed—for to retreat is as cowardly as it is fatal. Indeed, once landed, retreat is impossible. Americans do not surrender.... A pint of sweat will save gallons of blood.... God is with us.... We shall surely win."[18] They surely did. The Vichy French resistance had been spirited, but on 11 November, as Patton was about to launch his attack on Casablanca, they surrendered. Patton liked the French, and left the administration of Morocco largely in their hands.

It wasn't until March 1943 that Patton was called into action again—this time in Tunisia, as commander of II Corps after Rommel had mauled American units in the Kasserine Pass (among those taken prisoner was one of Patton's sons-in-law, the West Point–educated John Waters). In the ten days before going into action again, he gave II Corps the Patton treatment, requiring spit and polish and an aggressive attitude, even urinating in one commander's foxhole to show his contempt for going on the defensive. That commander, General Terry Allen, led the II Corps' 1st Infantry Division to victory a few days later, at Gafsa and El Guettar. Patton was promoted, shortly before the attack, to lieutenant general.

Next up for Patton was the invasion of Sicily as commander of the United States Seventh Army. In stiff fighting Patton's men took their beaches, seized Palermo (netting fifty thousand captured Axis soldiers; one hundred thousand by the end of the Sicily campaign), and won the race against British Field Marshal Bernard Montgomery's Eighth Army to seize the prize of Messina, which Patton entered, the victor, on the morning of 17 August 1943. If there were any doubts, since the Battle at Kasserine Pass, about the efficiency and fighting spirit of the American Army, Patton had dispelled them.

Patton's success and flamboyance had made him one of the most publicized and celebrated generals in the United States. But his slapping of two nerve-addled soldiers, in separate incidents in August 1943, when he was visiting wounded GIs (always an emotional experience for him), cost him the full confidence of his commander, General Dwight Eisenhower. Eisenhower was frank with journalists about the incidents but equally frank about how it wouldn't help the war effort if reporters publicized them and cost Eisenhower one of his best fighting generals. The reporters agreed, and Patton made a round of apologies to his men at large and to the soldiers he had slapped. As he waited for his next assignment, he sat in a metaphorical doghouse. The press's silence on the slapping incidents was broken in November 1943. Patton, amid the clamor of the press and public, was unrepentant, telling Secretary of War Henry Stimson, "I love and admire good soldiers and brave men. I hate and despise slackers and cowards."[19] He had no fear of reporters or public opinion, because his motives were pure and he was certain setbacks were temporary; in the end God would protect him and guide him to what he had to do.

"FARTHER AND FASTER THAN ANY ARMY IN THE HISTORY OF WAR"

For the nonce, Patton was kept occupied moving around Europe, his presence a feint to keep the Germans guessing where the United States might deploy its most successful general. In reality, Eisenhower had made no decision to deploy him at all, bypassing him for command of American forces in Italy (which went to General Mark Clark) and in Britain (which went to General Omar Bradley). What Eisenhower eventually had in mind for Patton, in January 1944, was to command the Third Army. After the Allies had stormed and secured the beaches at Normandy, Patton—under the eminently stable and trustworthy 12th Army Group commander General Omar Bradley—would be the tiger unleashed to drive the Germans out of France. Patton took the Third Army and formed it in the Patton style with deportment, drill, duty, and discipline. His officers were taught to encourage their men; to lead from the front; to keep plans aggressive, simple, and direct; to be ready to seize opportunities; and always to kill the enemy in big bleeding bunches. With Confederate General Nathan Bedford Forrest, Patton believed that war means fighting and fighting means killing; and an officer should make damn sure that it is the enemy that does the dying. He treated his officers as the gentlemen he expected them to be and spoke to the men as the profane, no-nonsense man of war he knew inspired confidence: a foul-mouthed, jocular but intimidating coach to fire up their fighting spirit.

At the end of July 1944, nearly two months after the Allied invasion of France, General Patton charged into battle, liberating Avranches, Normandy, from the Germans and then leading the breakout into Brittany and toward the Seine and Loire Rivers. In a 14 August diary entry, Patton noted, "In exactly two weeks the Third Army has advanced farther and faster than any Army in the history of war." His strategy was simple: *"L'audace, l'audace, toujours l'audace."*[20] By the end of the month, the Third Army was stalled, not because of lack of aggression or success, but from a lack of gasoline, which could not reach it swiftly enough from the supply depots. Patton believed he was only two days from plunging into

Germany, but Eisenhower gave priority to supplying Montgomery's advance toward Antwerp and the Rhine. On 8 September 1944, Patton wrote to his wife, "God deliver us from our friends. We can handle the enemy."[21] As German resistance to Patton's drive intensified after he crossed the Moselle River, the general told reporters, "Whenever you slow anything down, you waste human lives."[22]

But optimism was growing that the Germans were near defeat. One prominent doubter was Patton, who expected, when few others did, the December 1944 counteroffensive that became known as the Battle of the Bulge; and it was Patton who swiftly delivered—in an extraordinary shift of direction on snow- and ice-slicked roads— three divisions at lightning speed to break the German attack and rescue the 101st Airborne Division surrounded at Bastogne.[23] Patton judged the relief of Bastogne as "the most brilliant operation we have thus far performed and is in my opinion the outstanding achievement of this war."[24]

In March 1945, he courted controversy again when he sent a detachment of about three hundred soldiers on a daring mission behind enemy lines to liberate American prisoners of war from a camp in Germany, among whom there might be—he wasn't sure— his son-in-law, John Waters. The mission almost succeeded, but its failure led to press criticism that he had risked men's lives for the sake of his son-in-law—an accusation that roused Patton's contempt. If the liberation of the American prisoners had temporarily failed, Patton's Third Army nevertheless rounded up more German prisoners of war than any other—nearly a million men—and was the first to break open a concentration camp.[25] At Buchenwald, another concentration camp liberated by the Third Army, Patton was physically sick. "Honestly," he wrote his wife, "words are inadequate to express the horror of those institutions."[26]

Patton gloried in war but was nevertheless appalled by aspects of this one—the concentration camps; the Allied bombing of German civilians in their cities; the fact that Eisenhower was content to let the Communist Russians into Berlin. Patton was promoted to full general in April 1945. His armies entered Czechoslovakia, but, at Eisenhower's orders, were not allowed to liberate Prague. On 9 May 1945, the war in Europe ended with Germany's unconditional surrender.

Patton wanted a transfer to the Pacific war, and when that looked unlikely, dreamt of fighting the Russians, his putative allies, perhaps with the assistance of the Germans, his recent enemies, whom he considered excellent soldiers and whose people he quickly came to admire (the horrors of the concentration camps aside). As a peacetime administrator of part of Bavaria, he ruled with a lenient hand and thought the United States should look to reconcile with the Germans, not punish them further. He opposed denazification. He thought most Nazi Party members were not ideologues but had merely joined the party because they felt it was necessary.[27] They were needed now for efficient administration; to dismiss them would only increase the suffering of the German people. He opposed the prosecution of Nazi war criminals, which appeared to him as vindictive victor's justice, or, in his own words, "not cricket."[28]

He also expected his death—not because of ill health, but because he had a premonition that this was his fate, and odd occurrences (a Polish Spitfire pilot firing on his plane, a near fatal collision with an ox cart, a traffic accident) seemed to underline it. Especially after Japan's surrender, Patton believed he had outlived his usefulness. His duty was done, and his days therefore numbered. In October, he left the Third Army. His new assignment was command of the Fifteenth Army, which was not really an army at all, but a unit formed in Bad Nauheim to gather documents to write a history of the European war.

On 9 December 1945, an Army truck collided with Patton's car, leaving him with paralyzing, and eventually fatal, injuries. He died on 21 December 1945. In 1943, Patton had spoken at an Armistice Day service honoring American dead, saying, "I consider it no sacrifice to die for my country. In my mind we came here to thank God that men like these have lived rather than to regret that they have died."[29] These are words that apply most dramatically to the life of General George S. Patton.

CHAPTER FOURTEEN

GEORGE C. MARSHALL (1880–1959)

M arshall was born in Pennsylvania and his father hailed from Kentucky, but most of his bloodlines were Virginian, dating back to the colonial era. John Marshall, the fourth chief justice of the United States, was a distant cousin. His family was Episcopalian and prosperous, though a bad investment by his father made for tighter economic circumstances by the time young George reached the age of ten. His upbringing was small town; his pleasures largely rural; his terrors academic, for he was an outdoorsy boy, did not like to study, and entered public school at the age of nine humiliatingly unprepared by his previous tutors: his one good subject, as befitted his proud Virginian blood, was history.

Against his parents' wishes, Marshall wanted a military career. His path to that goal would not pass through West Point. His father doubted he had the smarts, and his father's politics—he was a conservative Democrat in a Republican state—did not look promising for winning a congressional appointment. Marshall's elder brother had gone to the Virginia Military Institute, as had earlier Marshalls, and though VMI graduates were not, at that time, guaranteed commissions, he decided that would be his route. His brother's and father's doubts about his intellectual capacity (his brother said that if he went to VMI he would disgrace the Marshall name), and his mother's self-sacrificing generosity (she sold two family properties to pay for his tuition), made him determined to succeed.

Academically, he passed muster, managing to stay in the top half of his class. Where he excelled was in military training and leadership, graduating as first captain, the highest-ranking cadet. Tall but light, he also played on the football team his senior year, and, almost as important, he met the woman who would become his wife, Elizabeth "Lily" Carter Coles, whose Virginia bloodlines matched his own, though her people had never left the state or descended into trade (she was a doctor's daughter; Marshall's father was a businessman).

"A MAN WHO WAS GOING TO BE
CHIEF OF STAFF OF THE ARMY ONE DAY"

Bearing a recommendation from the superintendent at VMI and from New York senator John Wise (a native Virginian, VMI graduate, and Republican ally of President William McKinley), Marshall strode into President McKinley's office without an appointment (covertly attaching himself to a father and daughter who had one) and strode out with an invitation to sit the examination to become an officer in the United States Army. He received his commission in January 1903, married in February, and reported for duty at Fort Myer with orders to join the 30th Infantry in the Philippines. Before the end of the year, he was back stateside, if not yet reunited with his wife, whose health was considered too fragile for the Philippines and, at least initially, for the Oklahoma Territory. He was stationed at Fort Reno. It was here, of all places, Marshall endured "the hardest service I ever had in the army,"[1] mapping the southwestern desert of Texas. The expedition, launched in the scorching heat of June 1905 and lasting until the end of August, left him sunburnt and thirty-five pounds lighter than when he started.

The formerly less-than-studious Marshall applied to the Infantry and Cavalry School (or Army School of the Line, as it was soon to be called) at Fort Leavenworth, hoping that additional training would advance his prospects for promotion. He aced the qualifying examination, and in August 1906 entered the school. No student worked harder than Marshall. In 1907, he was promoted first lieutenant and finished his first academic year at Leavenworth at the top of his class. After his second year, he was one of five officers invited to stay and become an instructor. In the Philippines, he had taken to riding as a form of exercise and a relief from the tedium of the tropics, when he wasn't fording crocodile-infested streams. At Leavenworth, riding became his chief recreation. Horses and dogs and the habits of a Virginia gentleman became his own on the plains of Kansas.

In 1910, he finished his tour of duty at Leavenworth and, given leave, took his wife on a tour of Europe. The intervening years until the United States entered the First World War were spent as a typically itinerant officer moving from one post to the next—from New

York to Texas, Massachusetts to Arkansas, Washington to the Philippines to California and elsewhere—but Marshall had already impressed his superiors with his talents as a staff officer, a man who was expert and expeditious at organizing and training troops and drawing up plans for field exercises. Indeed, another young officer serving in the Philippines, Hap Arnold, after watching First Lieutenant George Marshall issuing orders during a training exercise, "told my wife I had met a man who was going to be chief of staff of the army one day."[2] Other officers, including generals, were nearly as flattering, marking Marshall out as an exceptional officer—Lieutenant Colonel Johnson Hagood going so far as to say, in an efficiency report on Marshall, that "he is a military genius....and if I had the power I would nominate him to fill the next vacancy in the grade of Brigadier General."[3]

Such excellence came at a price. Marshall literally worked himself into the hospital from exhaustion at age thirty-three. But he learned his lesson. He tried to establish regular work hours that allowed him to ride in the morning, play tennis in the afternoon, unwind before bed, and take the occasional hunting trip. He managed it with no loss of efficiency.

Little more than two months after the declaration of war on Germany, Captain Marshall, now assigned as staff officer to General William Sibert, commander of the 1st Division, shipped out for France. When General Pershing criticized Sibert's management of the division before Sibert's staff officers, Marshall leapt to his commander's defense and, to the astonishment of everyone, gave Pershing a subordinate's equivalent of a tongue-lashing—and did so in such a way that Pershing respected him for it, and eventually appointed him to his own staff. Marshall, like any officer worth his salt, craved a field command, but General Robert Bullard, who took over for Sibert, recognized "Lieut. Col. Marshall's special fitness is for staff work and...I doubt that in this...he has an equal in the Army today."[4] As a staff officer, Marshall helped plan the American attacks at Cantigny and at Saint-Mihiel and throughout the Meuse-Argonne Offensive.[5] Marshall, with his tremendous grasp of logistics and tactics, was so successful that he earned the nickname of "the wizard."[6] Brigadier General Fox Conner, Marshall's immediate superior on Pershing's staff, had another name for him, telling Dwight Eisenhower that Marshall was "nothing short of a genius."[7] After the war, Pershing asked Colonel Marshall to become one of his personal aides, a position he held until Pershing's retirement in September 1924.[8]

At Marshall's request, his next assignment sent him to China as executive officer of the 15th Infantry Regiment stationed in Tientsin, a happy imperial posting that he held for three years and that afforded him freedom from a desk, a comfortable lifestyle (much enjoyed by his wife), a ringside view of the unfolding Chinese civil war, associates like future Generals Matthew Ridgway and Vinegar Joe Stilwell, and enough leisure time to learn Chinese. In the summer of 1927 he was back stateside as an instructor at the Army War College in Washington, DC, an assignment that thrilled his wife, though her joy was short-lived. She died in September 1927 after a thyroid operation. The Marshalls had been childless, and with no parental responsibilities to divert him from his mourning, he sublimated it into work. In October, he reported to the Infantry School at Fort Benning, Georgia, as assistant commandant. As he later noted, the "change to Benning was magical." It "caught me at my most restless moment, and gave me hundreds of interests, an unlimited field of activity, delightful associates, and all outdoors to play in."[9] And for all the image we have of Marshall as a master organizer, planner, strategist, and supreme desk commander rather than a battlefield leader, he had not joined the Army to be a bureaucrat. Working for Pershing after the war, when he had time to ride and take exercise, his wife noted that Marshall thrived: "he was hard as nails and black as an Indian. I've never seen him looking better."[10] Marshall liked being an Indian; he liked having "all outdoors to play in."

The play in this case was teaching tactics to infantrymen, which allowed him time in the field, time in the classroom, and time to stamp his ideas on the officers and men who passed through during his five-year tenure at Fort Benning. Among the Infantry School instructors were Joe Stilwell and future five-star general Omar Bradley.[11] Marshall wanted orders kept simple so that they could be quickly understood and enacted. He wanted an Army prepared for mechanized "open" warfare, a faster and more powerful version of the German invasion of France in 1914. He wanted soldiers drilled in the fundamentals of infantry combat: shoot, move, communicate.

While at Benning, Marshall found himself a wife. That had not been his intention, but the handsome widower was introduced to the Kentucky-born, English-trained former actress (and daughter of a Baptist minister) Katherine Boyce Tupper, herself a widow. She had, needless to say, stage presence; and so did he, in his quiet, commanding, military way. They met in 1929 and were married in Washington, DC, in 1931. Marshall became the stepfather to her three teenage children: Molly became a riding companion, and the boys, Clifton and Allen, hunting companions.[12]

In June 1932, Marshall was sent to command an infantry battalion at Fort Screven on Tybee Island, Georgia, a post that, he wrote General Pershing, "at least keeps me away from office work and high theory."[13] A year later he was given command of a regiment at Fort Moultrie in South Carolina and promoted colonel soon thereafter.

In addition to his normal military duties, he was deeply involved in the Civilian Conservation Corps, a liberal program of which the conservative Marshall approved. He saw it as military training by other means for America's young men.

To his dismay he was made senior instructor of the Illinois National Guard in October 1933. To him it seemed a pointless duty, and a potentially distasteful one, given the labor trouble in Illinois; but Douglas MacArthur, who assigned him there, tried to reassure him about the importance of the position. Marshall had worked successfully with Guard units in the past, and more than most officers in the Army, he had a rapport with citizen-soldiers. Marshall spent three years with the Guard before he achieved the long-sought rank of brigadier general and a new assignment, commanding a brigade in Washington State—a job that again included working with the Civilian Conservation Corps, which he loved.

In 1938, however, he was recalled to Washington, DC, to lead the general staff's War Plans Division and three months later became deputy chief of staff of the Army. At a meeting at the White House in November 1938, Marshall was the only officer present to criticize President Roosevelt's plan for increasing American air power. Marshall thought it unbalanced and unrealistic. Roosevelt ended the meeting, but not his relationship with Marshall, whose honesty he admired and whom he appointed Army chief of staff in 1939, making him a four-star general. Marshall was sworn into office 1 September 1939, the day Germany invaded Poland.

"TO PRODUCE THE MOST EFFICIENT ARMY IN THE WORLD"

Marshall's goal was to build up America's armed forces for what looked like a repeat—though on a greater and more destructive scale—of the Great War. He had to do so in spite of a Congress opposed to rearmament and a president cautious about pushing his luck. In the Great War, Marshall noted, the American Expeditionary Force, however quickly it was rushed into existence, had time to train in theater and in low-level combat, and thus, to find its feet. In this war, if the United States should enter it, the Army would have to be trained, armed, and ready at the outset—and large enough to make a difference. In 1939, the Army numbered fewer than 175,000 men; Marshall wanted to add more than a million men over the next two years. Roosevelt preferred air power to infantry and, at a meeting on 13 May 1940, rejected Marshall's proposal. Marshall shot back with a detailed defense, adding, "If you don't do something and do it right away.... I don't know what is going to happen to this country.... *you have got to do something and you've got to do it today.*"[14] Roosevelt complied with most of Marshall's requests.

Marshall was focused on the blitzkrieg success of Nazi Germany in Europe, but also on aggressive, expanding imperial Japan. Every officer who had served in the Philippines knew Japan as a potential American enemy. In 1940 Japan became an open ally of Nazi Germany and Fascist Italy with the Tripartite Pact. That same year, Marshall himself gained two important allies when President Roosevelt, a liberal Democrat, appointed conservative Republicans Frank Knox (a former Rough Rider and Army major in the Great War) secretary of the Navy and Henry Stimson (an Army colonel in the Great War and a friend of Marshall's) secretary of war. Knox and Marshall, and even more Stimson and Marshall, generally saw eye to eye even when Marshall and Roosevelt did not. The Army chief of staff and the president were divided by strategic vision, temperament, and even manners. Roosevelt favored assisting the British whenever possible; Marshall thought the priority should be America's own armed forces, not building up an ally that might fall, as France had done. In allotting resources, Roosevelt, who had been assistant secretary of the Navy under President Wilson, tended to give preference to the Navy; Marshall just as naturally thought the Army, which would have to fight the Wehrmacht, should come first. The president had a freewheeling, informal style of doing business; Marshall insisted on cold logic and professional formality.

Marshall could impress and sway Roosevelt with his logic, argument, and force of character; and he radiated credibility and integrity in his dealings with Congress, which was more easily swayed by the Army chief of staff's recommendations than the president's. With Marshall there was no taint of partisan politics—and there was no doubting his expertise or his honesty. When he said, "I have but one purpose, one mission, and that is to produce the most efficient Army in the world,"[15] congressmen knew that it was true.

As part of that drive for efficiency, Marshall ran his own office on a rigid timetable. He was at his desk by 7:30 a.m., usually after a morning horseback ride, and out the door no later than 5:00 p.m. After hours, he avoided social engagements (and when they were unavoidable, left early), preferring to go horseback riding (his primary release from the pressures of the office) or play tennis or simply go home, and aides knew better than to contact him at home unless absolutely necessary. A ruthless use of his time in the office—subordinates learned to be concise—and an insistence on making time for relaxation were, he thought, essential to his own efficiency.

In the Army as a whole, he was a keen judge of officers, determined to promote men of ability, regardless of seniority and, in the case of National Guard officers, regardless of their political clout. He had told a reporter in 1939,

The present general officers of the line are for the most part too old to command troops in battle under the terrific pressures of modern war. Many of them have their minds set in outmoded patterns, and can't change to meet the new conditions they may face if we become involved in the war that's started in Europe. I do not propose to send our young citizen-soldiers into action, if they must go into action, under commanders whose minds are no longer adaptable to the making of split-second decisions in the fast-moving war of today, nor whose bodies are no longer capable of standing up under the demands of field service.... They'll have their chance to prove what they can do. But I doubt that many will come through satisfactorily. Those that don't will be eliminated.[16]

In their place would be promoted men Marshall had thoroughly tested and who had proved their mettle, men who were currently colonels, lieutenant colonels, and majors, men whose names would soon become familiar to the American public: men like Patton, Eisenhower, Mark Clark, Lucian Truscott, and Omar Bradley.

INDISPENSABLE

After the Japanese attack on Pearl Harbor and Nazi Germany's declaration of war against the United States, Marshall accepted a Europe-first strategy and was a dogged proponent—against President Roosevelt and also against British prime minister Churchill and his generals—of a cross-Channel invasion of occupied France as soon as possible, as soon, indeed, as 1942. President Roosevelt and the British preferred the safer, if more indirect, option of an Allied invasion of Vichy-controlled French North Africa. This was an argument Marshall lost—at least until 1944.

In 1945 Churchill, Marshall's erstwhile rival for strategic influence on the president, famously said that Marshall was "the true organizer of victory."[17] Marshall, however, wanted to *lead* victory as a commander. Here again, he was foiled, in part because he refused to request the assignment, telling the president the decision was his as commander in chief. Roosevelt confessed he wanted Marshall "to be the Pershing of the second world war and he cannot be that if we keep him here."[18] Yet the president felt he had to "keep him here"; Marshall was indispensable as Army chief of staff. The president thus chose General Dwight Eisenhower, not Marshall, to be the supreme Allied commander for the cross-Channel invasion of Europe that Marshall had so consistently and strenuously advocated. As Roosevelt told Marshall in recompense, "I feel I could not sleep at night with you out of the country."[19]

Like his hero Robert E. Lee, Marshall was widely seen as a man of unimpeachable character and sound judgment. He was the indispensable man who ensured that America's armies were properly led and supplied. If he was not a leader in the field, he was nevertheless a leader at the highest level of command, working with the commander in chief, giving force and direction to America's global strategy. Like Lee, Marshall was a man of powerfully suppressed emotion. He consciously assumed a mask of command so that he constantly projected a George C. Marshall who was dispassionate, disinterested, logical, honest, and untiring—a man that congressmen, senators, his fellow officers, the commander in chief, and the public at large could trust. But the mask was not something to hide behind; it was a reflection of Marshall himself. He rejected honors and rewards when he could; he squelched would-be biographers (and never wrote a memoir); he gave informed, straightforward, detailed answers to questions; he supported his commanders in the field (there was between Marshall and Eisenhower none of the rivalry that had divided Army chief of staff Peyton March and commander of the American Expeditionary Force John Pershing in World War I); and he denied having any political ambitions, which he thought would be fatal to his work, with the quip, "My father was a Democrat, my mother a Republican, and I am an Episcopalian."[20] In 1944 President Roosevelt awarded him a fifth star and made him General of the Army.[21] In November 1945, two months after the surrender of Japan, Marshall resigned his position as Army chief of staff.

SHAPING THE POSTWAR WORLD

He was not left unemployed long. Indeed, it was but a single day before President Harry Truman called him with a new assignment. He wanted Marshall to go to China. The country—already divided, with American ally Chiang Kai-shek and his party the Kuomintang (and his affiliated warlords) against the Communists led by Mao Tse-tung—seemed certain to fall into civil war unless a coalition government (led by Chiang) could be negotiated. That was Marshall's job: achieve a democratic, non-Communist China that nevertheless included Communists in the government and reformed the corrupt Kuomintang. Marshall did the best he could in an impossible situation. In January 1947, he was recalled to Washington and named secretary of state.

Once he had led soldiers; now he led diplomats—some of the most famous in American history, including future Secretary of State Dean Acheson and future ambassador to the Soviet Union George Kennan. Acheson recalled, "The moment General Marshall entered a room everyone in it felt his presence. It was a striking and communicated force. His figure conveyed intensity, which his voice, low, staccato, and incisive, reinforced. It compelled respect. It spread a sense of authority and calm." To Acheson, Marshall said, "I shall expect of you the most complete frankness, particularly about myself. I have no feelings except those I reserve for Mrs. Marshall."[22]

Marshall and his team were agreed that the United States could not disengage from the war-shattered world; the United States would have to lead it, help rebuild it, and aid it; and to ensure American security, the United States needed military strength with a global reach; it was no longer insulated by the Atlantic and Pacific Oceans. George Kennan, who had developed the idea of "containment," of forcibly blocking an expansionist Soviet Union, had an ally in Marshall. During the Second World War, Marshall had kept his views as strictly military as possible, regarding the Soviet Union as an enormous military force arrayed against Nazi Germany and potentially against Japan. As secretary of state, he took Kennan's view, that the Soviets were internationally aggressive and responded only to tough talk and the threat of actual force. When the British government conceded that it could no longer afford to continue fighting Communists in postwar Greece or support Turkey against the Soviet Union, the Truman administration, Marshall included, believed the United States had to fill the gap.

In 1947 Marshall announced the principles for a European Recovery Program, which became known as the Marshall Plan, for the rebuilding of Western Europe. Marshall was also involved in the direction of the Berlin airlift (after the Soviets blockaded West Berlin in 1948), he encouraged the formation of a West German government, and he oversaw the creation of NATO (founded in 1949). Throughout the early Cold War period, Marshall had to play power politics against a massively militarized Soviet Union. America's own armed forces had been rapidly demobilized after the Second World War. Urged by foreign policy hawks "to give the Russians hell" in negotiations, Marshall lamented, "My facilities for giving them hell.... was 1⅓ divisions over the entire United States. This is quite a proposition when you deal with somebody with over 260 and you have 1⅓."[23]

Nevertheless, by 1948 Marshall was pleased to see Western Europe recovering and Soviet influence retreating; there the United States was winning the peace. The same could not be said of China. Marshall took what he considered the realist position: Chiang's Kuomintang was so corrupt and its hold on power so tenuous that it would require an unsustainable drain on American resources to support it. If China fell to the Communists, it would not, Marshall thought, pose a grave foreign policy risk to the United States; it was not Europe. China—however large it was and however large it loomed in the American imagination as a great field for missionaries and spreading democracy—was at best a regional power, and a chaotic and impoverished one. Even as a Communist state, it could be a rival rather than a satellite of the Soviet Union. Moreover, like the Soviet Union, it could be contained. George Kennan and Marshall believed that the answer to a chaotic or Communist China was not to intervene there but to build up Japan and the Philippines, just as the United States was rebuilding Western Europe. Containment did not mean rushing to fight the Communists everywhere but rather reinforcing potential Western strong points to inhibit Communist expansion. It also meant not creating opportunities for Soviet gains, which Marshall thought would be the result of the partition of Palestine into Zionist and Arab states—a partition that might inflame the Arab world and make it susceptible to

Soviet influence. President Truman recognized the new state of Israel anyway.

Marshall resigned after Truman's 1948 reelection, but in 1949 the president appointed him to lead the American Red Cross, a position that was meant to ease Marshall into retirement. The eruption of the Korean War in 1950, however, meant a return to the colors, not this time as a general, but as secretary of defense. Marshall wanted his term to last only six months—an emergency interim appointment to help with rapid mobilization—but was persuaded to extend it to a year. He took over as secretary of defense in September, a week after MacArthur landed his blow at Inchon. In the months that followed, as American fortunes in the war waxed and waned, and MacArthur and Truman butted heads over strategy, Marshall cautiously took the side of the commander in chief. Marshall knew MacArthur's merits, and he believed in giving autonomy to the officer in the field, but he also believed in a strict demarcation of military authority. MacArthur could argue for his strategy, but in the end he had to be subordinate to the authority of the president of the United States—and that, it appeared, MacArthur was unwilling to accept. MacArthur returned to the United States and a hero's welcome. Marshall, on the other hand, though he retained his dignity and stature, came under attack from Senator Joe McCarthy and his supporters, who portrayed him as a Communist-appeaser. In 1948, Marshall had written to a friend, "God bless democracy! I approve of it highly but suffer from it extremely. This incidentally is not for quotation."[24] Not for quotation, perhaps, but it illuminated how stoically he accepted the storms and tempests of public controversy.

After his resignation in September 1951, Marshall retired, save for fundraising work for VMI (which named one of the five arches in its barracks after him),[25] acting as chairman for the American

Battle Monuments Commission, and representing the United States at the coronation of Queen Elizabeth II. In 1953 he was awarded the Nobel Peace Prize. In his acceptance speech he noted, "There has been considerable comment over the awarding of the Nobel Peace Prize for 1953 to a soldier. I am afraid this does not seem as remarkable to me as it quite evidently appears to others. . . . The cost of war in human lives is constantly spread before me, written neatly in many ledgers whose columns are gravestones. I am deeply moved to find some means or method of avoiding another calamity of war." That means or method, he added, included the West having a "very strong military posture."[26]

Marshall was pleased to spend his retirement quietly—gardening, hunting (at least before bad health got in the way), and reading for pleasure (Westerns were favorites). He died in 1959 after a series of strokes. He had been something of an American Cincinnatus, pressed into long service but happy in private life and disdaining political ambition. American admirers compared him to George Washington for his dignity and strength of character. Winston Churchill took a longer view, or a more poetic one, saying of Marshall, "That is the noblest Roman of them all."[27]

CHAPTER FIFTEEN

EDDIE RICKENBACKER (1890–1973)

Eddie Rickenbacker, one of the great American heroes of the First World War, was a well-known figure up to his death. Since then he has been largely forgotten, which is too bad, because his was a great American story. He was the son of German-speaking Swiss immigrants who, however precarious their economic circumstances, were hugely patriotic about their new country. Nineteenth-century America had no welfare state but did have a highly effective culture for stamping Americanism onto newly arrived European immigrants. As one example: Rickenbacker's father, though over forty and a family man, sought to prove his zealous American patriotism by enlisting for the Spanish-American War. To his disappointment and his wife's relief, he was turned away.

Eddie Rickenbacker grew up in Columbus, Ohio, the third of eight children. His parents had the Germanic virtues—they were strict, strong, confident, and industrious—and Eddie put a turn-of-the-century American spin on them: he was a tough, enterprising, daredevil, fun-loving, rambunctious boy. He was ready with his fists, keen for a smoke, leader of a boyhood gang (more *Our Gang* than Crips and Bloods), and held a variety of odd jobs, including selling newspapers from the age of five. He once tried to "fly" a bike-plane (a bike with an umbrella attached) off the roof of a barn and managed to survive that and many other dangerous boyhood accidents, including, variously, crashing into a horse-drawn street car, falling headfirst into a ditch and knocking himself unconscious, and more than once barely escaping being run over by a train. He dodged death so often that he realized one day he wouldn't: "I could see time stretching on endlessly. As it continued, more and more wondrous marvels would be developed and become realities. But at some point along this interminable path, my life would stop, and time would flow on without me. In my despair, I would go off alone to the barn and sob for hours at a time."[1] His father dispelled Eddie's precocious sense of despair in the most practical way—he beat it out of him with a switch.

Resolved to make the best of things, he learned from his father the value of determined, orderly work and from his mother the healing power of prayer. Like his father, Eddie was handy with tools and liked to tinker and build, including a "push-mobile," a boy-sized horseless carriage he built for racing. When he was fifteen, his life took a more serious turn when his father was killed in a fight at a work site.

BUILDING CARS AND RACING THEM

Rickenbacker convinced his mother to let him drop out of school and take a full-time job; he didn't tell her when he lied about his age and education to employers. After a succession of jobs that ranged from working at a glass factory to polishing and carving grave stones (including his father's) to cleaning railcars to assisting at a bicycle and auto shop, he talked his way into a job at the Frayer-Miller automobile manufacturing plant. While there, he took a correspondence course in engineering, which led to his serving as backseat mechanic for Frayer's race cars. When Lee Frayer took a job designing cars for the Columbia Buggy Company, he brought the seventeen-year-old Rickenbacker with him. The dynamic, cheerful, can-do teenager swiftly moved up from managing a department of fifteen to regional manager of the company and a successful race car driver. By nineteen, he had grown to the size of a football player—six foot two and more than two hundred pounds.

Rickenbacker had made a habit of resigning from one job confident he could get the next one he wanted; this time he had his eye on the Mason Automobile Company, where he hoped to become a full-time racer. Instead, at least initially, they made him a mechanic and race car builder. Not for the first time, Rickenbacker accepted less money because he thought the prospects were better; though as it turned out, he found himself not only racing for the company, as he wanted, but also investing in it to keep it going. Racing cars became his profession—driving for the Maxwell Automobile Company and then for the Prest-O-Lite Company—and it made him a celebrity. It was reported that a silent film actress even sent him a telegram offering to marry him if he gave up racing. He politely declined her offer, remarking with Kiplingesque aplomb, "A woman is only a woman, but my soul mate is a racing car."[2]

In late 1916 Rickenbacker traveled to England to work for the Sunbeam Motor Works getting their racing cars ready for the 1917 racing season in the United States. Germany's declaration of unrestricted submarine warfare in February 1917, and warning to Americans in England to leave before the torpedoes were set loose, meant Rickenbacker had to return home. His stay in England had not been entirely pleasant. He had been shadowed by British detectives who suspected, because of his name, that he was a German spy, and he was put off by what struck him as British snobbery. Nevertheless, he returned convinced the United States should enter the war on the Allied side, gave public testimonials to that end, and organized a group of race car drivers to form a flying corps, the Aero Reserves of America. Rickenbacker knew something about aircraft engines, had flown and learned that his fear of heights disappeared when he was in the air, and was eager to put his auto racing skills to use in a plane. But Brigadier General George D. Squier of the U.S. Army Signal Corps, which ran the Aviation Section, dismissed the idea of race car drivers as pilots, telling Rickenbacker it would be unwise "for a pilot to have any knowledge of engines and mechanics. Airplane engines are always breaking down, and a man who knew a great deal about engines would know if his engine wasn't functioning correctly and be hesitant about going into combat."[3] What they needed were daredevils without brains.

FLYING ACE

Instead, after the United States declared war, Rickenbacker was tapped by a friend, Major Burgess Lewis, to join the American Expeditionary Force as a driver, receiving an immediate rank of sergeant. He embarked for France, where he was assigned to Colonel Billy

Mitchell. He soon talked his way into pilot training, earned his wings, was promoted to lieutenant, and became an engineering officer responsible for training new pilots under the command of Major Carl "Tooey" Spaatz. Spaatz wanted to retain him, but Rickenbacker was determined to attend Aerial Gunnery School and become a combat pilot. He got his wish. After training at the Gunnery School, he was assigned to the 94th Aero Pursuit Squadron, which became known as the "Hat-in-the-Ring" Squadron from the insignia they designed for their unit. He would be going into combat.

Rickenbacker's first kill was on 29 April 1918, after a series of flights where he had flown through anti-aircraft fire, been shot at by enemy planes, and mistaken two of his colleagues for enemy pilots, though he never fired his guns at them. On 8 May 1918, he became a flight commander after Captain Norman James Hall was shot down and made a prisoner by the Germans. On 28 May, Rickenbacker shot down his fifth plane, which made him an "ace," and two days later he rescued an American pilot and shot down two more German planes.

The American planes were castoffs from the French—Nieuports at first, which were eventually replaced by much more effective Spads—but the American pilots flew with the same sort of spirit that animated the doughboys on the ground. "It was this style of Indian warfare," Rickenbacker wrote of Quentin Roosevelt's dogfight tactics, which were similar to his own, "that had moved the German Intelligence Office to state that their training was indeed hopeless against American recklessness. German formation flying was admirable until an American joined it and moved in concert with it for fifteen minutes before shooting it up! One can imagine the disgust of the methodical Boches as they digested this latest trick of the Yank!"[4]

Rickenbacker's mechanical knowledge, careful pre-flight checks of his equipment (which didn't prevent his machine guns from jamming), fast reflexes, and wily combat techniques honed by a continual review of his previous dogfights made him a deadly effective combat ace who relished aerial duels and strafing enemy infantry. It was not bloodlust that drove him, but duty and competition. He was happy to see enemy pilots parachute to safety or scramble out from crashed planes: "I never wanted to kill men, only to destroy machines."[5] Even an ear infection and perforated eardrum that the doctors said would end his flying days could not keep him grounded, at least not for long.[6] In September he was promoted captain and made commander of the 94th Aero Squadron.

By the end of the war, Rickenbacker had fought through 134 "aerial encounters," shooting down at least 26 confirmed enemy aircraft. Those stats made him America's top fighter ace, "ace of aces," though as he noted, "One can hardly expect to get confirmations for all one's victories since nine-tenths of our combats were necessarily fought on the German side of the lines."[7] His 94th Aero Squadron was also the tops, with more flying hours and confirmed destruction of enemy aircraft than any other. When the Armistice became official, Rickenbacker was flying over the trenches and saw American and German soldiers celebrating in no-man's-land together, no longer enemies, but grateful survivors of the titanic struggle.

After the war, Rickenbacker wanted to stay with his squadron, but such was his celebrity that the War Department ordered him home, against his protests, to help sell Liberty Bonds. He was inundated with requests for commercial endorsements—and offers to make him a movie star—all of which he categorically refused. He had no intention of cashing in on his fame, but he did write a memoir of the war titled *Fighting the Flying Circus*, which gave him the opportunity to tell the story of the 94th Aero Squadron to a popular audience. His bond tour was successful (Damon Runyon, whom he had befriended when Runyon was a war correspondent, helped him prepare his remarks).[8] The tour was arduous and at the end of it he was promoted major—a promotion he felt he didn't earn; he continued to style himself Captain Rickenbacker—and discharged from the Army. He was fine being discharged into civvy street, but he was angry and dismayed that the U.S. government, in stark violation of the freedom for which he and his colleagues had just fought, was about to enforce Prohibition. He considered it a slap in the face of the returning soldiers, and a more obvious slap in the face of anyone with a German (that is, beer-drinking) heritage. He denounced the law and vowed not to abide by it.

COMMERCIAL VENTURES

He also vowed to find a position with a company that would actually put him to work and not merely capitalize on his name. He decided he wanted to build his own car and found financing to support it, establishing the Rickenbacker Motor Company in 1921. "Our car," Rickenbacker wrote, "would appeal to the white-collar worker, the junior executive, the fairly prosperous farmer and the woman of taste. Finally, it would earn the appreciation of anyone who recognized fine engineering and workmanship"[9]—and who might want the 94th Aero Squadron emblem on a car. Rickenbacker would leave economy cars to Henry Ford and luxury cars to the likes of Cadillac and Packard. His cars would simply be the best.

The project, however, would not have his undivided attention. He took another job—as California sales director for General Motors' new car, the Sheridan (a car and a job that only lasted for a year)—and he got married in 1922 to a divorcée named Adelaide Frost.[10] The couple honeymooned in Europe. In Germany, a former German fighter pilot invited the Rickenbackers to dinner. Among the group was Hermann Göring, another World War I flying ace, who was already predicting a new German Reich, this one founded on air power.

In Rickenbacker's own (commercial) empire, he took it as a point of pride that while the Rickenbacker Motor Company was growing rapidly, its profit margins were small, because that meant the buyer got more car for his money. He was also an innovator, producing the first commercial car with four-wheel brakes—which unfortunately proved to be his downfall. His competitors waged an enormous campaign alleging that four-wheel brakes, which had been used in race cars, were dangerous in passenger cars. The charge was ludicrous, but it was also effective; it forced the company into bankruptcy and Rickenbacker into a fortune's worth of debt.

While his company foundered, Rickenbacker testified for the defense at Billy Mitchell's court-martial and said bitterly after Mitchell's conviction, "That was his reward for the great service he had given his country."[11] Rickenbacker, luckily, found himself with a reputation that enabled him to raise money for another commercial venture. He credited his country: "Here in America," he wrote, "failure is not the end of the world. If you have determination, you can come back from failure and succeed."[12] He bought an engineering company (which he later sold to General Motors) and the Indianapolis Motor Speedway, saving it from property developers, and added a golf course to its attractions. To keep cash flowing to his family—the couple now had two adopted sons—and to continue paying off his debts, he took another sales job with General Motors.

He also got back into aviation. General Motors used him as an advisor in acquiring the American division of the German Fokker company (for which he became vice president of sales). He contributed stories for a syndicated newspaper cartoon about an American fighter pilot named Ace Drummond. He began flying again, including attempting—and failing—to break the transcontinental speed record; and he invested in Florida Airways, which was being established by a wartime buddy, and which went bust by pushing too hard to become a passenger airline when there was a dearth of willing passengers. Still, in 1930, President Herbert Hoover came through with a much-delayed medal, awarding Rickenbacker the Medal of Honor to go along with his nine Distinguished Service Crosses.

Rickenbacker remained an American hero, albeit at times a controversial one. He opposed the New Deal policies of Franklin Delano Roosevelt[13] and told reporters that Roosevelt's scheme—short-lived as it turned out—to use military aircraft to fly mail routes was "legalized murder."[14] The young pilots, who lacked proper training and flew aircraft unsuited to the task, routinely crashed in bad weather. He also warned—but found few listeners—about German military rearmament after a 1935 visit when he was given a tour of Germany's rapidly expanding air force, being built in violation of the Versailles Treaty.

At home, Rickenbacker's goal was to become a leader in commercial aviation. When he became general manager of Eastern Air Lines in 1935, he wanted to do more than deliver the U.S. mail. "Eastern Air Lines," he said, "is held up by government subsidy. I believe it can become a free-enterprise industry, and I will pledge all my efforts and energies to making it self-sufficient. But if this airline cannot be made to stand on its own feet and must continue to live on the taxpayers' money through government subsidy, then I want to be relieved of that job."[15] He even closed the company's office in Washington, DC. He didn't want lobbyists; he wanted employees who worked on and with the airplanes. In 1938, he bought Eastern Air Lines from General Motors.

Even before he bought the company, he managed it with a near-manic insistence on knowing everything he could about his planes, his employees, and his business; and he made sure everyone knew what "Captain Eddie" thought and wanted. He increased the number of flights, improved the aircraft, and boosted his employees' benefits while keeping his own pay static. By 1939, he had built Eastern Air Lines into a company that was making more than a million and a half dollars in annual profit.

In February 1941 he survived a plane crash (eight others on the plane didn't) but was hospitalized for four months, barely dodged easeful death (he felt it as a presence and realized he had to fight for life), and was left with a permanent limp. Surviving the crash was a personal triumph, but the Japanese attack on Pearl Harbor later that year struck him as a political failure. Rickenbacker was convinced that had the United States built a giant, world-class air force in the 1930s—something he had ardently, publicly advocated—the United States could have deterred Nazi and Japanese aggression. It would have been expensive, a billion dollars over five years by his estimation, but nothing in comparison to the nearly $300 billion and more than 400,000 lives that World War II cost the United States. As an America Firster, Rickenbacker thought that with proper preparation the United States could have avoided war.

In 1942 General Hap Arnold, chief of the Army Air Forces, tapped Rickenbacker for a special job, telling him, "I'm concerned about the reports I'm getting from combat groups in training. I'm told that they are indifferent, that they haven't got the punch they need to do the job they're being prepared for. I want you to go out and talk to these boys, inspire them, put some fire in them. And while you're there, I want you to look around and see what the problems are."[16]

ONE LAST ADVENTURE

After tours of bases stateside and in England, Rickenbacker set off for Canton Island in the Pacific in October 1942 with a top secret message from the president for Douglas MacArthur. Unable to find the island, and with fuel running out, the pilot of the plane was forced to make a crash—and as it turned out, expert—landing into the ocean. All eight men aboard survived the impact (though one died during their coming ordeal). Freeing themselves from the plane, they loosed its three rubber rafts and then bobbed amidst twelve-foot waves. What they had failed to secure from the plane was their stowed-away emergency food and water. They lived off rainwater, a handful of oranges someone had stuck in his pocket, a seagull, and a few fish that they managed to catch—for twenty-four days. The rafts, initially roped together, were later separated. Three of the men washed ashore on an island and were rescued by a missionary. The pilot, who was alone in a raft, was picked up by the U.S. Navy and directed Navy rescuers to Rickenbacker and the others. Rickenbacker not only survived (minus more than fifty pounds) but delivered his secret message (and it remains secret) to MacArthur.[17]

The American press had assumed Rickenbacker was dead; when they were proved wrong, headlines sang the praises of the apparently indestructible hero. He wrote the story of his ordeal for *Life* magazine, but only after Hap Arnold had authorized it and only on Rickenbacker's condition that his payment for the story go to the Air Force Aid Society. Because he had been on a taxpayer-funded mission, Rickenbacker felt he had no right to profit from the adventure.

He continued to go on inspection tours around the world, including a special mission to Soviet Russia to see what use they were making of lend-lease American planes.

After President Roosevelt's death, Rickenbacker welcomed the elevation of fellow Great War veteran Harry Truman to the presidency. He judged Truman a conservative Democrat who would "get us on an even keel again."[18] Rickenbacker changed his opinion of Truman, just as he had earlier changed his opinion of Roosevelt, going from supporter to critic, though not as violently, summing up: "Well, he knew how to swear. He knew how to drink bourbon. He knew how to make up his mind, and unfortunately made it up in the wrong direction. But on the whole, he wasn't too bad."[19]

In his own postwar return to normalcy, Rickenbacker sold the Indianapolis Motor Speedway, established a forty-hour work week and a retirement plan for his Eastern Air Line employees (while warning them that the plan in no way relieved them of their personal responsibility for their retirement welfare), and bought a ranch in Texas. Rickenbacker's eldest son, David, had seen wartime service in the Marines. His second son, Bill, after graduating from Harvard, joined the postwar Air Force and trained in Texas. This inspired Rickenbacker to acquire a piece of land that could be passed down in the Rickenbacker family for generations. In the event, however, he eventually donated the land to the Boy Scouts, and the Rickenbacker family settled in and around New York, Bill becoming an investment analyst and senior editor for the conservative magazine *National Review* and David working for the United States Trust Company.

In 1959, with some concerned about his age and autocratic management style, Rickenbacker was promoted from president to chairman of the board of Eastern Air Lines. That made him less involved in day-to-day operations—and spared him, as he saw it, from having to work around the unwelcome and ever-increasing bureaucratic regulation of commercial aviation. Nevertheless, Eddie Rickenbacker remained one of the most successful, and lowest-paid, airline executives in the country up until his retirement, at the direction of the airline's board of directors, at the end of 1963.

In retirement he traveled, wrote his memoirs, and was an outspoken lecturer against the socialist trends he saw in America. His sacred trinity was God, country, and freedom. He loathed President Kennedy's failure to follow through with the Bay of Pigs invasion and thought American involvement in the Vietnam War was a typical liberal Democrat mistake—though at the same time he loathed the leftist antiwar movement and argued that the best way to end the war was to win it. He died in 1973 of heart failure while on a trip to visit his ancestral Switzerland. Though he died abroad, Rickenbacker—America's World War One "ace of aces"—was a classic American through and through.

CHAPTER SIXTEEN

FRANCIS P. DUFFY (1871–1932) AND ALVIN C. YORK (1887–1964)

ather Francis Duffy, the most decorated United States Army chaplain, was actually born and raised, and earned his undergraduate degree, in Canada. Both his maternal and paternal grandparents were Irish immigrants, and his Irish bloodlines would guide his future. He accepted a teaching position at a Catholic school in New York City, decided to become a priest—eventually earning a doctorate at the Catholic University of America—and became a professor at St. Joseph's Seminary in New York. He got a brief taste of stateside chaplain's duty during the Spanish-American War when he ministered to soldiers returning from Cuba. Many of the soldiers suffered from tropical fevers; Duffy himself came down with typhoid and had to be hospitalized.

As a professor Duffy was popular with his students. But as an intellectual in the most intellectual of religious denominations and a relative liberal in the most conservative institution in the world—one dedicated to preaching eternal verities—he got into a slight bit of bother with the Church authorities who thought his views were tinged with unwelcome modernism. As a consequence, the magazine he edited was shuttered, and he was eventually removed from his professorship and assigned as a parish priest in the Bronx, starting up the Church of Our Savior, a converted store consecrated into a church.

THE FIGHTING 69TH

Tall, lean, and tough looking, in 1914 Duffy became chaplain of the 69th Infantry Regiment—the "Fighting 69th," a proudly and jealously "Irish" regiment—of the New York National Guard. In 1916 he wrote a frank letter to Cardinal John Farley asking for a transfer from his parish duties, saying that he wanted "a man's job—one big enough to tax my energies to the full."[1] He got that job, but not from Cardinal Farley. The Fighting 69th was mobilized (and Father Duffy with it) to join General John J. Pershing's expedition against Pancho Villa. In the event, the 69th never saw action against the banditos, but Father Duffy did have to defend the 69th's reputation against false allegations of drunken, brawling (Irish) behavior, and keep down the dander of his men who were suspicious at the arrival of non-Irish officers to the regiment. The 69th returned home in March 1917 to a parade, a hero's welcome, and a blessing from Cardinal Farley.

The Fighting 69th was proud of its fame in the War Between the States—whence came its moniker—but many of its Irish American volunteers were truculent and suspicious about the prospect, which became a reality in April 1917, of going to war alongside the dreaded English. Both Cardinal Farley and Father Duffy, however, were diligent in asserting that it was time for Irish Americans to once again prove their loyalty, their patriotism, and their willingness to fight for their adopted American home. Sure enough, new recruits came pouring in, many of them Irish Americans, others willing to fake it to join an esteemed regiment. When the 69th (now officially the 165th Infantry Regiment) was made part of the Rainbow Division, it was reinforced by other New York regiments—an unpopular move, but Father Duffy promised an Irish welcome to all who came into the regiment. He even helped arrange the transfer of poet and Catholic convert Joyce Kilmer, though only after he was convinced Kilmer wasn't a pantywaist poetaster[2] and Kilmer's enthusiasm overcame Father Duffy's doubts that the poet's place was at home with his wife and children (of whom he had five, one of whom died shortly before he officially joined the 69th).[3]

Sent to Camp Mills, Long Island, Father Duffy was a peacemaker among New Yorkers from rival boroughs and regiments, as well as between his own New Yorkers and the rough-hewn men of the 167th Regiment from Alabama, which had last met the 69th in the War Between the States. After the Rainbow Division shipped overseas, Father Duffy once again tamped down Irish tempers when the troops were sent British uniforms to replace their own tattered togs. (By compromise, they wore the uniforms but only after clipping off the British buttons and replacing them with American ones.)

On 1 March 1918 Duffy wrote down a sentiment that few European soldiers would have echoed at that stage of the war: "The trenches at last!" The men, he noted, "are happy at being on the front...and look on the discomforts as part of the game....Their main sport is going out on patrols...to cut wires, and stir things up generally. With our artillery throwing over shells from the rear and our impatient infantry prodding the enemy, this sector will not be long a quiet one."[4] German shelling took its toll on the regiment, picking off two sentries and collapsing a dugout that claimed the lives of twenty-one men of E Company.

Father Duffy reminded the men at a St. Patrick's Day Mass, "We can pay tribute to our dead, but we must not lament them overmuch." There was still fighting to do, and a just cause to be served. At least one soldier thought Father Duffy resembled St. Patrick himself, preaching to the converted heathen as the chaplain stood "erect on the hill-top beside his little improvised altar...[overlooking] the columns of men as they approached."[5]

The eventual colonel of the Fighting 69th, Frank McCoy—a West Pointer, veteran of the Spanish-American War, and former aide to President Theodore Roosevelt—noted how Father Duffy knew all the men of the regiment by name, cajoled the sick and wounded with jokes instead of mothering them with sympathy, and was good company at the dining table and a "very learned" man.[6] He was also a tireless, calm, and courageous one, insisting on serving at the front, under fire, slapping nervous soldiers on the back, offering words of martial encouragement, handing out cigarettes, helping to treat and retrieve the wounded, hearing confessions before battle, and helping bury the dead after. Once, in a tight spot, he disdained an offer of grenades, saying, "Every man to his trade. I stick to mine."[7]

By war's end the Fighting 69th (or the 165th as it was known during the war) had taken casualties of more than 50 percent of its force. So Father Duffy was kept busy, but not too busy to conspire to make his great friend the outstanding combat officer William J. "Wild Bill" Donovan colonel of the 69th, a position Donovan, commander of the regiment's 1st Battalion, had disdained during the war,[8] but now gratefully accepted to lead the regiment home. Father Duffy ended the war a lieutenant colonel and had earned the Distinguished Service Cross, the Distinguished Service Medal, the Conspicuous Service Cross, the Légion d'Honneur, and the Croix de Guerre.

After the war he returned to life as a parish priest, as rector and then pastor of Holy Cross Church in the area of New York City known as "Hell's Kitchen." Alexander Woollcott recollected of him, "This city is too large for most of us. But not for Father Duffy. Not too large, I mean, for him to invest it with the homeliness of a neighborhood. When he walked down the street—any street—he was like a curé striding through his own village. Everyone knew him."[9]

Father Duffy died in 1932, after an intestinal infection. An estimated twenty-five thousand people turned out for his funeral at St. Patrick's Cathedral in New York City, the streets lined with mourners. His best epitaph came perhaps from a New York police officer trying to move a woman who had positioned herself in a reserved spot outside the cathedral. The woman asserted her right to be there, saying she had been a personal friend of Father Duffy. The policeman replied, "That is true, Ma'am, of everyone here today."[10] Father Duffy was the Catholic intellectual who made his true mark not in learned journals but in the mud of the bloody trenches of France and in the counsel, sacraments, and sermons he delivered as a parish priest.

THE MARKSMAN

Alvin C. York made no pretense of being an intellectual, a philosopher, or a theologian—he was nevertheless one of the great

Christian heroes of the war, a man of conscience who spoke to America's conscience. He was an authentically log-cabin-born American from the hills of Tennessee, the son of a farmer who doubled as a blacksmith. York was the third of eleven children, and like his siblings he worked around the house or in the fields as soon as he was able. He also learned to hunt and to make every shot count—because ammunition cost money.

Schooling and church-going were often ignored in the mountains. While the mountain folk were religious and centered their social life on going to church, the pastors were too few and their churches too scattered to make it a regular affair; and education had to play second fiddle to the need for farm labor. Alvin's formal education ended after the third grade.

When his father was killed by a mule kicking him in the head, Alvin, nearly fourteen, took a variety of jobs to support the family. That was admirable, but to burn off steam from his labors he became a roughhouser—a card player, a drinker, a brawler. Handy with his fists, he was equally adept with knives and also strove to emulate the gunfighters of mountain legend, practicing with a revolver until he could "crack a lizard's head"[11] with a bullet fired from either hand. Drunk or sober, he was an impressive marksman who earned money (and meat) in shooting competitions.

By his mid-twenties, York had begun sobering up and attending church more regularly. He still enjoyed his prowess with guns but came to realize that trouble was something to be avoided, not dallied with in raucous drinking sessions. He had a conversion experience in January 1915, after which he put drinking and smoking, dancing and gambling—and their consequent dangers—behind him. In 1917 he got engaged to a girl thirteen years his junior (he had recognized her as his future wife from the moment he first saw her; they married immediately after his return from the war) and was so active in the life of his church that he even preached when the preacher was away (York's other special interest was establishing Sunday schools).

When conscripted for the war, York tried four times to get an exemption on religious grounds and was stunned that the authorities would not take his pacifistic reading of the Bible as...well, gospel. York made a good soldier, nevertheless, in that he was dutiful and an expert marksman before he was even handed his Army rifle. At the rifle range, he thought the targets were awfully large—much bigger than a turkey's or a lizard's head—and was amazed that "Them-there Greeks and Italians and Poles and New York Jews and some of the boys from the big cities...not only missed the targets, they missed the background on which the targets were fixed. They missed everything except the sky."[12]

Two kindly officers talked to York about his objections to fighting, gave him a different interpretation of Scripture than he had previously considered, guaranteed him a noncombat role if he requested it, and granted him leave to think it over. York went home and spent a night alone on the mountain praying. When he returned, he was convinced that God had no objections to his fighting in his nation's cause and that as long as he kept faith he would be preserved from all harm. York had always considered patriotism a virtue. His officers convinced him that America's cause in the First World War was just, and he knew in his gut, "If some feller was to come along and bust into your house and mistreat your wife and murder your children,"[13] a Christian man didn't have to just stand for it—he should defend himself and his family. He returned to his officers a calm, confident soldier, though he "couldn't help a wonderin' why there wasn't some other way to get peace except by fightin' for it."[14]

In May 1918, York shipped to France with the 82nd "All American" Division (a division with soldiers from every state in the Union). In action, he learned that "The only thing to do was to pray and trust God"[15]—and to get the enemy before he got you. York did that well enough that on 8 October 1918 he managed to knock out 35 enemy machine guns, kill 25 German soldiers, and round up and capture another 132. That extraordinary feat made him an American hero—the mountain sharpshooter whose facility with rifle and pistol, and cool-handed courage, seemed to make him a throwback to the days of the long-rifle men, a Davy Crockett of the Great War. Marshal Foch thought it the most outstanding individual action of the entire conflict. Woodrow Wilson felt obliged to meet York in Paris in December 1918. He shook the soldier's hand, talked to him briefly, but did not invite him to stay for dinner—indeed, he had the bemused York escorted away, as he was expecting other guests.

Though the events of October 1918 had made him famous, York was never entirely at ease with what he had done. He prayed not only for his fallen American comrades but for the souls of the Germans he had killed; he once said that the fighting in the Meuse-Argonne was "one of those things I want to forget";[16] and at the end of his life he asked his minister son how God would judge his actions of that day. For his own part, he believed that God had protected him and that the American Expeditionary Force had indeed served the role of peacemaker in the terrible war in Europe. When York returned stateside, he refused to capitalize on his fame—that didn't seem right to him—except in one respect. Having seen the big old world, he thought that some of it deserved to come to the mountains, and that perhaps he was the one ordained to help bring it there.

In his words,

> Before the war I had never been out of the mountains. I
> had never wanted to be. I had sorter of figured out that
> them-there mountains were our shield against the outside
> world. They sorter of isolated us and kept us together so
> that we might grow up pureblooded and resourceful and
> God-loving and God-fearing. They done that, too, but
> they done more'n that. They done kept out many good
> and worthwhile things like good roads, schools, libraries,
> up-to-date homes, and modern farming methods. But I
> never thought of these things before going to war. Only
> when I got back home again and got to kinder thinking
> and dreaming.[17]

HELPING THE MOUNTAINEERS

Sergeant York had learned a lot from the war. He had learned
about people very different from himself. He had learned about the
devastation of war; and he believed he had skirmished with the per-
ils of Vanity Fair immediately after it. But most of all, he had come
to accept his vocation: to devote whatever influence he had as a
famous soldier to improve the lot of his people. It wasn't easy,
because a grateful community handed him unexpected troubles. The
Rotary Club awarded him farmland that neither the club (which did
not raise enough money for the project) nor York could afford, let
alone stock and run, especially after the postwar agricultural bust.
It took him two years (until the end of 1921) of hard work, negotia-
tion, donation campaigns, and frankly embarrassment to dig his way
out of the hole that the club had unwittingly sunk for him. As York

said, "I could get used to most any kind of hardship, but I'm not fitted for the hardship of owing money."[18]

Nevertheless, once his farm was paid for he devoted himself not to it—though it was his main source of income, he regarded it as a sidelight—but to fundraising for a school that would emphasize vocational skills and Christian learning (as well as using his influence for other worthy projects, including roads). His work to build his school, however, rather than leading to immediate sweetness and light, resulted in years of political and legal wrangling. The school, the Alvin C. York Institute,[19] finally opened in 1929 as a public school, though because the subsequent Great Depression crimped the state budget, York often used his own funds to keep the school running. His governance of the school was frequently criticized, and he finally resigned as the school's president in 1935, though he continued to support the institution that bore his name and harbored his hopes to help his fellow mountaineers.

After the rise of Nazi Germany, York argued for military preparedness, which he thought might keep war from America's shores. He shared some of the isolationism of his countrymen—he had no interest in Americans fighting in another European war—but he also regarded imperial Japan as a direct and Nazi Germany as an indirect threat to the United States that had to be thwarted. By 1941 he ardently supported President Roosevelt's policy of materially supporting Great Britain against Nazi Germany and its allies.

Also in 1941, York became an inadvertent recruiter for Uncle Sam with the Warner Brothers film *Sergeant York*, starring Gary Cooper. Inadvertent, because York had initially, at least, envisioned the film as mostly about life and progress in rural Tennessee, rather than about his experiences in the Great War, and he had agreed to the film—after declining previous offers—in large part because he was trying to raise money for a Bible school. Nevertheless, by the time the film came out, York was hoping that it would help forge national unity against the threat of the expansive Axis Powers.[20]

When war came, York volunteered, and was commissioned a major, though he was found medically unfit for active service and instead served on the local Selective Service Board (which inducted two of his own sons) and threw himself into all the volunteer work he could find to support the war effort. He was appalled that so many of his fellow mountain Tennesseans—crack shots—were being rejected merely because they were illiterate. But he inspired other men, those under the commands of Generals Matthew Ridgway and Omar Bradley, with a lecture on how effective a good marksman can be.

York inevitably took a special interest in soldiers from his region, and particularly in their spiritual and moral welfare. As in World War I, he was a little unsure about Orientals—then mistaking Vietnamese for Chinamen, now advising in favor of interning the Japanese, "whether native or foreign born" because they "all look alike and we can't take any chances."[21] With such insights, it was inevitable that he occasionally toyed with the idea of running for elective office. He was a Democrat, and among the races he considered was running against Tennessee congressman Albert Gore, but alas he never did. He believed, fundamentally, that political problems are actually moral and religious problems (a core conservative insight), but he also believed that the challenge of the Soviet Union was best dealt with not by moral suasion, but swiftly, by means of the atomic bomb. One of York's takeaway lessons from World War II was the folly of letting aggressive dictators grow stronger and bolder. Rather than send American soldiers to fight in Europe again, better to drop a bomb on Soviet strongman Joseph Stalin and be done with him and his gangster crew—or so thought the Tennessee mountain man.

York remained stalwart, though his health was failing him, the IRS was hounding him, and his Bible school came a cropper. He had always been improvidently generous to others and neglectful of his own finances, and toward the end of his life he was bailed out by donations and by Congress's reining in the voracious demands of the IRS. When he died in 1964, eight thousand people turned out for the funeral in rural Pall Mall, Tennessee, and President Lyndon Johnson sent as his emissary General Matthew Ridgway. The old long-rifle huntsman had no interest in being interred in Arlington; he knew his place was, as it always had been, among his kin in Tennessee.

CHAPTER SEVENTEEN

HARRY S. TRUMAN (1884–1972)

Harry Truman was the only American president to have seen action in World War I. Franklin Roosevelt was assistant secretary of the Navy, and Dwight Eisenhower was an Army training officer, a brevet lieutenant colonel; but neither saw action overseas. Truman did. He went to war feeling like he was "Galahad after the Grail....I rather felt we owed France something for Lafayette."[1]

The thirty-three-year-old man who held such notions was born on a farm in southern Missouri. The metropolis to which his family moved when he was six was Independence, a city of unpaved roads and no public water supply or electricity but six thousand people. The Trumans moved there for the schools, as young Harry, though he had weak eyes and needed glasses, read constantly (the Bible from start to finish twice), and his mother had ambitions for her young son.

As an elder statesman who reveled in his reputation for hard drinking and hard swearing, he confessed, "I was never popular. The popular boys were the ones who were good at games and had big, tight fists. I was never like that. Without my glasses I was blind as a bat, and to tell the truth, I was kind of a sissy."[2] Actually, his peers thought him more "serious" than a "sissy"—an arbitrator who could straighten out their history when they were playacting as Jesse James or the Dalton brothers; a boy they would trust to umpire a baseball game. He was a good student at a school that taught a traditional, classical curriculum, an avid reader in a home that was well stocked with books,[3] a boy who preferred train-watching or playing the piano to rough-and-tumble sports (where his glasses might get broken) and who kept himself neat and clean. He enjoyed, as he remembered it, a blissful small-town boyhood.

His mother was well read and doted on Harry, the eldest of her three surviving children. His father was industrious, a dealmaker, a successful livestock trader, a respected man—though with an easily ignited, nasty temper—who maintained the family in relative comfort until Harry finished high school. Then some bad land investments put the family in straitened circumstances. The family's heritage was Southern, and Harry's boyhood heroes included Robert E. Lee (venerated by his mother) and Andrew Jackson. He often daydreamed of becoming a general (he hoped to go to West Point until he realized his eyesight disqualified him)—or, given the hours he practiced, a pianist.[4]

PAYING A DEBT

After high school he took courses at a commercial college, eventually seemed to have found his niche, at least temporarily, as a bank clerk, and in 1905 found an outlet for his military interests by enlisting in a National Guard artillery unit (memorizing the eye chart so his eyesight would not disqualify him). In 1906, he heeded a call from his father and took up work on a family farm—to which the family had retired—where he spent the next eleven years working the soil, an occupation he did not like, and reading or playing the piano in his few leisure hours. In 1911, after two three-year enlistments with the National Guard, he decided he could not justify the time away from the farm. That changed after April 1917, when he decided it was time to pay his debt to Lafayette.

There were other factors too. He had enjoyed his military service, he was a patriot, and, as an active Democrat who had won a couple of minor political appointments, he knew that spending time in uniform could advance his political career. He reenlisted in the National Guard, sneaking past the eye test again, was elected a first lieutenant, and showed, as he had in all his jobs, that he was a dutiful and dedicated soul. Before his unit had finished its training at Fort Sill, Oklahoma, he had been recommended for promotion to captain. By April 1918 he was in France and attending Advanced Artillery School. The curriculum's intellectual demands, long hours (seven in the morning to nine-thirty at night), and hard physical training prompted Truman to write, "When I come home I'll be a surveyor, a mathematician, a mechanical draftsman, a horse doctor, a crack shot, and a tough citizen if they keep me here long. We have periods of lectures and exams and everything just like West Point…and they sure give us thunder if we are late."[5] He graduated from the school, received his official promotion to captain, and was given command of a notoriously undisciplined artillery battery. "Give 'em hell Harry" got his start here, busting miscreants, promoting high performers, and surprising even himself with his success at managing and training a difficult lot of men: "Can you imagine me being a hard-boiled captain of a tough Irish battery?"[6] he wrote his girlfriend (and future wife), Bess Wallace.

Having come to pay his debt to Lafayette, Truman didn't particularly care for France or the French. Typical was his frustration with the dining habits of French officers: "It takes them so long to serve a meal that I'm always hungrier when I get done than I ever was before."[7] He was a diligent tourist when on leave, but flinty in his patriotism and utterly convinced of the superiority of Missouri to La Belle France, Kansas City to the City of Lights, and everything American to everything French.

He saw his first action in August 1918, amid the mud and mire of the Vosges mountain range in Alsace-Lorraine, firing an artillery barrage and being fired on in return. The captain stood his ground. Many of his men did not. He cursed them for it, and won their respect.

Forced marches in cold, bitter rain brought them to the Argonne Forest and the enormous offensive that would end the war. Truman remembered that the opening barrage, to which his battery contributed, belched out "more noise than human ears could stand. Men serving the guns became deaf for weeks after. I was deaf as a post from the noise. It looked as though every gun in France was turned loose and the sky was red from one end to the other from the artillery flashes."[8] The artillery followed the infantry, and at the end of it all, with the armistice in November, only one man in Truman's battery, Battery D, had been killed in action and only two others had been wounded, all of them while detailed to another command. He had performed exceptionally well. The war was the making of him.

With the war over, he wanted to go home, but he joked about his loyalty and affection for his artillery pieces: "If the government would let me have one of them, I'd pay for it and pay the transportation home just to let it sit in my front yard and rust. Men you know—gunners and section chiefs especially—become very much attached to their guns....It's like parting with old friends who've stood by me through thick and thin."[9] Bess Wallace had stood by him through thick and thin too. She married Captain Truman on 28 June 1919.[10]

POLITICS

He had no interest in returning to farming, so he set up store as a haberdasher. As a small businessman, he could not survive the postwar recession. Politics proved a better outlet for his talents. In 1922, supported by the Democrat political machine of Kansas City boss Tom Pendergast, he was elected a county judge.[11] He was swept away, however, by the Republican electoral coattails of Calvin Coolidge, elected to the White House in 1924. Not only did Truman have to make a living, but he was perilously deep into debt from several failed business enterprises. He managed membership sales for the Kansas City Automobile Club, and was quite good at it, but it hardly satisfied him.

Regarding business as a game of chance where luck was rarely on his side, he decided that he would rather face voters than creditors. He was not without idealism, but to make his way in politics he made himself a wheel of the Pendergast machine. Pendergast himself was not without a certain amount of idealism either. He believed himself to be a realist, he thought men's opinions were easily swayed by newspapers, he denied that laws could make men better, and he believed that politics was a business where the victor handed out patronage and jobs. Yet the machine also served, in its own corrupt way, as a sort of nondenominational Catholic relief service,[12] helping not just political friends, but the poor—who were expected to show their gratitude at the polls. In 1926 the machine returned Truman to office as presiding judge (which meant chief administrator) of Jackson County, a position he held for eight years. He did what he was expected to do as far as patronage was concerned, though he also did what he thought he ought to do to improve public services and run the county efficiently, never pocketing any extra money for himself.

Nevertheless, he felt his ambitions were thwarted. He wanted to run for governor; Pendergast said no. He had his eye on a congressional seat; Pendergast had promised the seat to someone else. But luck finally turned up trumps for Truman. The popularity of President Franklin Roosevelt made the U.S. Senate seat held by Republican Roscoe Patterson vulnerable. Moreover, the likely Democrat challenger came from a rival political camp to that of Pendergast. After riffling through his own roster of talent, Pendergast insisted that Truman run. Truman had just turned fifty. In the hours before he made "the most momentous announcement of my life"—to run for the United States Senate—he wrote, "I have come to the place where all men strive to be at my age and I thought two weeks ago that retirement on a virtual pension in some minor county office was all that was in store for me."[13] Fate had much more in mind.

Truman won an upset victory in the primary and went on to win big in the general election in 1934 as a supporter of Franklin Roosevelt's New Deal policies for ameliorating the economic depression. Still, for all his ambition—now apparently gratified—Truman was uncertain he could be reelected, fretted he was unworthy of the job, and knew the press, and possibly others, regarded him as the "rube from Pendergast land."[14] Democrat senator J. Hamilton Lewis of Illinois tried to reassure his new colleague: "Harry, don't start out with an inferiority complex. For the first six months you'll wonder how the hell you got here, and after that you'll wonder how the hell the rest of us got here."[15]

Truman was right that his reelection would be difficult; the chief problem was his loyalty to Pendergast, who was convicted of tax evasion in 1939. Truman refused to abandon his patron, convinced that Republican judges had railroaded Pendergast, though the FBI and IRS had provided a wealth of evidence against him. Truman even ranted against federal district attorney Maurice Milligan, claiming he was corrupt and a "personal appointment"[16] of President Roosevelt (whose policies Truman otherwise supported). The result was that in 1940 Truman ran for reelection with his patron in jail, the administration unsupportive, and the Missouri press opposed to him. He won anyway, though much more narrowly than before.

His signature issue became ferreting out waste in rearmament programs, which brought him public recognition (the Senate Special Committee to Investigate the National Defense Program even became known as the "Truman Committee"), congressional clout, and a grudging, annoyed respect from the administration, which accepted that Truman strongly backed the administration's policies even as he investigated embarrassing cost overruns and inefficiencies. The press rallied to him and declared that his committee was a major boost to the war effort, saving billions of dollars. It also shot him onto the 1944 Democrat ticket as the vice presidential candidate—his nomination regarded as the "Second Missouri Compromise," rallying conservative and moderate Democrats who opposed the sitting vice president, the very liberal Henry Wallace.

WARTIME PRESIDENT

Truman was vice president for only eighty-two days. Summoned to the White House on 12 April 1945, he was greeted by Eleanor

Roosevelt. With her hand on his shoulder, she announced, "Harry, the president is dead."

After a moment of stunned silence, Truman replied, "Is there anything I can do for you?"

The president's widow responded, "Is there anything we can do for you, Harry? For you are the one in trouble now."[17]

General Patton, in Europe, thought it was America that was in trouble now. He said of Truman, "It seems very unfortunate that in order to secure political preference, people are made Vice President who are never intended, neither by Party nor by the Lord to be Presidents."[18] In deeper trouble, however, were the Axis Powers. In less than a month, Germany surrendered. Japan had no hope for victory in the Pacific but was instead girding itself to make unconditional victory for the Allies extraordinarily costly.

In Truman's arsenal was one weapon of which he had known nothing when he was vice president: the atomic bomb. Another weapon that he hoped to use against Japan was Soviet military power. Truman met the Soviet leader, Marshal Joseph Stalin, at the Potsdam Conference on 17 July 1945. He liked him (he thought him a Slavic version of Tom Pendergast) and was convinced he could work with him, even as he regarded the Soviet Union as a police state and was bluntly opposed—in principle if not in force—to the export of Communism into Eastern Europe.

It took the dropping of two atomic bombs—one on Hiroshima on 6 August and one on Nagasaki on 9 August (the same day that the Soviet Union declared war and invaded Japanese-held Manchuria)—and a massive conventional air raid on Tokyo on 13 August before the Japanese issued a formal statement of surrender on 14 August. Truman had calculated that by dropping the atomic bombs he could end the war swiftly—and by ending it, save hundreds of thousands of lives.

THE TRUMAN DOCTRINE

Truman's great and immediate postwar challenge was how to handle the Soviet Union, which appeared intent on forcibly extending its totalitarian system everywhere, from North Korea to Eastern Europe. Truman had every intention of trying to find an accommodation with the Soviets, but their intransigence and global aggression left him fuming. To his secretary of state, James Byrnes, Truman vented his frustration at the Soviets' behavior in Poland, their imposition of Communist tyrannies on Romania and Bulgaria, and their occupation of northern Iran. "There isn't a doubt in my mind," he wrote, "that Russia intends an invasion of Turkey and the seizure of the Black Sea Straits to the Mediterranean.... Only one language do they understand—'how many divisions have you?' I do not think we should play compromise any longer.... I'm tired of babying the Soviets."[19]

That was in private. In public, he was more cautious. He introduced Churchill at Westminster College in Fulton, Missouri, where the former prime minister delivered his speech about a Communist Iron Curtain descending across Central and Eastern Europe. While Truman privately approved Churchill's remarks, his administration did not officially endorse them. Most of Truman's advisors shared and reinforced his strong anti-Communism, but there were others on the left of the Democrat Party, including his commerce secretary, former vice president Henry Wallace, who very much believed the Soviets deserved to be babied, indulged, and appeased.

In domestic policy, Truman had nothing but headaches, in part because of postwar circumstances, in part because of his attempt to tread a middle path. On the one hand, he knew he had to rapidly reduce government expenditures; on the other, he felt obliged to try to advance the liberal domestic policies of Franklin Roosevelt—including the creation of a national health insurance program—against strong congressional opposition. Truman understood the need to demobilize America's massive Army and Navy, to bring the boys home, but he worried about the foreign policy consequences and whether the postwar economy could absorb so many men without a spike in unemployment, and as commander in chief he fretted about the "disintegration of our armed forces."[20] He tried to play the arbiter between labor and management but pleased neither one, and the nation suffered from so many strikes, including among steelworkers (the largest in American history), that when the railway workers went on strike he tried to get Congress to approve legislation (the House actually did) that would allow him to draft striking workers into the military.

The 1946 election delivered a Republican majority to the House of Representatives for the first time since 1930. Instead of recoiling from the rebuke, he took fire from it. No longer would Truman worry about trying to hold the disparate factions of the Democrat Party together. He intended to go his own way and trust that if it was the right way, others would follow; he would be a leader rather than a conciliator. That did not mean that political calculations never entered into his considerations. They manifestly did; indeed, in Truman, as in most politicians, there was no stark divide between what he believed was right and what he believed was politically advantageous. He was a practical man.

In 1947, financially battered Britain informed the United States that it would have to withdraw British troops supporting the anti-Communist government in Greece and end its financial aid to Turkey, which was under pressure from the Soviet Union. In response, Truman enunciated what became known as the Truman Doctrine: that the United States should "help free peoples to maintain their free institutions and their national integrity against aggressive movements that seek to impose upon them totalitarian regimes. This is no more than a frank recognition that totalitarian regimes imposed upon free peoples, by direct or indirect aggression, undermine the foundations of international peace and hence the security of the United States."[21] Congress agreed to provide the requested aid to Greece and Turkey. But that was only the beginning.

In June 1947 in a speech at Harvard University, General George Marshall, now secretary of state, sketched the outlines of what became known as the Marshall Plan for the restoration of the economies of Europe, including the Soviet bloc, if the Communists would participate, which they would not. Truman, who had done his part to restore the peace of Europe in two world wars—as a captain of artillery and commander in chief—now committed the United States to the economic and political well-being of Europe and the containment of a hostile power larger and even more menacing in its ideological and geographical reach than the recently defeated Axis Powers.

In addition, Truman committed the United States to the creation of a Jewish homeland in a Palestine partitioned between Arabs and Jews, though in typical Truman fashion he lashed out at Jewish-American pressure on the administration: "Jesus Christ couldn't please them when he was on earth, so how could anyone expect that I would have any luck."[22] In May 1948 Truman issued a statement recognizing the new state of Israel. He was the first world leader to do so, and acted against the advice of the State Department.

In his 1948 campaign for president, Truman did not try to reconcile liberals and Southern conservatives in his own party. Instead
he split them, with leftists breaking off to support a run by Henry
Wallace, carrying the banner of the Progressive Party—or "Henry
Wallace and his Communists," as Truman called them[23]—and Southern conservatives backing South Carolina governor Strom Thur-
mond and his "Dixiecrats," who opposed Truman's support for
federal legislation to protect the civil rights of black Americans.

In foreign policy, Truman's warnings about Soviet aggression
appeared further vindicated when the Soviets blockaded Berlin
in 1948. The Western Allies responded with the Berlin airlift—
a bit of inspiring Cold War heroism that kept Berlin supplied
and eventually forced the Soviets to lift the blockade in 1949.

Americans supported the airlift, but they did not appear to support the commander in chief who ordered it. The Republican nominee, New York governor Thomas Dewey, was the sizable favorite
among the pollsters. But Dewey had lost to Franklin Roosevelt in
1944 and was not an ideal candidate: he had a stiff, uninspiring, and
unhelpfully dapper and conceited image. His moderate positions—
which drew no stark contrast to Truman—and his obvious belief
that he could coast to victory didn't help him either.[24] In the event,
he coasted to a stunning landslide defeat, with the Republicans also
losing both houses of Congress. A grinning Truman, in one of the
great moments of American politics, held up the front page of the
Chicago Daily Tribune with its glaring and egregiously wrong headline: "DEWEY DEFEATS TRUMAN."[25]

As the newly reelected president, Truman said he wanted to offer
Americans a "Fair Deal," which amounted to a laundry list of new or
expanded federal government programs to make life more equitable or
secure, or to promote, as he saw it, the common good. His domestic

agenda, however, was too liberal even for the Democrat majorities in Congress. His foreign policy agenda met with more success. In 1949, the United States founded the North Atlantic Treaty Organization (NATO) uniting the West in a military alliance stronger than any since the Reformation had divided Christendom.

Which is not to say that all was going swimmingly for American foreign policy. In fact, in short order the Soviets broke America's nuclear monopoly (thanks in part to Communist spies) by detonating their own atomic bomb, dubbed "Joe 1" by Americans; China fell to the Communists; and the Soviets' postwar occupation of North Korea, a country about which Americans knew little, looked to be no more temporary than their postwar occupation of Eastern Europe. The question for some administration critics was whether the administration was shot through with Communist spies and fellow travelers or simply blundering. The reality was a bit of both, combined with the fact that Washington could not control events around the world. (No one in the United States had "lost" China; America's Nationalist Chinese ally, Chiang Kai-shek, had managed that himself.) What Truman could do, and did, was authorize the development of the hydrogen bomb.

KOREA

In June 1950, the Cold War turned hot in an unexpected place, Korea. The Communist North invaded South Korea, which Secretary of State Dean Acheson, in a January speech to the National Press Club, had placed outside of America's national security interests in the Far East. American policy was that South Korea was of little strategic importance—but what was important was not giving a free hand to Communist aggression. Korea now seemed, in the words of Assistant Secretary of State Dean Rusk, like "a dagger pointed at the heart of Japan."[26] Truman was cautious but furious at the same time, and committed to stopping "the sons-of-bitches no matter what!"[27] The Soviet Union's boycott of the meetings of the United Nations Security Council (over the United Nations' refusal to recognize Communist China) allowed the United States to get a UN resolution condemning the attack and authorizing what became known as a "police action" to repel Communist aggression.

Without immediate American action, which meant deploying troops stationed in Japan to Korean battlefields, South Korea would have fallen. Even with American intervention, South Korea was nearly overrun. But under the command of General Douglas MacArthur, the South Korean and UN forces, chiefly American, drove the North Koreans back over the 38th parallel, which divided the two Koreas. Truman authorized MacArthur to keep going as along as neither the Soviets nor the Red Chinese intervened. But the Chinese did indeed come, troops pouring in by the tens of thousands, ultimately more than a million—and the apparently imminent Allied victory suddenly looked like the opening rounds of World War III. The prime objective of the Truman administration was to tamp down the war's flames so that they didn't engulf China, the Soviet Union, and the United States in a much greater war. That put the president at odds with his commander, Douglas MacArthur, who believed there was no substitute for victory. It says something about Truman's political unpopularity that MacArthur, returning stateside after Truman relieved him of duty for public dissent from administration policy, was greeted as a hero across the country and invited to address a joint session of Congress, where his speech was greeted with rapturous acclaim.

Hardly anyone was in raptures about Harry Truman's leadership. In May 1951, less than a quarter of Americans approved of his performance. Though his feistiness convinced an unimpressed American public that he would run for reelection, Truman thought eight years in the White House was enough. His second term, like many second terms, was mired in administration scandals; and he would leave the resolution of the Korean War, now stalemated, to someone else. His frustration revealed itself when he attempted to nationalize the nation's steel companies to stave off a national strike that he thought intensely unpatriotic when the country was at war, though he was much more sympathetic to the steelworkers (labor union Democrat voters) than to the companies, which refused to settle. The companies sued the president and won a judgment—endorsed by the Supreme Court—that the president had acted unlawfully. It was a stinging rebuke, a 6-to-3 ruling by justices who were all Democrat appointees.

Seeking someone to inherit his presidential mantle, Truman turned to General Dwight Eisenhower, then serving as NATO's supreme commander, to run as the Democrat nominee for president, apparently unaware—a tribute to Eisenhower's discretion—that Ike's own political leanings were considerably more conservative than Truman's. Eisenhower said he had no interest in running for office. Not much later, prominent Republicans like Dewey and Henry Cabot Lodge Jr. convinced Eisenhower that he needed to run, lest the GOP nomination be carried by the anti-internationalist, anti-NATO Robert Taft. Eisenhower beat Taft for the nomination and trounced the Democrat Party's nominee, Adlai Stevenson, in the 1952 election, taking not only Stevenson's home state of Illinois and Harry Truman's Missouri—along with thirty-nine other states (out of forty-eight)—but sweeping Republican majorities into both houses of Congress. In the presidential transition, Eisenhower and Truman's relationship was cold and curt.

"GIVE 'EM HELL HARRY"

Harry Truman, the man of the people—though the people didn't much care for him in January 1953—returned to Independence, Missouri. Loyal Democrat that he was, he campaigned against Eisenhower's reelection. Even though he didn't like the Democrat ticket of Adlai Stevenson and Estes Kefauver (toward whom he had a personal antipathy), he disliked Eisenhower more. Eisenhower, however, had ended the Korean War and was easily reelected.

Truman hated Richard Nixon—Eisenhower's vice president and the Republican nominee for president in 1960—and was chilly toward John F. Kennedy. Kennedy's father, Joseph P. Kennedy, had been Franklin Roosevelt's ambassador to Britain and a leading isolationist prior to America's entry into the Second World War. After the war, John F. Kennedy had supported, and his brother Robert had worked for, Senator Joseph McCarthy. Truman loathed McCarthy and disliked the Kennedys, *père et fils*. Truman thought John F. Kennedy too young to be president and thought it wrong to put a Catholic at the top of the Democrat ticket, though he commented, "It's not the Pope I'm afraid of. It's the pop."[28] He tried to block Kennedy from getting the nomination, but JFK's personal diplomacy eventually won him over; Truman's crotchetiness could be assuaged by deft, sincere flattery and shared policies. He approved of Kennedy's "New Frontier" domestic agenda and his Truman-like mixture of caution and committed anti-Communism in foreign policy.

In his post-presidential retirement, Truman lived humbly. He rejected offers to capitalize on his name, devoting himself instead to writing his memoirs and establishing his presidential library. He admired the example of Cincinnatus and George Washington, the hero who returns to his farm. Truman had no intention of farming again, but he was content, more or less, to live in his old home in Independence. He missed the limelight and mental stimulation of being at the center of power, but he traveled, and he corresponded with friends like Dean Acheson. He worked every day in his office until he was eighty-four and maintained an image as a straight-talking, no-nonsense, no-special-airs, common-man democrat.

He died on 26 December 1972, aged eighty-eight. He had, by then, overcome the poor reputation he had when he left office and become an iconic American figure. A few years after his death, *Give 'em Hell, Harry!*, a popular play and film, immortalized him as a tough, honest, tenacious statesman.[29] But of all the experiences that had shaped him, one stood out. It was his service in World War I. As a biographer noted, his war service "was the most successful and satisfying experience of Truman's first thirty-five years." He had demonstrated "an inner courage and an ability to lead other men," and Truman himself "frequently remarked that his political career was based on his military experience."[30] If Truman was "Give 'em Hell Harry," it was because he had first given the Huns hell as a captain of artillery in the Meuse-Argonne.

CHAPTER EIGHTEEN

WILLIAM J. DONOVAN
(1883-1959)

The grandson of Irish immigrants to Buffalo, New York, William Joseph (his confirmation name) Donovan grew up stereotypically Irish—pugnacious (his father set up a boxing ring for him in the backyard) and with a taste for poetry (though a mediocre student, he was excellent at declaiming). The Donovan home was full of books, and his parents were keen on their children's educational success. While his father had disdained going to college, being eager to make his way in the world, he was an autodidact who had worked himself out of the Irish ghetto and into the suburbs. He was also independent minded—a Republican among a sea of Irish Catholic Democrats.

Growing up, Will, as they called him, played football for Saint Joseph's Collegiate Institute (a Catholic high school) and then attended Niagara University (a Catholic college) for three years, where he mulled a priestly vocation before transferring to Columbia College (later University) in New York City with the thought that he might become a lawyer. Though an indifferent student, he had the gift of blarney, which suited him well as a debater and could be of use in a courtroom, and he played football (until an injury ended his career), rowed, and ran cross country. He completed his undergraduate studies in 1905 and enrolled in Columbia Law School, where he finally showed some academic moxie, graduating in two years.

His law degree didn't immediately translate into professional success. Indeed, he moved back to Buffalo, lived with his parents, and was uncertain what to do. He finally joined a well-respected and well-paying local law firm in 1909, when he was twenty-six. Two years later, he was bold enough to hang out his own shingle with a friend, Bradley Goodyear. After three years, they folded their law firm into that of John Lord O'Brian. At Columbia, Donovan, a soft-spoken, charming young man with dazzling blue eyes, had dated a string of socially prominent beauties. Now he was a partner of two socially prominent lawyers. O'Brian, nearly a decade Donovan's senior, was a politically ambitious and well-connected Republican. He had been a New York State assemblyman and was appointed district attorney by President Theodore Roosevelt.

Donovan was successful enough that he helped pay for the schooling of his younger siblings.[1] He was also a founding member of a National Guard cavalry unit set up by a group of local businessmen who wanted an excuse to ride and camp. Donovan was elected captain and made a hobby of reading up on military subjects. That was 1912. Two years later he married Ruth Rumsey, heiress to a fortune from her late multimillionaire father.[2] Three years later he was preparing for war.

"THE LINE IS THE REAL PLACE"

Donovan first saw the Great War in Europe in 1916 representing the Rockefeller Foundation, which was trying to bring war relief to the continent; and his military skills were polished that same year when his National Guard cavalry unit, Troop I, was dispatched to Texas for Pershing's punitive campaign against Pancho Villa's banditos. In 1917, he joined the Fighting 69th, New York City's Irish National Guard regiment, which became part of General Douglas MacArthur's 42nd "Rainbow" Division. Given charge of a battalion, he knocked it into shape with cross country runs and boxing competitions.

He looked the part of a soldier: fit, quietly commanding, with "eyes like blue ice that drilled straight through you." The chaplain of the Fighting 69th, Father Francis Duffy, had his eye on Donovan as an eventual colonel, a proper Irish Catholic officer for the regiment who was "cool, untiring, strenuous," of "fine character," with an "alert and eager intelligence."[3] Donovan worked hard at the Field Officers' School in France and pooh-poohed any disappointment that he was not swiftly made a colonel. In January 1918 he wrote his wife, "The line is the real place. And truly the Major has the best job in the war. It is low enough so that you still have touch with the men and high enough so that you can use your intellect."[4]

Donovan and his men moved into the trenches at the end of February 1918. He was a diligent and conscientious officer and expected the same virtues from his platoon commanders. He was also aggressive. Advancing with his 3rd Battalion in late July 1918 at the Battle of the Ourcq River, he pressed forward despite the battalions on his flanks failing to keep up. He suppressed enemy fire with well-placed machine guns and snipers, while his men darted ahead in ones, twos, or threes, dropped, got up, and darted again. Donovan and his men had scant regard for the Germans, regarding them as dirty fighters who would surrender when things got tough. During the Battle of Saint-Mihiel, the doughboys swept through the enemy, collecting so many thousands of prisoners that Donovan worried about keeping his own men disciplined and sharp.

During the Meuse-Argonne Campaign, Father Duffy noted of Donovan, "He goes into [battle] in exactly the frame of mind that he held as a college man when he marched out on the gridiron before a football game, and his one thought throughout is to push his way through. 'Cool' is the word the men use of him and 'Cool' is their highest epithet of praise for a man of daring, resolution and indifference to danger."[5] In his first action, Donovan had helped dig men out of a bunker that had been buried under a German bombardment—and won a Croix de Guerre, which he refused to accept until a Jewish sergeant of his unit was awarded one too. For his work at the Battle of the Ourcq he had been awarded a Distinguished Service Cross. He came to the Meuse-Argonne a highly regarded young officer who had been gassed, wounded by shrapnel, and shown the right stuff as a battlefield commander, earning the nickname from his men of "Wild Bill"—referring not to his manner, which was not wild at all, but to his courage and toughness.

Now he was a lieutenant colonel commanding the 1st Battalion and charged with breaching the *Kriemhilde Stellung*. His men had advanced the farthest, but the offensive was stalled, and Donovan, trying to press on, had been shot through the leg. Nevertheless he stayed on the field, directing his men until loss of blood forced him to accept evacuation. A month later the war was over. In January 1919, Donovan, now recovered, was assigned as a staff officer to the provost marshal general, policing American occupation troops. It was uncongenial duty. In April he was shipped home and restored to his old regiment as colonel of the Fighting 69th. He told his brother Vincent, "When I think of all the boys I have left behind me who died out of loyalty to me, it's too much."[6] When he was awarded a belated Medal of Honor in 1923, he left it to the regiment, citing the sacrifices of those who had died in its service.

INTELLIGENCE WORK

Donovan had promised his wife a trip, a sort of second honey-moon, which took them to Asia and allowed Donovan to do a little freelance intelligence work on Japan's imperial ambitions and on the civil war in Russia. Indeed, he was far more absorbed with gathering intelligence, which became a postwar hobby for him, than with spending time with his wife; she returned home alone. If Donovan was not a dutiful husband, he was certainly ambitious. He often traveled abroad on further business-building and intelligence-gathering jaunts,[7] while assuming a nascent political career as well. In 1922 he was named U.S. attorney for western New York, including Buffalo, where he gained a reputation as a tough enforcer of Prohibition laws—even against the social elite who presumed they were immune—and ran as the Republican candidate for lieutenant governor (he lost). In 1924 he became an assistant attorney general at the United States Department of Justice. Herbert Hoover, elected president in 1928, liked Donovan, had employed him as a speech-writer and campaign advisor, and promised to promote him to attorney general (Donovan had often been the de facto acting attorney general in the Calvin Coolidge administration). But ranged against Donovan were a wide variety of political enemies—Democrats, of course; anti-Catholics (including Prohibitionists who doubted someone like Donovan could sincerely be on their side); and perhaps most important, J. Edgar Hoover, director of the Justice Department's Bureau of Investigation. The colorful high-flyer Donovan and the scheming bureaucrat J. Edgar Hoover shared a deep personal antipathy for each other. In the midst of all this, President Hoover backed down and offered to make Donovan governor of the Philippines; instead, Donovan resigned.

In 1929, Donovan moved to New York City and started another law firm, which became hugely successful. In 1932, he was the Republican candidate for governor of New York but was trounced in what was a very Democratic year. Donovan had hoped to use the governorship as a springboard to become the first Catholic president of the United States. He made do with enjoying the perks that came with being a wealthy lawyer. He liked living in high style; he also took a keen interest in military and foreign affairs. As American diplomat Hugh Wilson said of him, "Colonel Donovan has played an active part in American political life and is one of the leading lawyers of the country, but he has a hobby and that hobby is war." Donovan, he added, was "not happy if there is a war on the face of the earth, and he has not had a look at it."[8]

There would soon be plenty of war, and plenty of opportunity for Donovan to pursue his hobby. At first, though, personal tragedy intervened. Donovan had always been distant from his wife and son, living a largely separate life, but he had a strong rapport with his daughter, who took his wife's place at many social functions. When she was killed in a traffic accident in 1940, aged twenty-two,

Donovan's grief was profound. He was a shattered man; his hair rapidly went white. War and intelligence gathering were now more than a hobby; they were a means of escape.

Donovan had been an outspoken opponent of President Franklin Roosevelt's domestic policies, but like Roosevelt he wanted the United States prepared for war, if war should come. President Roosevelt had appointed Republicans Frank Knox as secretary of the Navy and Henry Stimson as secretary of war to generate bipartisan support for his foreign policy. He tapped Donovan too, sending him on a fact-finding mission to Britain; Donovan returned an enthusiast for helping arm the British Empire to fight the war in Europe. Frank Knox asked Donovan to join him for an inspection of America's Pacific Fleet in Hawaii. Donovan became a private citizen emissary for the administration's military and foreign policies.

Donovan's own ambition was a return to the colors and eventual combat command; the British, however, made a concerted effort to enlist Donovan as their advocate in Washington, even arranging a meeting with Prime Minister Winston Churchill, who outlined his war plans. Donovan traveled through the Balkans and the Middle East, which both he and Churchill thought strategically vital, with the message that the United States intended to support Great Britain with aid and military supplies. He also hit the speaking circuit in the United States, arguing for military preparedness and American aid for Britain.

In 1941, Roosevelt appointed him coordinator of information—a vague title and unpaid position, but both Donovan and the president intended to make the COI the unofficial director of American intelligence. They did this against the opposition of J. Edgar Hoover, head of the Federal Bureau of Investigation; Army chief of staff George Marshall, who thought the military's intelligence role would be usurped; and the half dozen other intelligence agencies reporting to the president. Donovan ran agents, broadcast propaganda abroad, and built up an unconventional team of often brilliant, socially well-connected men—some of whom maintained businesses while they dabbled in intelligence—who supplied him with information, which he assembled, edited, and delivered to the president, eventually at regular intervals three times a day, along with his own assessments and ideas, one of which was to create an independent commando army. Donovan had not given up on the idea of a battlefield command.

Donovan suspected the Japanese would attack the United States, but he was surprised when the blow came at Pearl Harbor on 7 December 1941. Late that night, in a meeting at the White House, the president told Donovan, "It's a good thing you got me started on this,"[9] referring to Donovan's development and organization of American intelligence. Accurate intelligence would be crucial in the war to come. A failure of intelligence had left the United States unprepared for the attack on Pearl Harbor—something for which Donovan could not blamed, because his men had been focused on Europe and his intelligence assets in Asia were too few.[10] Others, including military and naval intelligence and Hoover's FBI, came under closer scrutiny.

Donovan built an intelligence agency out of whatever materials came to hand—not just Ivy League lawyers and wealthy businessmen but academics, criminals, expatriates with possibly valuable overseas links, and anyone of whatever background with skills that might come in useful. Donovan's COI was a bit like an intelligence version of Theodore Roosevelt's Rough Riders, though with fewer cowboys and more men wearing spectacles and carrying briefcases. He relied on no elaborate security clearances, but on his own whim, others' recommendations, and the cooperation of companies—and the Vatican—that encouraged their employees to assist Donovan's undercover assignments. Some gathered information, others analyzed it (the "chairborne division"); some engaged in sabotage, others designed weapons for saboteurs and spies. Donovan stood above it all, an ideas man of expansive imagination, blithely independent of the bureaucracy, with an enormous appetite for cloak-and-dagger operations. Roosevelt liked Donovan—his ideas were entertaining, if nothing else—and protected him from his many critics who thought him an irresponsible amateur.

THE OSS

To meet that criticism, Donovan lobbied to have his organization brought under the Joint Chiefs of Staff. It meant less independence, but it also meant that the COI's reports might be taken more seriously and that the COI would survive the number crunchers who regarded it as reckless and free-spending and largely unaccountable. The transfer was approved, and the COI—stripped of the Foreign Information Service[11]—became the OSS, the Office of Strategic Services, in June 1942.

Later that year, the OSS was assigned to undermine Vichy resistance to the Allied invasion of North Africa. OSS agents supplied worthwhile intelligence but failed to stiffen the backbone of potential Vichy defectors and Free French partisans. Donovan expected to do better in future guerrilla operations—starting perhaps by dropping agents in the Balkans.

In March 1943, Roosevelt made Donovan a brigadier general. The promotion did not come with a battlefield command, but Donovan planned to use his rank, when necessary, to better fight bureaucratic battles at home and rivalries with British intelligence abroad. Donovan was an Anglophile; he had used his intelligence reports to back Churchill against virtually every military advisor to Roosevelt in supporting the attack on North Africa rather than a direct assault on Nazi-occupied France; and he had been a great, licit conduit of intelligence to the British. But he also resented the British Empire's sense of superiority in its military and intelligence branches. He thought his OSS was at least an equal to British intelligence in many theaters and superior in some where British imperial motives might be questioned. The British reluctantly acceded to OSS operations in Greece, Romania, and Bulgaria. They were hostile, however, to the OSS dropping agents into Yugoslavia, where British operations were well established and the political alignments were complex and fragile.[12] Similarly, the British were opposed to the OSS meddling in Nazi-occupied Western Europe, particularly France, where they feared that Donovan's amateurs, as they regarded them, might put British intelligence assets at risk. If OSS agents were subordinated to the British (as they sometimes were), cooperation might be possible, but the British were adamant that Donovan should not run independent operations. Donovan was equally adamant that he should. In the end, Donovan won.

"HAPPY AS A CLAM"

Not only did he win the bureaucratic battle with the British, but he managed to insert himself as one of two members of the OSS to land with American troops during the invasion of Sicily (the other was there to interrogate prisoners). On shore, he convinced General Theodore Roosevelt Jr. to lend him a jeep and a driver. Donovan promptly saw combat against an Italian patrol, which he subdued himself with a light machine gun. His driver, Captain Paul Gale, a combat veteran, remembered that Donovan "was happy as a clam"[13] after the firefight. Donovan landed with the invasion force on Salerno as well, and, perhaps hoping to re-create his adventures in Sicily, he asked General Mark Clark for a jeep and a weapon. Clark obliged.

Donovan even convinced Generals Marshall and Eisenhower to let the OSS have a crack at organizing partisan guerrilla operations in German-occupied Corsica, supporting an invasion of fifteen thousand Free French. The OSS officer in charge, Major Carleton Coon (a prewar professor of anthropology), remembered that "Far from being the great victory which…has been portrayed in the papers," the Allied operation was "largely an act of occupying territory which the Germans did not want." The Germans "left as early as, if not actually when, they wanted to leave, and the French moved in afterward." All the OSS and its allies did was "annoy them on their way out."[14] Still, the OSS was annoying quite a lot of people—and not just the Nazis and the British and Donovan's bureaucratic enemies. Donovan's operations had gone global, from Europe, North Africa, and the Middle East to war-torn China and British India. He traveled incessantly, even into the depths of the Burmese jungle to check on OSS training of Kachin guerrillas. J. Edgar Hoover and President Roosevelt blocked Donovan from establishing a formal intelligence exchange with the Soviets,[15] and Douglas MacArthur kept all but a few OSS men out of the southwest Pacific (Donovan was one of the few, landing with MacArthur at Hollandia, Dutch New Guinea), but these were the exceptions to Donovan's ever-expanding intelligence empire that by the middle of 1944 numbered eleven thousand operatives.

Of course, the giant mission in 1944 was Overlord, the invasion of Normandy. By D-Day, 6 June 1944, the OSS and the British

Special Operations Executive (SOE) had parachuted teams—the famous Jedburghs—into France to help organize and supply the French resistance, the Maquis. The OSS performed other, more standard, intelligence operations as well, such as advising on German targets for Allied bombing. General Marshall had issued an order that Donovan should not land with the invasion force, but the irrepressible Irishman finagled a berth on a ship pounding the German coastline defenses with its big guns on 6 June, and then hitchhiked aboard smaller vessels to land ashore on 7 June, coming under Messerschmitt and German machine gun fire that pinned him to the ground—and reminded him that he had forgotten his poison suicide pills. He gallantly told the OSS London station chief, Virginia aristocrat Colonel David K. E. Bruce, who was pinned down with him, that as senior officer he would shoot Bruce first and then himself if they were in danger of being captured. Luckily for them both, Allied air cover drove the Germans back. Donovan was promoted to major general in November 1944.

The OSS helped Communist partisans fight the Germans, but as the war entered its final phase, Donovan recognized the Soviets as a potential future enemy, given their scarcely disguised hostility to the United States and the West. At home, he fought a bureaucratic turf war to establish a postwar intelligence organization. His rivals were J. Edgar Hoover at the FBI and the offices of military intelligence. President Roosevelt had loved gossip and hence intelligence. His successor, President Harry Truman, did not, having a healthy skepticism of and distaste for domestic spying. While Truman admired Donovan's war record in the Great War, he did not approve of highflying Republicans in a Democrat administration and initially gave short shrift to organizing a postwar intelligence service.

"THE LAST HERO"

Supreme Court Justice Robert Jackson, charged with prosecuting Nazi war criminals, eventually helped convince Truman otherwise. Donovan—who wanted revenge on the Nazis who had tortured and executed his agents during the war—provided OSS personnel and reams of useful information to help Jackson's investigations. In turn, Jackson, a Democrat, helped convince the president that the spy chief and his plans had their merits.[16] That, however, was not enough to save the OSS. Truman closed it down in September 1945. He planned to create his own intelligence service, not inherit Donovan's, and eventually did so with the Central Intelligence Agency in 1947.

Instead of leading America's intelligence service after the war, Donovan returned to practicing law—without much serious interest, mainly as a means to pay off his six-figure debts. His boredom and ambition led to another run for office, this time for the Republican nomination for U.S. senator from New York in 1946. New York governor Thomas Dewey, a liberal Republican at odds both personally and politically with the "reactionary" Donovan, made certain he didn't get it. In 1952 Donovan campaigned for Eisenhower. The newly elected president passed him over for appointment as director of Central Intelligence, the job Donovan wanted. As a consolation prize he was offered the ambassadorship to France, which he declined. But when Secretary of State John Foster Dulles asked Donovan to become ambassador to Thailand, he accepted—albeit already with plans (which in the end coincided with Eisenhower's) to transform the position into a seat of covert regional anti-Communist counterinsurgency and propaganda operations. He enjoyed his time in Thailand, but he was starting to feel his age, and in 1954 he asked to be relieved of the assignment. He still hoped to be a freelance troubleshooter in Southeast Asia but focused, for the nonce, on replenishing his once-again-drained financial coffers.

The intelligence chief's mind, however, began to deteriorate. By 1957, he found it virtually impossible to work, then virtually impossible to walk unaided; hospitalized, he alternated between periods of lucidity and bouts of dementia. He died 8 February 1959 at Walter Reed hospital. His brother Vincent, a priest who had helped recruit sacerdotal informants for the OSS, presided over his funeral, but it was President Eisenhower who summed up Donovan's life in two sentences: "What a man! We have lost the last hero."[17]

CHAPTER NINETEEN

THE ROOSEVELTS
THEODORE ROOSEVELT JR. (1887–1944), KERMIT ROOSEVELT (1889–1943), ARCHIBALD ROOSEVELT (1894–1979), QUENTIN ROOSEVELT (1897–1918)

All four sons of former president Theodore Roosevelt served in the Great War. One, the youngest son, Quentin, was killed in it; two others, Theodore Jr. and Archie, were badly wounded. They had been raised to be men of action as well as intellect. They certainly passed that test.

The Roosevelt household was famously rambunctious, with hiking, swimming, shooting, and games playing, all involving their father, who was a regular roustabout of creative and athletic energy—and it is not every household where the father has been governor of New York and president of the United States. At least three of his sons could remember when their father had been a rough-riding colonel in the Spanish American War. All knew him as a big-game hunter and as a master spinner of chilling ghost stories. He could converse, energetically, on any subject, and was interested in everything—from military history to poetry, from zoology to politics; but whatever the affairs of state, he was interested most of all in his children. He raised his brood to be joyful Spartans, relishing the natural world, uncomplaining, ready for any duty, any hardship, and following the credo his own father had given him: "Whatever you do, enjoy it."[1]

There were six children all told. Roosevelt's two daughters were Alice,[2] who became a famous Washington hostess and wit, and Ethel, who was actually the first Roosevelt in a war zone in World War One, serving as a nurse in France (her husband was a surgeon). Theodore Jr., the eldest son, from a young age aspired to be his father, and their careers had modest parallels, with junior serving, as his father had done, in the New York State Assembly and (after the Great War) as undersecretary of the Navy. Though all the boys were vigorous outdoorsman, none was more so than second son Kermit, who, though sickly as a child, became his father's aide-de-camp for adventure, accompanying him, as a Harvard undergraduate, on a yearlong safari to Africa and then a few years later on a near-fatal journey into the Amazonian jungle. Literary-minded and facile with foreign languages, Kermit was, unlike his brothers, moody and sub-dued; his father sometimes worried about Kermit's depressive spirits. Archie, like all the Roosevelts, was animal loving, and among his menagerie was an ill-tempered pet badger, which, as his father noted, was "usually tightly clasped round where his waist would have been if he had one," with the badger looking like "a small mattress, with a leg at each corner."[3] Like many animal-loving people, Archie could be reserved with others, and he had, in an exceedingly strong way, the Roosevelt streak of moralism, which in his father was overshadowed by boisterousness, but in the son, as his father conceded, could appear an "excess of virtue...but it is a fault on the right side, and I am very proud of him."[4] Quentin was the golden boy—the hilarious juvenile terror of the White House, funny, fearless, academically gifted, mechanically brilliant, and personally charming.

LARGER-THAN-LIFE FAMILY LIFE

All the Roosevelt boys learned to shoot from a relatively early age, and they became better shots than their big-game-hunting father, who once had to confess, when asked whether he was a good shot, "No, but I shoot often."[5] Ted was given his first rifle at age nine. To prove to his son that it was a real rifle, Roosevelt shot a small, neat hole in the ceiling and pledged young Theodore not to tell his mother. That was the sort of house Roosevelt kept. He had designed Sagamore Hill, the family home, for a large family before he had one, intending it to be a specially memorable place for the children, with its extensive grounds giving them "every benefit of the freedom of wild places."[6] Once they were old enough to go hunting on their own—or actually with old friends—he helped them plan their trips out West.

The Roosevelts were literary as well as outdoorsy. Father and all his children, if they were not gripping reins or a rifle, hiking or running, swimming or boxing, were probably reading. Roosevelt was a great memorizer and reciter of verse, and fifteen-year-old Kermit, playing on his father's weakness for poetry, asked if dad, then president, could find a job for the poet Edwin Arlington Robinson. He had sent his father a volume of Robinson's verse, which Roosevelt admired. The president took action: "I hunted him up, found he was having a very hard time, and put him in the Treasury Department. I think he will do his work all right, but I am free to say that he was put in less with a view to the good of the government service than with a view to helping American letters." He wrote his son, "You will be pleased to know that Robinson, your poet, has been appointed and is at work in New York."[7]

As for their formal education, the boys attended public schools for their early years before they were sent to boarding school (Groton, from which Archie was expelled), and then the Ivy League (Harvard). Along with their rustic hunting trips, this gave the boys a proper admixture of democratic experience and aristocratic demands. Among those aristocratic demands was military service in time of war. Ted had actually sought a military career, but Roosevelt had denied him permission to go to West Point or the Naval Academy, wanting him to go to Harvard. Roosevelt, for all his own martial nature, thought of military service as an aspect of a man's life, not a career, for there were too few opportunities for exceptional, individual achievement in a peacetime military, and too much invitation to mediocrity, waiting around for seniority and promotion.

THE ROOSEVELTS GO TO WAR

But with the U.S. declaration of war in April 1917, not only did Roosevelt himself try to return to the colors (only to be denied by order of President Wilson), but every one of his sons took a commission. All had taken prewar officer training as part of the Plattsburgh Movement for military preparedness, though Kermit, who had been working at a bank in Buenos Aires, had the least. Theodore Jr.—a successful businessman, married, with three children (a fourth would come in 1919)—was commissioned a major, and

Archie, who married shortly after the declaration of war,[8] was commissioned a first lieutenant. They were on the first troop transport
to France. Kermit, thinking that it would take too long for American
troops to go into action, used his father's assistance to be commissioned in the British army, and did so, typically, not out of a sense
of martial ardor, but of somber duty, confessing to his father that
the "only way I would have been really enthusiastic about going
would have been with you"[9]—as if the war were another safari
across Africa or trek into the South American jungle. Kermit did,
however, have a dramatic role in view: he wanted to fight in the
Near East and see the fall of Constantinople from the Turks to the
British. To that end he became a captain in the British army and was
sent to Mesopotamia. He brought his wife and son (three more
children would be born in due course) across the Atlantic with him,
despite the danger of U-boats, and housed his family in Spain, where
his wife's father was ambassador.

Quentin, meanwhile, dropped out of Harvard, became engaged
to the granddaughter of Cornelius Vanderbilt, eluded the restrictions
of an Army physical examination (by memorizing the eye chart and
lying about a serious chronic back injury), and, after his Flying Corps
training, was commissioned a first lieutenant.

To their father's disapproval, Ted and Archie arranged to serve
together in the 26th Infantry Regiment of the 1st Division. Ted,
despite his amateur standing in the eyes of the professional officers
with whom he served, proved himself an excellent trainer of troops,
applying Roosevelt family–style competition (pitting units against
each other) and exacting discipline and standards of physical fitness
(endless push-ups and pull-ups, especially as punishments), along
with practicality and an obvious concern for the well-being of the
men. Aristocrats they might be, with a deep sense of noblesse oblige,

but Ted and Archie quickly dispelled suspicions that they were spoiled rich man's sons. Their toughness, enthusiasm to pitch in, and generosity (including buying farmers' produce for the troops when government rations weren't up to snuff)[10] won them admiration and respect. Kermit and Quentin were not long behind Ted and Archie, with Quentin being among the first American air officers to arrive in France, in August 1917. Like his brothers, he proved himself an extremely capable officer with a manner that inspired confidence and affection. Eddie Rickenbacker remembered him as "Gay, hearty, and absolutely square in everything he said or did.... [He] was one of the most popular fellows in the group.... He was reckless to such a degree that his commanding officers had to caution him repeatedly about the senselessness of his lack of caution. His bravery was so notorious that we all knew he would either achieve some great spectacular success or be killed in the attempt.... But Quentin would merely laugh away all serious advice."[11] Quentin was more than a dashing flyboy; he was also a gifted administrator—which might not have been suspected in someone so apparently lighthearted and high-spirited—and could ably turn a wrench with the oil-spattered mechanics. He charmed the locals, too, with his fluent French.

Kermit was less interested in charming Iraqi Arabs, but he quickly made himself fluent in Arabic and commanded an armored car (built by Rolls Royce). He adopted a British swagger stick as part of his kit and used it, rather than a revolver, to demand the surrender of Turkish soldiers he confronted after busting down a door during the battle for Baghdad. They complied, and Kermit won a British Military Cross for his courage, just as Archie won a French Croix de Guerre (and two Silver Stars), and Ted was later awarded the Croix de Guerre and Chevalier de la Légion d'Honneur (and the American Distinguished Service Cross). With American troops moving into the battle line, Kermit sought and received a transfer to the American Army, where he was commissioned a captain of artillery.

"THEY HAVE DONE PRETTY WELL, HAVEN'T THEY?"

Roosevelt knew his boys were brave, but he also cautioned them against taking unnecessary risks, saying on more than one occasion that if, after the boys saw action, their superiors deemed them more useful as staff officers than combat officers, they should not decline the posting "merely because it is less dangerous."[12] Nevertheless, they lived the dangerous life. Archie had an arm broken and a knee-cap shattered by shrapnel; Ted was gassed and shot in the left leg and never regained feeling in his left heel.

Quentin, though not in action, had already broken an arm and reinjured his back crash-landing a plane and had been hospitalized for pneumonia. On 6 July 1918 he had his first dogfight and came back elated. In combat against three German planes, he had shot one down and evaded the other two. His proud father wrote, "Whatever now befalls Quentin, he has had his crowded hour, and his day of honor and triumph."[13] That pride, however, was admixed with anxiety. Quentin considered himself an extremely well-trained pilot who could survive any aerial challenge. If any Roosevelt son should die, however, he openly mused that he should be the one because he had no children—though of course he wanted to live, marry his fiancée,[14] and have a family of his own. On 14 July, Quentin was shot down. At first he was listed as missing, but on 20 July came confirmation that he had been killed. Quentin's Croix de Guerre was awarded posthumously.

Roosevelt was devastated by his son's death. At one point he was spied on his rocking chair murmuring, "Poor Quinikins! Poor

Quinikins!" But he was contemptuous of wealthy or powerful men who kept their sons out of harm's way, and maintained a brave face, writing Bob Fergusson, a friend from Rough Rider days, "It is bitter that the young should die... [but] there are things worse than death.... They have done pretty well, haven't they? Quentin killed...over the enemy's lines; Archie crippled, and given the French war cross for gallantry; Ted gassed once...and cited for 'conspicuous gallantry'; Kermit with the British military cross, and now under Pershing."[15]

Roosevelt himself, though touted by some as the likely Republican nominee for president in 1920, was a physical wreck. He had never recovered from his arduous and disease-ridden 1913–1914 expedition into the Brazilian jungle, and in November 1918 his numerous ailments led to an extended hospitalization. At Sagamore Hill for Christmas and the New Year, he was no longer the unstoppable dynamo, but a tired old man barely able to walk. He had lived long enough to see Archie come home, Ted promoted to lieutenant colonel (in September 1918), and victory in the war; he died on 6 January 1919.

THE OLDEST MAN ON UTAH BEACH

His sons were not done with fighting. When World War II came, all of them wanted to be a part of the action. Ted rose highest. A founder of the American Legion, failed Republican gubernatorial candidate for New York (in 1924), former governor of Puerto Rico and the Philippines, and accomplished business executive (at Doubleday, the publishers, and American Express), his true métier was as a soldier. In 1941, he became an active-duty Army colonel commanding his old unit, the 26th Infantry Regiment of the 1st Infantry Division, and was promoted to brigadier general before the end of the year. He won a second Croix de Guerre fighting in North Africa, campaigned in Sicily, and was, along with his commander, Major General Terry Allen, relieved of command for the reckless, rowdy behavior of their troops. He served as a liaison officer in the Italian theater and then was assigned to the 4th Infantry Division, commanded by Major General "Tubby" Barton, which was preparing for Operation Overlord, spearheading the American assault on Utah Beach.

Ted insisted on landing with the first assault wave at Utah Beach. Hobbling along with a cane—he had arthritis and a heart condition (which he kept secret)—he was the oldest man on the beach, the only general to land with the first troops, and the only soldier to have a son (Quentin II) landing on another Normandy beach (Omaha). He calmly directed the assault, and when General Barton came ashore, certain that the insanely brave Roosevelt must surely be dead, he was astonished to see his friend not only alive but prepared to give him a thorough briefing on the progress of the attack. General Omar Bradley thought Roosevelt's performance the most courageous he had ever seen. Orders had been prepared for Roosevelt to take a new command as a major general when he died of a heart attack on 12 June 1944. He was awarded the Medal of Honor, posthumously, in 1944; his father received a posthumous Medal of Honor in 2001. The only other father and son to win Medals of Honor were another veteran of World War I, Douglas MacArthur, and his father, Arthur MacArthur.

As with the First World War, Kermit was impatient to get into the Second, and rather than wait for America's entry he finagled a commission in the British army with the help of Winston Churchill. Between the wars Kermit had been a global adventurer, helped build a steamship company, and proved himself a gifted writer. But the

Great Depression was more than a financial calamity for him—it was an apt phrase to describe his own mental state. Kermit had become a profound alcoholic, to the cost of his marriage and his health. Back in uniform he was usually sober, and could still do good work. But his body was too ravaged to keep him in uniform long. He served with the British in Norway and North Africa before being sent home with a medical discharge (which he contested).

He sought a commission in the American Army and insisted that he be given an assignment that offered a chance of combat. Being a Roosevelt, he got it, with General George Marshall assigning him to Alaska, where he accompanied bombing raids against the Japanese and helped train an Aleut and Eskimo militia. It rejuvenated him for a while, but his body rapidly failed. A forcibly retired captain in the British army, a barely functioning major in the American Army— with, he thought, little hope of seeing combat—he committed suicide on 4 June 1943 with a Colt .45 pistol.

BOOKENDS

Archie, though considered 100 percent disabled from his wounds in the First World War, would not be denied an opportunity to fight in the Second. Between the wars he had been an oil and financial executive. After the Japanese attack on Pearl Harbor, he employed sheer Rooseveltian gumption to be commissioned a lieutenant colonel and awarded a combat command in New Guinea, where he proved he still had the audacious Roosevelt fighting spirit. Archie was fearless in the face of enemy fire. He told one young soldier who was cowering while Roosevelt stood erect, "Don't worry. You're safe with me. I was wounded three times in the last war, and that's a lucky charm." It was for a while, at least, before an enemy grenade exploded into the same knee that had been hit with shrapnel in France. He served in New Guinea from 1943 to 1944 and was invalided out of the service, the only American soldier to be declared 100 percent disabled in two wars. He returned to his brokerage business and dabbled in right-wing causes. In 1971 his wife died in a car crash, in which he was driving, and he secluded himself in Florida, where he died in 1979.

All the brothers were valiant, each in his own way, and it was their father, and their experiences in the Great War, that defined them. In 1918 Ted remarked, "Quentin's death is always going to be the greatest thing in any of our lives." That he was right was confirmed by his sister Alice, who wrote a half century later, "All our lives before and after have just been bookends for the heroic, tragic volume of the Great War."[16]

PART V

THE VICTORY

CHAPTER TWENTY

IN DUBIOUS BATTLE

The fighting wasn't over. While American troops on the Western Front celebrated the end of the Great War, in the frozen depths of northwest Russia, American doughboys—and their de facto allies, British, Canadians, and French—were fighting against the Bolsheviks. The number of Allied troops involved was relatively small,[1] but the fighting was fierce, even if their mission was confused, not least because of the usual wavering of President Wilson. But the goal of more clear-sighted leaders, like Churchill, was sound—to strangle the monster Bolshevism in its cradle.[2]

To Churchill, the Bolsheviks represented a greater threat to civilized Europe than did the reeking tube and iron shard of the Kaiser's

Reich. Bolshevism, he declared in the House of Commons, was "not a policy; it is a disease. It is not a creed; it is a pestilence." The Germans had smuggled Bolshevik leader Vladimir Lenin into Russia "in the same way that you might send a phial containing a culture of typhoid or of cholera to be poured into the water supply of a great city, and it worked with amazing accuracy." Churchill's policy after Germany's surrender was to "Kill the Bolshie and Kiss the Hun" because, as he noted in April 1919, "Of all tyrannies in history, the Bolshevik tyranny is the worst, the most destructive, and the most degrading."[3]

Such virile language was certainly not in Wilson's repertoire, but the American president was eventually and temporarily browbeaten by British, French, and Italian support for intervention in the summer of 1918. After the Bolshevik Revolution, which removed Russia from the war, the British, French, and Italians were intent on reestablishing an Eastern Front. After the German surrender in November 1918, Churchill continued to press the cause of combating the Bolsheviks, but he did not carry a majority of the British Parliament or the sentiments of a war-weary British people. Yet his warnings, as the victors set about establishing peace after the Great War, were prescient. If the Bolsheviks succeeded, if the monarchist White Russians were not restored to power, then a new and terrible regime dedicated to international revolution, and possibly allied with German militarism and even Japanese nationalism, would extend "from Yokohama to Cologne in hostility to France, Britain, and America."[4]

Wilson, unlike Churchill, was no friend of monarchy and had welcomed the liberal socialist revolution of March 1917. After the Russian provisional government—led first by the liberal Prince Lvov and then by the socialist Alexander Kerensky—was deposed by the Bolsheviks in the October Revolution, he remained hopeful. While

Wilson disdained the lawlessness and violence of Bolshevism, he trusted that it might be moderated, that it was an understandable if extreme reaction to the authoritarianism of the Russian czar.

BREST-LITOVSK

There was, however, a practical wartime problem. The Bolsheviks, unlike the provisional government, were eager to exit the World War so they could concentrate on slaughtering their opponents at home. They reached an armistice with Germany and the Central Powers in December 1917, which culminated in the Treaty of Brest-Litovsk in March 1918, officially withdrawing Russia from the Great War, turning over vast swathes of czarist Russian territory and its resources to the Germans, and freeing forty German divisions to join the Western Front. Some, including French prime minister Georges Clemenceau and British prime minister Lloyd George, considered the Bolsheviks de facto allies of the Germans. The Bolsheviks had repudiated all debts, leaving French investors—not just financiers, but more than a million average Pierres—with a collective several-billion-dollar fortune of now-worthless government bonds that had been meant to put a ribbon on the diplomatic ties between czarist Russia and the French Republic. Moreover, the Bolsheviks' internal reign of terror appalled those who did not embrace Bolshevism—as many unfortunately did—as the inevitable wave of the future. In the estimate of author William Manchester, the subsequent Russian Civil War of 1917 to 1922, "the Bolshevik holocaust—five years of fighting, pestilence, and famine—cost fifteen million lives,"[5] nearly as many as were lost globally in the Great War.

Wilson was not entirely blind to Communist excesses or to pragmatic Allied interests in Russia. Before the German surrender, those interests had included the reestablishment of an Eastern Front and the recovery of Allied military supplies that could fall into the hands of the Germans—or into the hands of the Bolsheviks who might give them to the Germans. Churchill wanted direct military intervention on the side of the White (pro-monarchist and other anti-Communist) Russians against the Reds, something that was not on Wilson's agenda.

But Wilson could let his liberal heart bleed a little for the Czech Legion, a body of troops now marooned in Russia yet still willing to fight for the Western Allies in the hopes of winning national self-determination for Czechoslovakia (part of the Austro-Hungarian Empire) after the war. The Bolsheviks had initially agreed to let the Legion evacuate to Vladivostok and from there make its way to France. But under pressure from the Germans, Leon Trotsky, the Bolshevik commissar of war, reneged on the agreement. He gave orders to disarm the Legion, deny its men rail transport, and otherwise prevent them from fighting for the Allied cause. The Legion then determined to slug its way out. Wilson thought it appropriate to help them.

IDEALIST INTERVENTION

On 17 July 1918, Wilson issued an *aide-mémoire* to the Allied ambassadors, which, in the words of historian John Toland, "preached idealism and disinterestedness while ignoring reality."[6] Wilson underlined his previous, and to some degree continued, opposition to intervention in Russia, stating that it was "the clear and fixed judgment of the Government of the United States...that military intervention would add to the present sad confusion in Russia rather than cure it, injure her rather than help her, and that it would be of no advantage in the prosecution of our main design, to win the war against Germany. It cannot, therefore, take part in any such intervention or sanction it in principle." He, then, confusingly, authorized a limited intervention: "Military action is admissible in Russia, as the Government of the United States sees the circumstances, only to help the Czecho-Slovaks consolidate their forces and get into successful cooperation with their Slavic kinsmen and to steady any efforts at self-government or self-defense in which the Russians themselves may be willing to accept assistance." Wilson then added to the confusion by saying that the only legitimate role for Allied or American troops would be "to guard military stores which may subsequently be needed by Russian forces and to render such aid as may be acceptable to the Russians in the organization of their own self-defense."[7] Nowhere did Wilson say which Russians were to be aided. The Czech Legion, meanwhile, with about sixty thousand men, had essentially annexed Siberia to itself, and unlike President Wilson, the Legion had no qualms about allying itself with the White Russians: when the Legion seized Vladivostok, it raised the Czar's flag.

The American commander destined for Vladivostok was Major General William S. Graves. As British author and fellow major general Clifford Kinvig has noted, "If ever there was a commander who regarded his instructions as a cage rather than springboard it was General Graves."[8] His instructions were merely Wilson's *aide-mémoire*, delivered to him in a sealed envelope at a train station by Secretary of War Newton Baker, who dallied no longer than to say, "This contains the policy of the United States in Russia which you are to follow. Watch your steps; you will be walking on eggs loaded with dynamite. God bless you and goodbye."[9] This, surely, would have been enough to confuse any man, let alone an officer who had hoped to see, and was better suited to, straightforward action against a straightforward enemy on the Western Front.

General Graves assembled an American army of more than eight thousand men at Vladivostok. The city hosted a cosmopolitan array of uniforms, including British, French, and Italian, but in small numbers—except that is, for the Japanese, who landed more than seventy thousand soldiers and swiftly assumed command of all Allied troops, save for those of the affiliated power, the Americans. An ally of Britain and France, but a recent combatant against the Russians (in the Russo-Japanese War of 1904–1905), Japan's was the only government, beside the contending Russian forces, that had territorial designs on Siberia. These were inhibited, however, by the necessity of keeping in step with Japan's Western allies. Indeed it seems that part of President Wilson's calculation in sending American troops to Siberia was to dissuade Japanese annexations of Russian territory.

ADVANTAGE REDS

Graves faced a situation for which chaos would be a polite word. Aside from the Czech Legion, Siberia was awash with disparate White armies, unaffiliated independent warlords and raiders, Cossacks, freed prisoners of war, and of course the Reds. Because they controlled the Russian heartland, were united by a clear ideology, and could commandeer peasants and provide guaranteed meals to soldiers (who might otherwise starve), the Reds had the advantage over the White Russians, whose leadership and armies were divided and who represented an awkward coalition ranging on a political spectrum from monarchist to socialist to freebooter. Graves dismissed the local White Cossack leader, for instance, as a "murderer, robber, and a most dissolute scoundrel."[10]

The British, Canadians, French, and Italians, despite numbering only about five thousand men, were eager to join the White Russians against the Reds. This Graves would not do—or at least not until his men were forced into fighting the Bolsheviks. Graves was charged with protecting the Trans-Siberian Railway for the Czech Legion. The Bolsheviks attacked the Americans in the summer of 1919, prompting Graves to finally make common cause with the Allies and the Whites in a short, limited, anti-Bolshevik campaign.

More than 3,600 miles away, in northwestern Russia, American troops had been sent to guard Allied stores and secure the railway at the port of Archangel. They were thrown into fighting the Bolsheviks much sooner, and with far less restraint. In part, this was because they were under a British commander, Major General Frederick C. Poole; in part it was because a handful of American sailors and Marines who landed in August 1918 had loaded a railway car, chased retreating Soviet forces, and got into a firefight.

Just over 5,700 American soldiers—including engineers, medical staff, and infantry—were sent to Archangel, arriving in September 1918. Poole left a detachment to guard the city while he took a combined force of ten thousand men (British, Americans, and others), divided it into two columns, and plotted an advance four hundred miles to a rail link with the Trans-Siberian Railway. They didn't make it. The lead elements advanced about two hundred miles before they turned back, stymied by bad maps, freezing temperatures, difficult, swampy terrain, running battles against Bolshevik troops, and a casualty rate among the American troops, from start to finish of the northern Russian expedition, of almost fifty percent.[11]

Poole's army was not the most impressive to have taken the field for the Allies. It was composed largely of British troops deemed unfit for duty on the Western Front, British-officered Slavic forces (some of whom turned on their commanders), war-weary Frenchmen, a smattering of American sailors and Marines, and mystified American soldiers, the bulk coming from the 339th Infantry, "Detroit's Own," made up of draftees, mostly from Wisconsin and Michigan, who assumed they would be fighting in France. They had received scant training but were proud enough to resent being placed under British command. Their own American commander, Colonel George Evans Stewart, was nearly as mystified about their mission as they were.

After securing a perimeter around Archangel and advancing along the rail line and the Dvina River against stiff Bolshevik resistance, six hundred Americans, Scots, and Canadians fought a three-day battle at the village of Toulgas, repulsing a Soviet attempt to storm the Allied position. Though the Communists outnumbered the defenders and were supported by river gunboats, a brave and clever American counterthrust drove them back, killing at least five hundred Soviets by battle's end, more than ten times the number of Allied dead. The battle was begun on 11 November 1918. The American troops remembered it sardonically as "The Battle of Armistice Day."

With winter setting in, there was no chance of advancing farther into Russia. There was also no opportunity to extricate the Allied force, as the port at Archangel had frozen over. American and British troops made fighting retreats in the snow against a Bolshevik army that might lack uniforms but not numbers. In 1919, the Red Army was 3 million strong.

President Wilson did not need much convincing that the American intervention no longer served any useful purpose, if it ever had, and in February 1919 he ordered an American withdrawal from Archangel, effective whenever the weather would allow. The Western forces of the Archangel expedition had no objective now except to beat back the enemy and survive until they could be evacuated, beginning with the spring thaws of April. By June, the Americans were gone. The British remained until September. The Soviets seized Archangel from the White Russians in February 1920.

Meanwhile the Siberian front devolved from chaos to calamity with the Czech Legion eventually trading White Russian leader Admiral Alexander Kolchak and a train full of gold to the Soviets in exchange for safe passage home. It rapidly became clear that unless the reluctant General Graves was prepared to fight the Communists, the Americans would have to leave as well. Orders to that effect came in January 1920, and the evacuation was completed in April.

Churchill foresaw what would follow. On 14 May 1919, he gave a speech at Dundee, Scotland, where he advised, "Our policy must be directed to prevent a union between German militarism and Russian Bolshevism, for if that occurred these tyrants and tyrannical masses would swiftly crush the little weak States which lie between, and they would then form a combination which would stretch from China to the Rhine, which would be unspeakably unfriendly to Britain and to the United States and France, and to all that those free democracies stand for."[12] Churchill believed that at relatively minimal cost—no more than forty thousand men deployed at Archangel by July 1918—the Russian Civil War could have been tipped to the Whites, and a peaceful and secure postwar world, for which the Allies had fought, could have been achieved. But that would have required a military and a moral commitment that President Wilson and the Western Allies refused to make.

CHAPTER TWENTY-ONE

THE VICTORS AT VERSAILLES

The Russian sideshow was but one part of America's introduction to international statecraft. The main stage was Paris and the postwar negotiations that would culminate in the Treaty of Versailles. America's negotiating position had been staked out well before the end of the war. On 8 January 1918, in a speech to a joint session of Congress, President Wilson enunciated his Fourteen Points to guide the postwar world. He announced, before getting down to particulars, that "What we demand in this war, therefore, is nothing peculiar to ourselves. It is that the world be made fit and safe to live in; and particularly that it be made safe for every peace-loving nation which, like our own, wishes to live its own life, determine its own institutions, be assured of justice and fair dealing by the other peoples of the world, as against force and selfish aggression."

The president's tone was resolutely progressive and internationalist: "All the peoples of the world are in effect partners in this interest, and for our own part we see very clearly that unless justice be done to others it will not be done to us."

"The program of the world's peace, therefore, is our program," Wilson declared, "and that program, the only possible program," was of course his Fourteen Points, which were:

1. An end to secret diplomacy and treaties. Everything henceforth was to be done in the open so that people knew what their leaders were committing them to as a nation.
2. Freedom of the seas, outside of reservations for territorial waters and the enforcement of international covenants.
3. Free trade, long the liberal shibboleth for establishing perpetual peace.
4. International arms reductions to the barest of minimums.
5. A liberal adjustment of colonial claims, taking into equal consideration the interests of the colonial powers and the interests of the native populations. Wilson used the word "imperialist" as a condemnation, applying it frequently to Germany, though Britain had by far the larger empire—the largest in world history in fact, which reached its zenith immediately after the Great War.

6. Ironically, given his future dispatch of troops to Russia, he called for all foreign powers (meaning most especially the Central Powers) to leave Russia alone to determine her own destiny, taking an optimistic view that if greeted with good will and disinterested assistance, Russia would gravitate in a liberal direction. Like many a liberal before and after him, Wilson believed that revolts against reactionary monarchies tend naturally toward the triumph of liberal values.

7. The restoration of an independent Belgium.

8. The restoration of France's territorial integrity, plus the return of Alsace-Lorraine to French sovereignty.

9. An adjustment of Italy's frontiers to incorporate neighboring ethnic Italians within Italy's borders.

10. "The peoples of Austria-Hungary, whose place among the nations we wish to see safeguarded and assured, should be accorded the freest opportunity of autonomous development." In other words, the collapsed Habsburg Empire should be divided among its constituent nationalities on the grounds of "national self-determination," another liberal shibboleth. In practice, it meant the forcible, violent shifting of peoples into ethnic safe havens.[1]

11. This point built on the previous one with a few particulars, including that Serbia's borders should allow it access to the sea, and that the Balkan states should work in "friendly counsel" while protected by "international guarantees."

12. The Ottoman Empire was to be carved up. The Turks would have their state, but their other territories

should be granted national self-determination. In addition, "the Dardanelles should be permanently opened as a free passage to the ships and commerce of all nations under international guarantees."

13. Something that had not existed for more than a hundred years—an independent Poland—was to be re-created, with borders that gave it territorial access to the sea. Its "political and economic independence and territorial integrity" was to be "guaranteed by international covenant."

14. The creation of a League of Nations, which would develop the international agreements for the Fourteen Points to become effective, provide the many necessary international guarantees, and perpetuate a liberal world order.

As for Germany, Wilson said, "We wish her only to accept a place of equality among the peoples of the world—the new world in which we now live—instead of a place of mastery." He closed with a rousing, or, according to taste, ridiculous peroration:

An evident principle runs through the whole program I have outlined. It is the principle of justice to all peoples and nationalities, and their right to live on equal terms of liberty and safety with one another, whether they be strong or weak.

Unless this principle be made its foundation, no part of the structure of international justice can stand. The people of the United States could act upon no other principle, and to the vindication of this principle they are ready to devote their lives, their honor, and everything that they possess. The moral climax of this, the culminating and final war for human liberty has come, and they are ready to put their own strength, their own highest purpose, their own integrity and devotion to the test.[2]

The "final war for human liberty," presaged the end, in Wilson's mind, of the corrupt old order. He was a prophet of the world to come, a new world order for a Europe that had nearly destroyed itself. For many Europeans, Wilson's idealism vindicated their sacrifices. They regarded him as a moral hero. Aside from the Bolsheviks with their rhetoric of world revolution, he was the only statesman whose thinking and proclamations were not grounded in national interest. Or, as Wilson himself preferred to think, America had been the only disinterested party in the world conflict and would be the only disinterested party in the making of the peace.

THE PARIS PEACE CONFERENCE

It seemed as if the man and his moment were met as delegates from around the world descended on Paris in December 1918. Through the first six months of 1919, they asserted nationalist aspirations, progressive nostrums, and hopes for new republics—and Wilson was at the center of the negotiations. The other two of the "big three" statesmen at the conference were regarded, in comparison, as representing European cynicism and *Realpolitik*, though they were hardly defenders of the old order. They were, in fact, men of the political Left. Georges Clemenceau, the prime minister of France, was an anti-clerical radical and nationalist; David Lloyd George, prime minister of Great Britain, was a Welshman, a Liberal, and an architect of Britain's nascent welfare state. Neither Wilson nor Clemenceau nor Lloyd George had any interest in re-creating the Congress of Vienna of a hundred years before, playing the roles of the conservative statesmen Castlereagh, Wellington, and Metternich, and effecting a world restored; they wanted a world remade. Truth be told, though, the reactionaries of 1814–1815 did their job better, preserving a longer peace, than did the liberals of 1919.

Of course Clemenceau, Lloyd George, and Wilson faced a daunting task. Even as they and all the other delegates sat down to their deliberations, borders and governments were being decided in tumult, anarchy, and armed conflict. Most of the crowned heads of Europe had been deposed. The Czar and his family had been murdered. The Kaiser was in exile in the Netherlands. Bavarian king Ludwig III had given way to a socialist revolt. Austria and Hungary had declared themselves republics, making Charles I an emperor without an empire (he would eventually go into exile in Switzerland, and later Madeira).[3] The states of Poland, Lithuania, Latvia, Estonia, and Finland were reemerging from the past. Communist red flags popped up, however briefly, at points in the heart of Europe. German mercenary armies, the Freikorps, fought Bolsheviks in Germany, saving the secular, socialist Weimar Republic—and even tried to annex the Baltic States, in secular emulation of the Teutonic Knights.

None of this dented Wilson's idealism—and it was his idealism and France's insistence on taming Germany that dominated the Peace Conference. Led by Wilson, the peacemakers sought not only to reform Europe but to create an international settlement that encompassed the world. The fighting, after all, had stretched from Europe to Africa, the Middle East, and the Pacific; the European powers had overseas empires; and the Ottoman Empire, which before the war had extended from Mesopotamia and Armenia through the Middle

East to the borders of Bulgaria and Greece, was kaput, and new borders were being drawn by scimitar and rifle (not to mention British Arabists and French diplomats). The challenges facing President Wilson and his colleagues were economic, diplomatic, and military. Famine and disease were stalking victims in lands where farms had been wrecked and factories destroyed, political arrangements were being settled by force, and while all might be quiet on the former Western Front, elsewhere in allegedly postwar Europe, bullets were still flying.

Wilson disdained to visit the now-quiet battlefields of France and Belgium. He had never been interested in military details. His goal was to shape a liberal peace that used international institutions to defend national self-determination, a byword for democracy and progressivism.[4] To this end, America's five delegates to the Paris Peace Conference were himself—never before had a president gone abroad to negotiate a peace treaty—his perpetual emissary Colonel House; his secretary of state, Robert Lansing; the president's rarely consulted military advisor, General Tasker Bliss; and Henry White, who had been President Theodore Roosevelt's ambassador to Italy and France and later became a supporter of President Wilson.

Conspicuously absent from Wilson's delegation were any Republican representatives. Wilson, a highly partisan man, thought they would only get in the way. He paid scant consideration to the possibility that he might later need their support, though Republicans held majorities in both houses of Congress and had no shortage of senior statesmen, including former president William Howard Taft (who had also been governor of the Philippines and a secretary of war), Henry Cabot Lodge (an ally of Theodore Roosevelt and his aggressive brand of foreign policy, soon to be chairman of the Senate Foreign Relations Committee), and former senator Elihu Root (who had also been secretary of state and secretary of war). Wilson, however, did not suffer political opponents gladly. He had campaigned against Republicans in the 1918 elections, charging them with obstructing the war effort. He had warned the American people that returning Republican majorities would be seen abroad as a repudiation of his leadership—and the American people went ahead and repudiated him anyway.[5] Undaunted, Wilson continued to equate progress with Wilsonian idealism, announcing in Boston in February 1919, that "Any man"—by whom he meant, though he did not say, Lodge and other likeminded Republicans—"who resists the present tides that run in the world will find himself thrown upon a shore so high and barren that it will seem as if he had been separated from his human kind forever."[6] The one Republican he did tap was Herbert Hoover, who was placed in charge of Allied relief and saved countless lives across the continent until declaring in the summer of 1919 that the Europeans were now ready to stand again on their own feet—an estimate that significantly exaggerated their recuperative powers.

"A MISSIONARY...TO RESCUE THE POOR EUROPEAN HEATHEN"

Republicans weren't the only ones who felt Wilson's condescension and were subject to his suspicion. He was sniffy to the British—warning them that they and the United States were not kindred nations. He thought the French were trying to subject him to emotional blackmail by arranging for him to see the battlefields of the Western Front. He identified himself with the hidden aspirations of "the people" of Europe, about whom he knew very little, while being wary of the actually elected leaders of the major Western powers.

Lloyd George and Clemenceau felt equally distant from Wilson, though they all grew somewhat closer as the negotiations wore on. The British prime minister noted, "I really think that at first the idealistic President regarded himself as a missionary whose function it was to rescue the poor European heathen from the age-long worship of false and fiery gods." Lloyd George continued,

> His most extraordinary outburst was when he was developing some theme—I rather think it was connected to the League of Nations—which led him to explain the failure of Christianity to achieve its highest ideals. "Why," he said, "has Jesus Christ so far not succeeded in inducing the world to follow His teachings in these matters? It is because He taught the ideal without devising any practical means of attaining it. That is the reason why I am proposing a practical scheme to carry out His aims." Clemenceau slowly opened his eyes to their widest dimensions and swept them around the Assembly to see how the Christians gathered around the table enjoyed this exposure of the futility of their Master.[7]

Christian forgiveness was not much on offer. The French had one great idea, and that was to use any peace treaty—and the League of Nations—to put shackles on Germany. With Russia no longer a counterweight to German power, the French supported the creation of small nations between Russia and Germany—a *cordon sanitaire* against the bacillus of Bolshevism and an expansive Germany. Wilson was no friend of the French, but with his penchant for tutoring nations, he agreed that "The world had a moral right to disarm Germany and to subject her to a generation of thoughtfulness."[8] It apparently did not occur to him that "thoughtfulness" might exercise itself as resentment.

It also did not appear to occur to him that without military power to give its sanctions force, the League of Nations was a league of weak sisters. The British preferred to entrust their security to the Royal Navy. Wilson, the president who kept the United States an affiliated rather than an Allied Power, was equally dismissive about the United States participating in an international military body: it was unconstitutional and yet another tiresome proposal of the French against the Germans. The important thing was for the League to establish the principle of forgoing aggression and of unanimous international decision making. There would be no recourse to military power. The League, after all, was meant to do away with war. Germany, as part of its encouragement to thoughtfulness, would initially be excluded from membership.

Wilson, the anti-imperialist, opposed France's desired to expand her empire by annexing former German possessions in Africa. The French wanted these colonies not just for the *gloire* of France but for their potential military manpower. Instead, Wilson was taken by the notion, advanced by Jan Smuts of South Africa, of League "mandates" that would give specified League members responsibility for the temporary governing of territories that could not govern themselves—essentially territories without European majorities. Germany would lose its colonies and be given no mandates. Germany, in Wilson's view, and in the view of the Allies, was guilty of starting the war; and Germany's harsh exactions from its conquered provinces overseas and in Europe from Belgium to Bolshevik Russia did not encourage sympathy. Wilson, not surprisingly, thought the Germans needed to be taught a lesson. While the president and Lloyd George proclaimed they sought justice, not vengeance, Wilson had doubts about the French, doubts that Clemenceau fed, telling Wilson, "The President of the United States disregards the depths of human nature. The fact of the war cannot be forgotten. America did not see this war at a close distance for its first three years; during this time we lost a million and a half men.... You seek to do justice to the Germans. Do not believe that they will ever forgive us; they only seek the opportunity for revenge. Nothing will destroy the rage of those who wanted to establish their domination over the world and who believed themselves so close to succeeding."[9]

PUNITIVE MEASURES

There was general agreement that Germany should be disarmed, but to what degree—especially given the Bolshevik menace—was a matter of heated debate. In the end the victors attempted to almost completely demilitarize what had been a highly militaristic German society. The German army was limited to one hundred thousand men and the navy to fifteen thousand, police forces were limited to prewar levels, and school cadet corps were eliminated. Beyond that, Germany was denied an air force, a tank corps, submarines, heavy artillery, and much else besides. The German military would amount to a constabulary force that might be able to handle domestic Bolshevik revolutionaries, but not much else.

There was also general agreement that Germany should be made geographically smaller, and there were several countries, not just France, that were eager to assist in this scheme, including Poland, Lithuania, and Denmark. France laid claim not only to Alsace-Lorraine but to the Rhineland—wanting either to annex it, make it independent (a second Belgium), or at the very least occupy and demilitarize it—and even to the coal-rich Saarland, which by any reasonable definition was entirely German. No matter how it was sliced and diced, Germany would still dwarf France in population. Even so, the French wanted to erect as many obstacles as possible to ensure that Germany could never again invade France.

But this was to neglect the role that resentment can play in human affairs. Germany, stripped of the trappings of a sovereign nation and a great power, was then stuck with the bill for the Great War. Germany bore the costs because Germany bore the guilt, as stated in Article 231 of the Treaty of Versailles (written by two Americans, Norman Davis and John Foster Dulles): "The Allied and Associated Governments affirm and Germany accepts the responsibility of Germany and her allies for causing all the loss and damage to which the Allied and Associated Governments and their nationals have been subjected as a consequence of the war imposed upon them by the aggression of Germany and her allies." Austria and Hungary signed treaties with similar clauses, but it was Germany on whom the brunt fell.

Lloyd George put the case for imposing financial reparations on Germany: "Somebody had to pay. If Germany could not pay, it meant the British taxpayer had to pay. Those who ought to pay were those who caused the loss."[10] Lloyd George had trained as a lawyer. For him it was a simple matter of damages and liabilities. He was also insistent that his client, Great Britain, get its fair share of any financial settlement, which, to get near the level of French demands, would have to include pensions for British war widows and orphans. Nevertheless, the British share of German payments was set at only slightly more than half of what the French were to receive.

The Americans were creditors, and though they sought no reparations payments for themselves, they did want repayment on wartime loans. The British were technically creditors too, but their loans to Russia, Italy, and other countries, including France, were unlikely to be repaid, and, in turn, the British owed the United States $4.7 billion. In 1923 Britain reached an agreement on a repayment schedule, with interest, to the United States. Writing many years later, after the conclusion of yet another world war, Winston Churchill noted, "The basis of this agreement was considered, not only in this island, but by many disinterested financial authorities in America, to be a severe and improvident condition for both borrower and lender. 'They hired the money, didn't they?' said President Coolidge. This laconic statement was true, but not exhaustive."

Churchill had a further point: "Payments between countries which take the form of a transfer of goods and services, or still more of their fruitful exchange, are not only just but beneficial. Payments which are only the arbitrary, artificial transmission across the exchange of such very large sums as arise in war finance cannot fail to derange the whole process of world economy. This is equally true whether the payments are exacted from an ally who shared the victory and bore much of the brunt or from a defeated enemy nation."[11] Magnanimity, in other words, was the better course politically and economically. This was a minority view in 1919, especially among the French, who saw German reparations payments as another shackle on German recovery, and hence on Germany's potential for aggression. One who shared Churchill's view was economist John Maynard Keynes, who believed in canceling debts and encouraging free trade, which in the end would benefit everyone. Keynes attended the Paris Peace Conference as an advisor from the British Treasury and returned as one of the most influential critics of the Treaty of Versailles. In the end, however, the total bill presented to the Germans—$34 billion   was a large but not fantastical sum, rather smaller than the more than $17 trillion the United States owed to its creditors in 2013.[12]

On 25 March 1919 Lloyd George's staff drafted a memorandum that he presented to the Council of Four (the United States, France, Italy, and Great Britain). The "Fontainebleau Memorandum" tried to carve out a moderate middle ground, stripping Germany of her colonies, demanding reparations payments, and demilitarizing the Rhineland, but otherwise warning against further punitive exactions. We "cannot," he said, "both cripple" Germany economically and "expect her to pay" reparations. The victors could not surround Germany with small states carved out of her own territory without creating a "cause for a future war" with "large masses of Germans clamouring for reunion with their native land."[13] Finally, he warned, as Churchill had, that "The greatest danger I see in the present situation is that," if punished too severely, "Germany may throw in her lot with Bolshevism and place her resources, her brains, her vast organizing power at the disposal of the revolutionary fanatics whose dream is to conquer the world for Bolshevism by force of arms."[14] Wilson agreed, Clemenceau was furious, and Prime Minister Vittorio Orlando of Italy was irrelevant. Clemenceau, however, won further concessions, including a limited French occupation of the Rhineland with a phased withdrawal over fifteen years; French ownership of the Saarland's coal mines, in reparation for Germany's destruction of France's coal industry; and a League of Nations mandate over the Saar, with the disposition of the country eventually to be settled by a popular vote.[15]

NATION-BUILDING

More difficult was determining the borders of the countries of Eastern Europe. Few Americans thought they had fought the Great War to settle the fate of Ukrainians, Ruthenians, Poles, Czechs, Slovaks, Latvians, Lithuanians, Estonians, Serbs, Slovenes, Romanians,

Croats, or the countless other ethnic groups whose futures were being determined in the faraway deal-making in Paris. Nevertheless, these groups and others canvassed for public support in the big cities of the United States, tapping into ethnic immigrant communities and affirming the Wilsonian ideals of national self-determination—or some variant thereof, given that it was impossible to draw borders that did not incorporate other nationalities. Small countries, the peacemakers soon realized, could be just as aggressive in asserting their dominion over territory as had been the defeated Central Powers. Trying to come up with proper borders, the Big Four, led by Wilson, literally crawled over a giant map on the floor. President Wilson was not always scrupulous on the matter of self-determination. He turned over a quarter of a million German-speaking citizens of Tyrol to the Italians, for example. This was an act of appeasement, but it did not stop Italian prime minister Vittorio Orlando from storming out of the Peace Conference, incensed at Wilson's blocking Italian territorial claims in the Adriatic—claims against the newly formed state of Yugoslavia, which had Wilson's sympathy. In June Orlando's government fell from power.

Wilson found the negotiations all very trying. He was in bad health and perhaps suffered a minor stroke during the six months spent hammering out the peace in Paris. Though European matters dominated the agenda, decisions made over other parts of the world cost him equal political strife—in particular, allowing the Japanese to take over the German concessions at Shantung, China, on a presumed temporary basis and with restrictions. China had declared war on Germany with the understanding that China would regain Shantung, the birthplace of Confucius. The Chinese thought Shantung should be theirs, and a good portion of the American public, which looked kindly on China as a great missionary field, agreed.

Wilson, however, needed Japan's support for the League of Nations and did not think he could get it otherwise.

For Wilson, the League was everything. Whatever shortcomings were left from the peace treaty the League would iron out through international cooperation and liberal, democratic principles. Wilson's understanding of democratic principles, however, fell short at home, where Republicans in the Senate thought the Treaty of Versailles a badly botched job and raised a particular protest over Wilson's concession to the Japanese on Shantung and China's consequent refusal to endorse the Versailles Treaty.

There were also doubts about the mandate system. As with China, American Protestant missionaries had been active in Armenia. It was assumed by some, including many Armenians, that when it came to divvying up the Ottoman Empire (against which America had never declared war), the United States might take responsibility for governing Armenia under a League of Nations mandate. Armenian representatives wanted this; Wilson, anti-Turk and pro-Armenian in sentiment, accepted the mandate—but subject to the approval of the United States Senate, which he assumed would not be given. It was hard for Wilson to imagine the American people accepting a de facto imperial role in the Near East, no matter how sympathetic they were to Armenia, and he was right about that.

Then there was the Holy Land. Wilson had appointed a commission, led by Henry Churchill King, president of Oberlin College, and Charles R. Crane, a wealthy businessman, diplomatic dilettante, Wilson supporter, and Arabist, to advise him on what should be done with certain non-Turkish areas of the former Ottoman Empire, chiefly the territories of modern Syria, Lebanon, Jordan, and Israel. (Anatolia was also within the commission's remit, but its fate would be decided in the Greco-Turkish War of 1919–1922, which essentially drove all non-Turks out of the region.) The commission completed its report at the end of August 1919, and it was ignored by all.

The King-Crane Commission stated that the ultimate and rightful ambition of the Arabs was independence. But this, for the nonce, was impractical and unwise. The best course and the one preferred by the Arabs themselves was an American mandate over the Middle East. The Arabs' second choice as a mandate power was the British, because most Arabs, with exception of the Maronite Christians of Lebanon, were Francophobes. The King-Crane Commission opposed a Zionist state, to which the British were committed by the Balfour Declaration (1917)—arguing that it could only be created and supported by military force.

In the event, American influence in drawing up the map of the Middle and Near East was practically nil. It was the British who took charge, creating the region's modern borders and granting France control of Syria and Lebanon while Britain assumed tutelage over Mesopotamia, Jordan, and Palestine. In 1922 the United States Congress passed a joint resolution affirming support for a Jewish homeland in Palestine, in accord with British policy.

But while drawing new borders was fun, the nub of the peace treaty—without which it was meaningless—was getting Germany's signature on the document. When the Germans arrived at Versailles in the spring of 1919, they were appalled at the treaty's terms and harrumphed at Woodrow Wilson's hypocrisy. The first of his Fourteen Points insisted on diplomacy being conducted in public, with "open covenants of peace, openly arrived at." But the reality was that the treaty had de facto been decided by Wilson, Lloyd George, and Clemenceau. The Germans were expected to sign and shut up, though as a face-saving measure they were granted a fortnight to study the treaty (it was the size of a book) and comment on it. By the end of May, the Germans had thoroughly annotated their objections. Many in the British delegation, including Lloyd George, and some Americans, including Herbert Hoover, had second thoughts (or first thoughts—because most had never seen the entire document themselves), but the signing of the treaty went ahead on 28 June 1919 at the palace of Versailles.

The reparations owed by Germany were, in fact, ratcheted down several times, but this had no effect on German resentment or on Germany's default on the debt in 1933.[16] In the end, according to historian Sheldon Anderson, "The Germans paid less in relative terms than the French did in 1871" following the Franco-Prussian War.[17] It was not reparations that sank Germany's economy during the Great Depression of the early 1930s, but something far more mundane, according to historian Richard Vinen: "Germany's problems sprang mainly not from reparations, which rarely amounted to more than 3 percent of her gross national product, but from a tradition of high state spending, compounded by the welfare commitments of the Weimar government and the financial legacy of the Great War."[18] Reparations and the military limitations placed on Germany crumbled away as the British and French declined to enforce them.

AMERICA BOWS OUT

The Americans were no longer involved at all—not because they were excluded, but because they had decided that they had paid their debt to Lafayette with more than 320,000 American military casualties, more than 116,000 of them dead. Their duty was done. In the Senate, the Republican majority had long warned Wilson that it would not accept a League of Nations that interfered with an independent American foreign policy; a treaty that obliged America to belong to such a league would be fatally flawed. This was not Wilson's attitude, of course. He thought the Treaty of Versailles a victory—he told his wife that "as no one is satisfied, it makes me hope we have a just peace"[19]—and he fought for it with such vigor that he brooked no compromises with, and would accept no amendments or revisions from, the United States Senate. On 10 July 1919 he challenged the Senate to approve the treaty, saying, "Dare we reject it and break the heart of the world?"[20]

It looked as though the Senate, to Wilson's astonishment and rage, was prepared to do just that. So he embarked on a whistle-stop campaign to rally the American people to the treaty. His health was failing, and the campaign nearly killed him. His doctors finally forced him to stop. But in his own righteous way he was prepared to risk his life for what he and Lloyd George and Clemenceau had wrought in Paris. Wilson suffered a terrible stroke on 2 October, which left him physically and mentally debilitated, though Wilson's wife tried to keep the effects hidden.

Republicans in the Senate would not ratify a treaty that committed the United States, without the consent of Congress, to protect the territorial integrity of threatened League states. Wilson, who by November had regained some of his strength, again refused any alteration of the treaty. He won the Noble Peace Prize but failed to get what he really wanted. In November 1919, the Versailles Treaty was put up for a vote in the Senate, once with amendments, once without—and both times it failed to gain the necessary two-thirds majority. On 19 March 1920 another vote was held on an amended version of the treaty, but Wilsonian Democrats who refused to countenance any changes helped sink it. In 1921, after Wilson was out of office, the United States reached a separate peace with each of the chief Central Powers—Germany, Austria, and Hungary—but disdained joining the League of Nations.

Wilson had the United States enter the Great War as an "associated power" rather than an "ally." Perhaps it should have been no surprise that despite his best efforts the United States wrapped up its postwar business in similar fashion, on its own terms. Wilson was asked in his last cabinet meeting what he would do now. Pedagogical to the last, he announced, "I am going to try to teach ex-presidents how to behave."[21]

APPOINTMENT AT ARLINGTON

ilson died in 1924. Fifteen years later came the most telling
refutation of his postwar vision: an even greater war than the
Great War had been. The peace of the world was not overturned by any statesmen he knew. It was overturned by a failed
postcard painter; but for Adolf Hitler, the Great War was unfinished
business.

In the Great War Hitler had been a regimental dispatch runner, a
moustached corporal disdained by his fellow soldiers as an apple pol-
isher yet considered unpromotable by his officers. A loner, unsociable,
impractical, and a dreamer whose twin passions were art and politics,
he spent much of his time in the rear but got close enough to the front

Epilogue

lines to be wounded by shrapnel in October 1916 and to be temporarily blinded by mustard gas in October 1918. He was still recuperating in hospital when news of the Armistice arrived in November. He had welcomed war in August 1914—"I sank down on my knees and thanked Heaven from an overflowing heart"[1]—and now, in shock and despair at Germany's defeat, he envisioned another war. "When I was confined to bed, the idea came to me that I would liberate Germany, that I would make it great. I knew immediately that it would be realized."[2]

A NEW ARMISTICE

On 22 June 1940, Hitler the corporal was now Hitler the Führer, the dictator of a third German Reich and supreme commander of the Wehrmacht. His destination was a railway car on the tracks near the forest of Compiegne, France, the very same railway car in which German representatives had agreed to the Armistice of 1918. Hitler had ordered the railway car removed from a museum (German engineers blew out a wall to get at it) and returned to the exact spot where the 11 November 1918 Armistice had been signed. The site of the surrender was now a memorial commemorating France's victory. It was transformed by Hitler into a revanchist historical tableau.

A guard of honor from the SS was there to welcome him. A monument to France's recapture of Alsace-Lorraine (an Allied sword plunged into the breast of a German eagle) was partly obscured by a draped Nazi flag. Not obscured was a separate granite tablet, raised three feet from the ground, on which were inscribed the words: "Here on the eleventh of November 1918 succumbed the criminal pride of the German Empire.... Vanquished by the free peoples which it tried to enslave." Hitler read the inscription and struck the prototypical fascist pose, as described by CBS radio reporter William

Shirer, an eyewitness: "He swiftly snaps his hands on his hips, arches his shoulders, plants his feet wide apart. It is a magnificent gesture of defiance, of burning contempt for this place now and all that it has stood for in the twenty-two years since it witnessed the humbling of the German Empire."[3]

The railway car had belonged to Marshal Ferdinand Foch, supreme commander of the Allied armies at the end of World War One. Hitler entered the railway car and sat in Foch's chair. When the French delegates arrived, General Wilhelm Keitel, chief of the *Oberkommando der Wehrmacht*, read out the preamble to the terms of the new armistice, which was all Hitler wanted to hear. He left the railway car, not bothering to listen to the recitation of the terms themselves. He knew them well enough: most important, the Germans would occupy northern and western France, the entire Atlantic coast—with the occupation costs paid by the French. The new French government, eventually centered on Vichy and led by a French hero of the First World War, Marshal Philippe Pétain, would represent a pliant vassal state. Keitel could wrap up the details; there would be no negotiations. In six weeks Hitler had achieved what Kaiser Wilhelm II had failed to do in more than four years of titanic battle. Shirer summarized the dramatic event by saying, "The whole ceremony in which Hitler has reached a new pinnacle in his meteoric career and Germany avenged the 1918 defeat is over in a quarter of an hour."[4] As Joseph Goebbels told Hitler, "The disgrace is now extinguished. It's a feeling of being born again."[5]

"THE UNNECESSARY WAR"

That feeling, of course, would not last, but the sense that the Second World War was the inevitable outcome of the First remains.

Winston Churchill, who surely has some standing on the issue, had a different opinion. He wrote that the Second World War was "the Unnecessary War." "There never was," he noted of World War II, "a war more easy to stop than that which has just wrecked what was left of the world from the previous struggle."[6] Churchill foresaw the coming of the war, yet knew it did not have to happen. There was nothing ineluctable about the Second World War; it did not occur as a clanking Hegelian *deus ex machina* to tie up the loose ends of the Great War. Neither the Versailles Treaty nor the United States Senate's rejection of the League of Nations put Hitler in power. What put Hitler in power was a popular vote of the German people, making the National Socialists the largest party in the Reichstag, and the political miscalculation of German president Paul von Hindenburg—Germany's chief of the general staff in the First World War—who was pressured by his political allies into making Hitler chancellor. Hitler thought of himself as a man of the future—and too many Germans shared that belief. He thought of Hindenburg as a reactionary old fuddy-duddy who had to be tolerated until he died (which happened in 1934). Hindenburg, for his part, recognized Hitler as a violent upstart and a would-be dictator. Even while finally capitulating to many of Hitler's demands, Hindenburg thought he could restrain Hitler's excesses, but he was too old to be the guardian of a German republic he defended out of obligation while yearning for a restored monarchy. Events over the next half dozen years that led to Poland's partition between the National Socialists of Germany and the Communists of Russia, which triggered the declaration of war by Britain and France, were not preordained; they were the result of the free actions of individual statesmen and their governments.

America's doughboys of the First World War were not responsible for the rise of Hitler. They won a great and honorable victory, and others squandered the peace. American intervention was decisive in defeating the Second Reich's attempt to dominate the European continent. When British foreign minister Arthur Balfour laid a wreath on George Washington's grave at Mount Vernon on 29 April 1917, shortly after America's declaration of war, he commented on "the immortal memory of George Washington, soldier, statesman, patriot, who would have rejoiced to see the country of which he was by birth a citizen and the country his genius called into existence fighting side by side to save mankind from a military despotism."[7] Balfour, the Tory statesman and former prime minister, had it exactly right.

ARLINGTON

If Hitler thought he had an appointment to keep at Compiegne, President Warren G. Harding had another appointment to keep on Armistice Day 1921 at Arlington National Cemetery. Little more than a fortnight earlier, on 24 October 1921, Sergeant Edward F. Younger, a twice-wounded veteran of the First World War and holder of the Distinguished Service Cross, had stood alone in a chapel in France. Before him were four coffins containing the remains of unidentified American soldiers. His job was to place a bouquet of white and pink roses on one of the coffins, marking that anonymous soldier for internment at Arlington in a new monument dedicated to the "Unknown Soldier."[8] He walked around the coffins until he finally felt an almost physical pull toward one of them. He placed the roses upon the casket, marking that soldier to be transferred back home along with French soil to line the bottom of his grave.

On 11 November 1921, the soldier and his casket were removed from the Rotunda of the United States Capitol building, where he had been lying in state, and placed upon a horse-drawn caisson for the journey to Arlington. Accompanying him were President Harding, Vice President Calvin Coolidge, former President Wilson, the justices of the Supreme Court, and General Pershing, as well as other elected officials, military officers, and dignitaries. At the gravesite, Harding placed a Medal of Honor and Distinguished Service Cross on the casket. A British representative added a Victoria Cross. The Belgian representative, a general, ripped his own Medal of Valor from his uniform and awarded it to the dead American soldier. President Harding led the assembly in the Lord's Prayer. Chief Plenty Coups, a Crow Indian, placed his war bonnet and coup stick by the soldier's tomb and offered up another prayer, this one to the Great Spirit acknowledged by his people. A salute was fired, taps was played, and the soldier's coffin was lowered to its resting place. The tomb would bear the inscription: "HERE RESTS IN HONORED GLORY AN AMERICAN SOLDIER KNOWN BUT TO GOD."[9]

For as long as the United States exists, he will be there, a guard from the 3rd United States Infantry Regiment (The Old Guard) keeping watch. The doughboys paid our debt to Lafayette. The question the Unknown Soldier might ask us is whether we have adequately paid our debt to the generation of Americans who fought the Great War, who forged the American Century, who defined for the world what it meant to be an American. Are we the nation of Sergeant York and Eddie Rickenbacker? Are we the same people, with the same mores, the same ambition, and the same spirit? If so, he'll rest easy. If not, perhaps we should return to study his generation's example, to remember what it was like to live "in the time of the Americans."[10]

NOTES

PROLOGUE

1. How American infantrymen gained this name is unclear, though it is usually thought to date from the sand-and-dust-covered soldiers tramping through deserts in the Mexican War.

2. Quoted in David D. Lee, *Sergeant York: An American Hero* (Lexington: University Press of Kentucky, 1985), 35.

3. All quotations are from Tom Skeyhill and Richard Wheeler, eds., *Sergeant York and the Great War: His Own Life Story and War Diary* (San Antonio: Vision Forum, 2011), 162–63.

4. This is how Byron Farwell quotes the famous exchange in *Over There: The United States in the Great War, 1917–1918* (New York: W. W. Norton, 2000), 310.

5.   Woodrow Wilson's speech seeking a congressional declaration of war, 2 April 1917.

6.   Ernest Hemingway, *A Farewell to Arms* (New York: Charles Scribner's Sons, 1957), 185.

7.   Quoted in Bruce D. Porter, *War and the Rise of the State: The Military Foundations of Modern Politics* (New York: Free Press, 1994), xvi.

CHAPTER ONE: THE CLASH OF EMPIRES

1.   Quoted in S. L. A. Marshall, *The American Heritage History of World War I* (New York: Simon and Schuster, 1964), 19.

2.   Quoted in David Fromkin, *Europe's Last Summer: Who Started the Great War in 1914* (New York: Vintage, 2005), 155.

3.   Quoted in D. J. Goodspeed, *The German Wars, 1914–1945* (New York: Bonanza Books, 1983), 11. Goodspeed notes that Bismarck often repeated this aphorism, which he first delivered in 1878, and over time the musketeer became a grenadier. He also predicted in 1897 that if Europe plunged into a continent-wide war, it would be because of "some damned foolish thing in the Balkans." This is quoted in many sources, including Tom Gallagher, *Outcast Europe: The Balkans, 1789–1989, From the Ottomans to Milošević* (New York: Routledge, 2001), 60.

4.   Quoted in Goodspeed, *The German Wars, 1914–1945*, 11.

5.   Albeit of a very German sort given that his maternal grandfather and great-grandmother were German.

6.   Quoted in James Barr, *Setting the Desert on Fire: T. E. Lawrence and Britain's Secret War in Arabia, 1916–1918* (New York: W. W. Norton, 2009), 5.

7.   President Theodore Roosevelt earned a Nobel Prize for mediating a treaty to end the war.

8.   The French, in turn, pledged to help the British patrol the Mediterranean, not that the British needed any help. The real purpose of the agreement was to place the Royal Navy athwart Germany's North Sea fleet.

9.   Quoted in Robert K. Massie, *Nicholas and Alexandra* (New York: Random House, 2011), 268.

10.   Serbia had mobilized on 25 July and Austria had followed the next day, but Austria was focused on Serbia, not on a greater war against Russia as well.

11.   This idea is explored at length in Sean McMeekin, *The Russian Origins of the First World War* (Cambridge: Belknap Press of Harvard University Press, 2011). Sazonov's famous exclamation is quoted on page 54.

12.   Bismarck had recommended against annexing Alsace-Lorraine on these very grounds—that it would give the French a permanent grievance against Germany—but was overruled. Most of the population of the annexed territories spoke German.

13.   Field Marshal Lord Kitchener, who joined the British cabinet as secretary of state for war in 1914, had long predicted an Anglo-German war, which he laid at the feet of weak statesmanship. He believed it would last at least three years, and that there would be no winners, except perhaps the growing peripheral powers of the United States and Japan. He told a stunned cabinet that he would need more than a million men to fight the war. "We must be prepared," he said, "to put armies of millions in the field and maintain them for several years." Quoted in Sir Philip Magnus, *Kitchener: Portrait of an Imperialist* (New York: E. P. Dutton, 1959), 284. See also the discussion of Kitchener's views in John Pollock, *Kitchener: Architect of Victory, Artisan of Peace* (New York: Carroll & Graf, 2001), 375–76.

14.   The Russians were particularly shortsighted; they had been forced to suppress a revolution only a decade earlier—in 1905, in the wake of the Russo-Japanese War.

15.   "The Younger" was to distinguish him from his famous uncle, Field Marshal Helmuth von Moltke (the Elder) (1800–1891), a great soldier, strategist, and longtime chief of the Prussian general staff.

16.   Britain was not bound by treaty to defend France, and the cabinet was divided about whether Britain should go to war on France's behalf. The German invasion of Belgium decided the issue.

17.   Yes, *that* John Foster Dulles, later secretary of state under President Eisenhower.

18.   Quoted in John Terraine, *The Great War* (Ware: Wordworth Editions, 1998), 11.

19.   Quoted in ibid.

CHAPTER TWO: TWO AND A HALF YEARS HARD

1.   Quoted in Martin Gilbert, *The First World War: A Complete History* (New York: Henry Holt, 1996), 43.

2.   Quoted in Michael A. Palmer, *The German Wars: A Concise History, 1859–1945* (Minneapolis: Zenith Press, 2010), 57.

3.   Though they have received relatively little scholarly attention, German newspapers at the outset of the war were full of stories of Russian atrocities in East Prussia.

4.   See Michael Walzer, *Just and Unjust Wars: A Moral Argument with Historical Illustrations* (New York: Pelican Books, 1984), 240–42, for a discussion of the chancellor's remarks before the Reichstag on 4 August 1914.

5.   Though he had been chief military historian for the general staff, he was officially retired when he wrote this book. He returned to command in the Great War.

6.   Friedrich von Bernhardi, *Germany and the Next War*, trans. Allen H. Powles (New York: Longmans, Green, 1912), 10, 6, 14, 13.

7.   Stephen Jay Gould cites the account of the American entomologist and evolutionist Vernon Kellogg, who worked on Belgian relief efforts before the United States entered the war. Gould noted that "Night after night, [Kellogg] listened to dinner discussions and arguments, sometimes in the presence of the Kaiser himself, among Germany's highest military officers.... [Kellogg] arrived in Europe as a pacifist, but left committed to the destruction of German militarism by force. Kellogg was appalled, above all, at the justification for war and German supremacy advanced by these officers, many of whom had been university professors before the war. They not only proposed an evolutionary rationale but advocated a particularly crude form of natural selection, defined as inexorable, bloody battle." See Stephen Jay Gould, *Bully for Brontosaurus: Reflections in Natural History* (New York: W. W. Norton, 1991), 424.

8.   Barbara W. Tuchman, *The Guns of August* (New York: Ballantine Books, 1994), 174.

9.   Both of these oft-quoted remarks of Schlieffen can be found in Tuchman, *The Guns of August*, 25.

10.   The French were not unusual in relying on massed infantry attacks; both sides considered them the only way to mount a breakthrough before the Western Front became a war of trenches.

11.   Quoted in Gilbert, *The First World War*, 36.

12. Good background to the story of the Angels of Mons is provided in Mark Girouard, *The Return to Camelot: Chivalry and the English Gentleman* (New Haven: Yale University Press, 1981), in particular pages 284–85.

13. Quoted in Michael Neiberg, *The Second Battle of the Marne* (Bloomington: Indiana University Indiana Press, 2008), 26.

14. Quoted in James A. Ramage, *Gray Ghost: The Life of Colonel John Singleton Mosby* (Lexington: University Press of Kentucky, 1999), 336. Mosby said this more than a year before America's entry into the war, which he did not live to see; he died in May 1916.

15. Alan Seeger, *Letters and Diary of Alan Seeger* (New York: Charles Scribner's Sons, 1917), 12, 31.

16. Seeger is quoted in Douglas Porch, *The French Foreign Legion: A Complete History of the Legendary Fighting Force* (New York: HarperCollins, 1991), 352.

17. Seeger, *Letters and Diary of Alan Seeger*, 167.

18. Paul Rockwell survived the war to protest about scurrilous novels (written in the 1930s) about the Legion.

19. See for instance Philip Warner, *Field Marshal Earl Haig* (London: Cassell Military Paperbacks, 2001), 56–59.

20. After the war, when he was Lord Lieutenant of Ireland, the IRA tried to murder him. They failed.

21. George H. Cassar, *The Tragedy of Sir John French* (Cranbury, NJ: Associated University Presses, 1985), 198.

22. The losses appalled French as well, and he was a regular visitor to military hospitals: "Horribly sad and very pathetic to see how good and cheery and patient the dear fellows are...I hate it all so! ... such horrible sadness and depression." Quoted in John Keegan, *The First World War* (New York: Alfred A. Knopf, 1999), 288.

23. The Tommies called it "Wipers."

24. The Germans had attempted to use poison (tear) gas on the Eastern Front at the Battle of Bolimów in January 1915. The freezing weather made it ineffective. They tried again, with more effect, on the Western Front, in April 1915, with chlorine gas at Ypres.

25. He cannot really be faulted for this. He had volunteered for the Franco-Prussian War, and his was a military family.

26.   Foch and his family were politically conservative, intensely patriotic, and
      ardently Catholic—the usual combination, but interesting nevertheless given
      the anti-clericalism of the French Republic. Foch's brother was a Jesuit priest,
      a fact that slowed Foch's promotion. Joffre, by contrast, ate meat on Fridays
      to reassure his political masters (and perhaps because he liked to eat—he
      always looked rather well fed).

27.   Quoted in Michael S. Neiberg, *Foch: Supreme Allied Commander in the Great
      War* (Dulles, VA: Brassey's, 2003), 25.

28.   Quoted in Gilbert, *The First World War*, 270.

29.   Though the popular image of the First World War is of men in trenches charg-
      ing over the top to be mowed down by machine gun fire, it was artillery that
      was the great slayer of men. In the Second Battle of Champagne, September–
      November 1915, the French alone fired 4,967,000 artillery rounds. In six
      months at Verdun, the combined totals were 40 million rounds. Artillery was
      not an efficient way to inflict casualties, but in World War One, it was the
      preferred way.

30.   Most sources conclude that each side suffered over three hundred thousand
      casualties.

31.   The classic book on the battle is Alistair Horne, *The Price of Glory: Verdun
      1916* (New York: Penguin, 1993), where he renders Nivelle's order as "You
      will not let them pass!" See page 292.

32.   Hussein led the Hashemite clan, which claims descent from the Prophet
      Mohammad.

33.   The Russians had actually vetoed Greek participation in the Dardanelles
      Campaign, lest the Greeks occupy Constantinople, which was a Russian war
      aim.

34.   Churchill had actually tried to convince the cabinet to grant him a field com-
      mand in October 1914 when, as First Lord, he inspected the defenses of
      Antwerp.

35.   Keegan, *The First World War*, 306.

CHAPTER THREE: WOODROW'S WAR

1.   Quoted in Joshua David Hawley, *Theodore Roosevelt: Preacher of Righteous-
      ness* (New Haven: Yale University Press, 2008), 251.

2.   It was an electoral college landslide, but won with less than 42 percent of the popular vote: Theodore Roosevelt took more than 27 percent, Republican incumbent William Howard Taft won more than 23 percent, and the Socialist Eugene Debs achieved 6 percent of the popular vote.

3.   Quoted in John Milton Cooper Jr., *The Warrior and the Priest: Woodrow Wilson and Theodore Roosevelt* (Cambridge: Belknap Press of Harvard University, 1983), 221.

4.   His colonelcy was purely honorary; he had never served in the military and was a small man with a most unmilitary mien.

5.   House's influence waned after the war, but before then Wilson could wax lyrical about the remarkable Mr. House, calling him "my second personality. He is my independent self. His thoughts and mine are one." See John Milton Cooper Jr., *Woodrow Wilson: A Biography* (New York: Alfred A. Knopf, 2009), 192. House recorded that Wilson told him that "we had known each other always, and merely came in touch then [at their first meeting], for our purposes and thoughts were one." Quoted in Louis Auchincloss, *Woodrow Wilson* (New York: Viking, 2000), 39.

6.   Quoted in Cooper, *The Warrior and the Priest*, 275.

7.   The War College Division, General Staff Corps, "A Statement of a Proper Military Policy for the United States," September 1915, published by the Government Printing Office, 1916, 8.

8.   Quoted in Martin Gilbert, *The First World War: A Complete History* (New York: Henry Holt, 1996), 13.

9.   Quoted in Martin Gilbert, *A History of the Twentieth Century* (New York: William Morrow, 2002), 78.

10. Godfrey Hodgson, *Woodrow Wilson's Right Hand: The Life of Colonel Edward M. House* (New Haven: Yale University Press, 2006), 100.

11. House had launched his own diplomatic initiative in the late spring and early summer of 1914 to prevent the looming war. His gambit was to create an Anglo-Saxon alliance between Germany, Britain, and the United States, which would simultaneously end Germany's fear of encirclement by hostile powers, put a damper on Anglo-German suspicions, and invite both powers to cooperate with the United States in helping to develop Latin America and other parts of the world. House actually met with the Kaiser, who "spoke of the folly of England forming an alliance with the Latins and the 'semi-barbarous' Slavs,"

and argued that in terms of demography and *Weltpolitik*, the great danger was Asia and the Yellow Peril. Nothing came of House's efforts, but after the war, the Kaiser mused that had it been given more time to develop, House's diplomatic overture might have prevented the war—though such sentiments spring easily from catastrophe. See Hodgson, *Woodrow Wilson's Right Hand*, 98–100. During the war, while America was neutral, House tied to broker a negotiated peace.

12.   Quoted in Edmund Morris, *Colonel Roosevelt* (New York: Random House, 2010), 378, 382–83.

13.   Quoted in Kathleen Dalton, *Theodore Roosevelt: A Strenuous Life* (New York: Vintage, 2004), 194.

14.   Quoted in H. W. Brands, *T. R.: The Last Romantic* (New York: Basic Books, 1997), 750.

15.   Quoted in LeRoy Ashby, *William Jennings Bryan: Champion of Democracy* (Boston: Twayne Publishers, 1987), 142.

16.   For instance, while Wilson was an enthusiast for a Pan-American pact that would guarantee "undisturbed and undisputed territorial integrity and…complete independence under republican forms of government," he continued and expanded American intervention in Nicaragua, the Dominican Republic, and Haiti as the only alternative to chaos. For a discussion of this aspect of Wilson's administration, see Cooper, *Woodrow Wilson*, especially pages 237–49.

17.   Quoted in Cooper, *Woodrow Wilson*, 190. Colonel House commented cynically that Palmer "wants to be Attorney General to advance his own fortunes as he thinks it would be possible for him to obtain lucrative practice after four years of service."

18.   Quoted in James P. Tate, *The Army and Its Air Corps: Army Policy toward Aviation, 1919–1941* (Maxwell AFB, AL: Air University Press, 1998), 3.

19.   Like all good stories and etymologies, this one is disputed.

20.   At least in theory and up to a point: he upheld racial segregation and in politics accepted a spoils system of appointments.

21.   Quoted in Patrick Devlin, *Too Proud to Fight: Woodrow Wilson's Neutrality* (New York: Oxford University Press, 1975), 143.

22.   Woodrow Wilson, "Jackson Day Address," Indianapolis, 8 January 1915. This was no new idea for Wilson. In a 4 July 1914 speech in Philadelphia, he had said that America's "flag is the flag, not only of America, but of humanity."

23. Burton J. Hendrick, *The Life and Letters of Walter H. Page*, vol. 1 (Garden City, NY: Doubleday, Page, 1922). Tyrrell's interview with the president is recounted on pages 203–5.

24. Republican senator Elihu Root's words weighed on Wilson's conscience: "American children will go through life fatherless because of the action that we are to approve tonight, and when these children, grown to manhood, turn back the page to learn in what cause their fathers died, are they to find that it was about a quarrel as to the number of guns and the form and ceremony of a salute, and nothing else?" Quoted in Devlin, *Too Proud to Fight*, 124.

25. A Mexican exile, he was jailed and died in the United States in 1916.

26. Woodrow Wilson, message to Congress, delivered to the Senate 19 August 1914. A more prosaic purpose was to keep Americans of different ethnic heritages from taking sides.

27. Quoted in Morris, *Colonel Roosevelt*, 389.

28. Quoted in H. W. Brands, *T. R.*, 750–51.

29. Quoted in H. C. F. Bell, *Woodrow Wilson and the People* (Garden City, NY: Country Life Press, 1945), 178.

30. The manifest of the *Lusitania* included as cargo empty shell casings, nonexplosive fuses, and small arms cartridges that were deemed, by the port authorities, *not* military ammunition.

31. Theodore Roosevelt thought this an outrage and said that if he were president, he would have an armed escort put the German ambassador on the *Lusitania*.

32. Woodrow Wilson speech at the Convention Hall, Philadelphia, 10 May 1915.

33. Quoted in Samuel Eliot Morison, *The Oxford History of the American People*, vol. 3, *1869 to the Death of John F. Kennedy, 1963* (New York: Mentor, 1972), 179.

34. Quoted in Brands, *T. R.*, 756.

35. Theodore Roosevelt statement to the press, 8 May 1915, quoted in Morris, *Colonel Roosevelt*, 419.

36. Quoted in Brands, *T. R.*, 756.

37. In a speech of 20 April 1915; it is quoted in part in Cooper, *Woodrow Wilson*, 278.

38. Chad Millman, *The Detonators: The Secret Plot to Destroy America and the Epic Hunt for Justice* (New York: Little, Brown, 2006), 24.

39. The phrase comes from Rudyard Kipling's poem "Recessional."

40.   Quoted in Allan R. Millett and Peter Maslowski, *For the Common Defense: A Military History of the United States* (New York: Free Press, 1994), 347.

41.   Quoted in Edward J. Renehan Jr., *The Lion's Pride: Theodore Roosevelt and His Family in Peace and War* (New York: Oxford University Press, 1998), 126.

42.   This is the translation in Mike Sharp, Ian Westwell, and John Westwood, *History of World War One*, vol. 1, *War and Response, 1914–1916* (Tarrytown, NY: Marshall Cavendish, 2002), 271.

CHAPTER FOUR: THE ROAD TO CANTIGNY

1.   The Senate voted for war on 4 April; the House of Representatives followed two days later.

2.   The pace did pick up, however, and by the end of 1917, seven hundred thousand volunteers had enlisted.

3.   Pershing had actually been recommended by Major Douglas MacArthur. In February 1917 MacArthur brought the news to President Wilson and Secretary of War Newton Baker that General Frederick Funston, their first choice to lead an American Expeditionary Force, had died of a heart attack. Baker asked MacArthur whom the Army would prefer as a commander; MacArthur answered that while he could not speak for the Army, he thought Pershing easily the best available man.

4.   One exception was the "Buffalo Soldiers," black troops of the American 92nd and 93rd Divisions who served under the French, and hence were actually the first American divisions to see combat, thought they weren't officially part of the American Expeditionary Force.

5.   Baker rather effetely called his work "a happy confusion. I delight in the fact that when we entered this war we were not, like our adversary, ready for it, anxious for it, prepared for it, and inviting it. Accustomed to peace, we were not ready." Quoted in Edward J. Renehan Jr., *The Lion's Pride: Theodore Roosevelt and His Family in Peace and War* (New York: Oxford University Press, 1998), 160.

6.   Quoted in Edward M. Coffman, *The War to End All Wars: The American Military Experience in World War I* (Lexington: University Press of Kentucky, 1998), 32.

7.   Quoted in Byron Farwell, *Over There: The United States in the Great War, 1917–1918* (New York: W. W. Norton, 1999), 104.

8. This meant that troops trained on American artillery (the standard three-inch gun) stateside had to be retrained for the differently operated French artillery pieces (chiefly their 75mm gun).

9. John J. Pershing, *My Experiences in the World War*, vol. 1 (New York: Frederick A. Stokes, 1931), 44.

10. Quoted in Laurence Stallings, *The Doughboys: The Story of the AEF, 1917–1918* (New York: Harper & Row, 1963), 15. Whatever elation the French felt—and however flattered the doughboys were with all the attention they received—once the American troops were billeted, they were appalled at French ideas of hygiene and sanitation. The *mademoiselles* might be pretty, but the *man-sewers* were indeed just that.

11. Quoted in Robert B. Bruce, *Pétain: Verdun to Vichy* (Washington. DC: Potomac Books, 2008), 57.

12. Quoted in Farwell, *Over There*, 71. Sims took command of U.S. Navy forces fighting in British and European waters. He ended the war as a vice admiral.

13. British objections were not entirely irrational. The British system had been to attempt to secure shipping lanes. Convoys, in comparison, were slow; when they arrived they could overburden a port; and they required the cooperation of fractious merchant seamen. But the convoy system worked, and the British system didn't. The British, however, should be credited with devoting some of their shipping to transporting doughboys across the Atlantic—even if it meant that imports of food for British civilians made way for imports of troops.

14. Ironically, the first officer killed was a doctor, Lieutenant William T. Fitzsimmons, hit during a German bombing raid on Base Hospital Number 5 on 4 September 1917. Three American privates died with him.

15. The entreaties of Major Theodore Roosevelt Jr., stationed in France, and son of the former president, helped bring it to an end.

16. Quoted in Farwell, *Over There*, 114.

17. Gough, a veteran of the Boer War, came from a celebrated Anglo-Irish military family. His brother, his father, and a nephew, all generals, each won the Victoria Cross, Britain's highest decoration for bravery.

18. It was codenamed Operation Georgette.

19. American divisions were larger than their French counterparts.

20. The lieutenant, Oliver J. Kendall, was presumed to have been tortured. His body was found after the war, July 1919; his throat had been slit.

21.   The effect of the tanks was more psychological than real. The Germans in this
       sector had not fought tanks before, but none of the awkward vehicles reached
       Cantigny.

CHAPTER FIVE: BELLEAU WOOD: "RETREAT, HELL. WE JUST GOT HERE!"

1.   The Marine Corps' slogan "First to Fight" dates from the First World War.
2.   Quoted in Joseph H. Alexander with Don Horan and Norman C. Stahl, *The
       Battle History of the U.S. Marines: A Fellowship of Valor* (New York: Harp-
       erCollins Perennial, 1999), 35.
3.   A famous story of the Marine Corps' spirit in World War I was of an American
       woman visiting a field hospital. Scanning a row of wounded Frenchmen, she
       spied the apparent figure of a doughboy: "Oh, surely you are an American!"
       The laconic reply: "No ma'am, I'm a Marine." The story can be found in many
       sources, including John W. Thomason Jr., *Fix Bayonets!* (Naval and Military
       Press, no date), ix.
4.   A. W. Catlin and Walter A. Dyer, *"With the Help of God and a Few Marines"*
       (New York: Doubleday, Page, 1919), 18–19.
5.   Both quoted in Matthew C. Price, *The Advancement of Liberty: How Ameri-
       can Democratic Principles Transformed the Twentieth Century* (Westport, CT:
       Praeger, 2008), 10–11.
6.   Williams also prudently sent a message to his battalion commander that he
       had countermanded the French officer's orders to fall back, and added, "kindly
       see that the French do not shorten their artillery range." Quoted in Dick Camp,
       The Devil Dogs at Belleau Wood: U.S. Marines in World War I (Minneapolis:
       Zenith Press, 2008), 63. Several Marines have claimed credit for Williams's
       famous rejoinder, as Camp discusses on page 64. Lieutenant Colonel Frederick
       "Fritz" Wise had a similar experience (see pages 60–61) arguing with a French
       officer urging him to retreat: "I have come to fight the Germans and this is
       where I intend to do it—and that is that, by God!"
7.   Quoted in Robert B. Asprey, *At Belleau Wood* (Denton: University of North
       Texas Press, 1996), 89.
8.   Quoted in Camp, *The Devil Dogs at Belleau Wood*, 64.
9.   Thomason, *Fix Bayonets!*, 9.
10.   Elton E. Mackin, *Suddenly We Didn't Want to Die: Memoirs of a World War
       I Marine* (Novato, CA: Presidio Press 1993), 18.

11. George B. Clark, *Devil Dogs: Fighting Marines of World War I* (Novato, CA: Presidio Press, 2000), 104.
12. Thomason, *Fix Bayonets*, 23.
13. Quoted in Camp, *The Devil Dogs at Belleau Wood*, 90.
14. Ibid., 107.
15. Thomason, *Fix Bayonets!*, 27.
16. See Alan Axelrod, *Miracle at Belleau Wood: The Birth of the Modern U.S. Marine Corps* (Guilford, CT: Lyons Press, 2010), 143–46, for a good discussion of Daly and his battle cry.
17. Quoted in John S. D. Eisenhower, with Joanne T. Eisenhower, *Yanks: The Epic Story of the American Army in World War I* (New York: Touchstone, 2002), 146.
18. The Germans allegedly referred to the Leathernecks as "dogs from hell."
19. Quoted in Camp, *The Devil Dogs at Belleau Wood*, 124.

CHAPTER SIX:
CHÂTEAU-THIERRY, "THE ROCK OF THE MARNE," AND SOISSONS

1. Quoted in Allan R. Millett, *Semper Fidelis: The History of the United States Marine Corps* (New York: Macmillan, 1980), 304.
2. Quoted in Geoffrey Perret, *Old Soldiers Never Die: The Life of Douglas MacArthur* (Avon, MA: Adams Media, 1996), 95.
3. Quoted in Robert B. Bruce, *A Fraternity of Arms: America and France in the Great War* (Lawrence: University Press of Kansas, 2003), 228.
4. Georges Clemenceau, who inspected these positions, found that the men "burned with an invincible resolution" even though, exposed as they were, they "had abandoned all chance of surviving to the triumph for which they offered their life." As author Robert B. Bruce notes in his book, *A Fraternity of Arms: America and France in the Great War*, the discipline of the men in these forward positions belies "the commonly held assumption that the French soldier of 1918 was a dispirited, dejected, and near-mutinous soldier." See page 230 for the Clemenceau quotation and Bruce's analysis.
5. Quoted in Laurence Stallings, *The Doughboys: The Story of the AEF, 1917–1918* (New York: Harper & Row, 1963), 138.

6. Quoted in John S. D. Eisenhower, with Joanne T. Eisenhower, *Yanks: The Epic Story of the American Army in World War I* (New York: Touchstone, 2002), 153.

7. These quotations can be found in Stallings, *The Doughboys*, 119.

8. Quoted in Stallings, *The Doughboys*, 134.

9. Quoted in Eisenhower, *Yanks*, 157. Laurence Stallings quotes Captain T. C. Reid expressing his regret to McAlexander that he had been "too busy" directing his troops to kill any Germans himself. See *The Doughboys*, 135.

10. Soon to be re-designated III Corps.

11. Replacements and supply troops brought the number to about 350,000.

12. Quoted in Douglas V. Johnson II and Rolfe L. Hillman Jr., *Soissons 1918* (College Station: Texas A&M University Press, 1999), 41.

13. Quoted in Byron Farwell, *Over There: The United States in the Great War, 1917–1918* (New York: W. W. Norton, 1999), 183–84.

14. On the second day of battle, 19 July, Marine Lieutenant Daniel Bender reconnoitered for enemy gas shells. He was wounded, and sent back this brief report: "No gas. Shot in the ass. Bender." Quoted in Johnson and Hillman, *Soissons 1918*, 103.

15. These quotations come from Johnson and Hillman, *Soissons 1918*, 125.

16. Fighting of course raged on, and Soissons itself was not taken until 2 August.

17. Quoted in Farwell, *Over There*, 184.

18. Quoted in Johnson and Hillman, *Soissons 1918*, 138.

CHAPTER SEVEN: SAINT-MIHIEL AND THE MEUSE-ARGONNE OFFENSIVE

1. While taking on this field command, he maintained his status as commanding general of the American Expeditionary Force.

2. The fourteen-inch guns were served by American sailors under the command of Rear Admiral Charles P. Plunkett. Helping them find their targets was infantry captain Edwin P. Hubble, who later became a celebrated astronomer.

3. Edward G. Lengel, *To Conquer Hell: The Meuse-Argonne, 1918; The Epic Battle That Ended the First World War* (New York: Henry Holt, 2009), 69.

4. Quoted in Lengel, *To Conquer Hell*, 71.

5. Edward M. Coffman, *The War to End all Wars: The American Military Experience in World War I* (Lexington: University Press of Kentucky, 1998), 300.

6.   Quoted in John S. D. Eisenhower, with Joanne T. Eisenhower, *Yanks: The Epic Story of the American Army in World War I* (New York: Touchstone, 2002), 207.

7.   Quoted in Byron Farwell, *Over There: The United States in the Great War, 1917–1918* (New York: W. W. Norton, 1999), 223.

8.   The German defenses were organized on three east-west lines: the *Etzel-Giselher Stellung*, which included Montfaucon; the stronger *Kriemhilde Stellung*; and the last-ditch *Freya Stellung*, five miles farther north.

9.   That historian is Edward G. Lengel in *To Conquer Hell*, 61.

10.   W. Kerr Rainsford, *From Upton to the Meuse: With the Three Hundred and Seventh Infantry* (Charleston, SC: Forgotten Books, 2012), 158–59.

11.   Quoted in John Toland, *No Man's Land: 1918, The Last Year of the Great War* (Lincoln: University of Nebraska Press, Bison Books, 2002), 464.

12.   Alexander, the son of a judge, chucked an incipient legal career and enlisted in the Army as a private in 1886. He earned an officer's commission three years later. He had many critics who thought perhaps he should have been busted back to his previous rank.

13.   Quoted in Thomas W. Johnson and Fletcher Pratt, *The Lost Battalion* (Lincoln: University of Nebraska Press, Bison Books, 2000), 93.

14.   Quoted in Richard Slotkin, *Lost Battalions: The Great War and the Crisis of American Nationality* (New York: Henry Holt, 2005), 333.

15.   Among those killed trying to relieve the lost battalion was Captain Eddie Grant, a Harvard-educated professional baseball player (his major league career spanned 1905 to 1915). A lawyer in civilian life, he had enlisted in 1917.

16.   Laurence Stallings, *The Doughboys: The Story of the AEF, 1917–1918* (New York: Harper & Row, 1963), 294.

17.   Douglas MacArthur, *Reminiscences* (New York: Crest Books, 1965), 76.

18.   Quoted in Eisenhower, *Yanks*, 262.

CHAPTER EIGHT: JOHN J. PERSHING (1860–1948)

1.   Quoted in Richard O'Connor, *Black Jack Pershing* (New York: Doubleday, 1961), 11.

2.   Colonel Baldwin also noted of Pershing, "You did some tall rustling, and if you had not we would have starved...." Quoted in Frank E. Vandiver, *Black*

Jack: The Life and Times of John J. Pershing, vol. 1 (College Station: Texas A&M University Press, 1998), 211.

3. Quoted in Richard Goldhurst, *Pipe Clay and Drill: John J. Pershing; The Classic American Soldier* (New York: Reader's Digest Press, 1977), 105.

4. Quoted in Jim Lacey, *Pershing* (New York: Palgrave Macmillan, 2008), 34.

5. Twenty years after the loss of his wife and daughters, visiting guests asked him why he appeared so melancholy. His answer: "Today is my daughter's birthday." See Donald Smythe, *Guerrilla Warrior: The Early Life of John J. Pershing* (New York: Charles Scribner's Sons, 1973), 217.

6. Orders of the Secretary of War Newton Baker to Major General John J. Pershing, AEF, reproduced in William R. Griffiths, *The Great War* (Garden City Park, NY: West Point Military History Series, Square One Publishers, 2003), 202.

7. Lacey, *Pershing*, 142.

8. It was also answered by Field Marshal Paul von Hindenburg, who concluded that "The American infantry in the Argonne won the war." Hitler agreed, incidentally. Both are cited in John Mosier, *Cross of Iron: The Rise and Fall of the German War Machine, 1914–1918* (New York: Henry Holt, 2006), 26–27.

9. John J. Pershing, *My Experiences in the World War* (New York: Frederick A. Stokes, 1931), 255.

10. It was this commission that created the American military cemeteries in France.

CHAPTER NINE: PEYTON C. MARCH (1864-1955)

1. These were the comments of his colonel, cited in Edward M. Coffman, *The Hilt of the Sword: The Career of Peyton C. March* (Madison: University of Wisconsin Press, 1966), 10.

2. Quoted in ibid., 12.

3. Quoted in ibid., 17.

4. Quoted in ibid., 32.

5. March was initially appointed as acting chief of staff under the nominal direction of General Tasker Bliss. He took on the full role in May.

6. Quoted in Byron Farwell, *Over There: The United States in the Great War, 1917–1918* (New York: W. W. Norton, 2000), 65.

7. In March 1918, a new air base for pilot training—March Field, in Riverside, California—was named in honor of March's son, Peyton C. March Jr.

8.   Quoted in Coffman, *The Hilt of the Sword*, 69.

9.   In his General Order No. 80, 1918, March, with the approval of Baker, made this explicit, the order reading in part: "The Chief of Staff by law (Act of May 12, 1917) takes rank and precedence over all officers of the Army, and by virtue of that position and by authority of and in the name of the Secretary of War, he issues such orders as will insure that the policies of the War Department are harmoniously executed." Quoted in John S. D. Eisenhower, with Joanne T. Eisenhower, *Yanks: The Epic Story of the American Army in World War I* (New York: Touchstone, 2002), 134.

10. Quoted in Coffman, *The Hilt of the Sword*, 92.

11. John S. D. Eisenhower notes that March lacked "the social manners that were generally considered prerequisite for a successful military career: his style was ruthless and abrasive. That had never held him back, however, especially when he had been called on to perform difficult jobs. His superior officers viewed him as a troubleshooter...." See *Yanks*, 90.

12. Coffman, *The Hilt of the Sword*, 151.

13. MacArthur achieved much of what March wanted, though Congress insisted on West Point remaining a four-year college. MacArthur remained a March favorite. March recommended MacArthur's appointment as Army chief of staff and thought him the right man for the job in the Korean War. MacArthur, in turn, was effusive in his praise of March.

14. Quoted in Coffman, *The Hilt of the Sword*, 189.

15. Quoted in ibid., 249.

CHAPTER TEN: DOUGLAS MacARTHUR (1880–1964)

1.   This was a taste he shared with Texas-born, Kansas-raised Dwight Eisenhower, who loved Western novels, and with VMI graduate George C. Marshall. For men of action, Westerns aren't bad preparation.

2.   Douglas MacArthur, *Reminiscences* (New York: Crest Books, 1965), 23.

3.   When Spain declared war on the United States in 1898, MacArthur considered chucking his studies to enlist, but his parents dissuaded him. Douglas MacArthur's father was himself soon off to the Philippines as a brigadier general of volunteers.

4.   Other nicknames, listed by William Manchester in *American Caesar: Douglas MacArthur, 1880–1964* (New York: Dell/Laurel, 1983), 103, were "the Beau

Brummell of the A.E.F." and "the Fighting Dude." Officers not in the 42nd Division were not always so complimentary, thinking him a glory hound.

5. Geoffrey Perret, *Old Soldiers Never Die: The Life of Douglas MacArthur* (New York: Random House, 1996), 84.

6. William Manchester, *American Caesar: Douglas MacArthur, 1880–1964* (New York: Dell/Laurel, 1983), 103.

7. Perret, *Old Soldiers Never Die*, 87.

8. Manchester, *American Caesar*, 104.

9. Quoted in ibid., 110.

10. MacArthur, *Reminiscences*, 66–67.

11. He was sent off with a gold cigarette case inscribed to "The bravest of the brave."

12. MacArthur, *Reminiscences*, 68.

13. Both quotations can be found in Richard B. Frank, *MacArthur* (New York: Palgrave Macmillan, 2007), 9.

14. Quoted in Edward G. Lengel, *To Conquer Hell: The Meuse-Argonne, 1918; The Epic Battle that Ended the First World War* (New York: Henry Holt, 2009), 329. Lengel also quotes the reaction of one soldier who heard of MacArthur's promise to risk 100 percent casualties: "Generous son of a bitch, ain't he?"

15. MacArthur and Summerall quoted in Byron Farwell, *Over There: The United States in the Great War, 1917–1918* (New York: W. W. Norton, 1999), 230.

16. Had this happened, and it is testimony to their incompatibility that she suggested it, one can imagine after the great crash of 1929, MacArthur declaring, indomitably, "Our yields shall return!"

17. MacArthur, *Reminiscences*, 93.

18. She went on to marry and divorce two more men. When MacArthur became a four-star general, she was married to the actor Lionel Atwill, prompting her memorable comment, "It looks like I traded four stars for one."

19. Later, in the Philippines, he would munch a head of lettuce while he did so. He was Spartan in diet, and his daily pacing likely added up to several miles of walking.

20. Quoted in Carlo D'Este, *Eisenhower: A Soldier's Life* (New York: Henry Holt, 2002), 226—though the most famous Eisenhower comment on MacArthur came in response to a woman's question of whether Ike had ever met him:

"Not only have I met him, mam: I studied dramatics under him for five years in Washington and four years in the Philippines." Quoted in Manchester, *American Caesar*, 182

21. Though in ill health, she even shipped out to the Philippines with her son in 1935, lived in a suite next to MacArthur's in the Manila Hotel, and died there. Throughout her life she did everything she could to advance her son's career.

22. And for a short time he kept a young Eurasian mistress, until he broke off the affair, realizing that it was a mistake in and of itself—and lest Mother should find out.

23. Hoover liked MacArthur as well, urging him to run for president against Franklin Roosevelt in 1944 and Truman in 1948.

24. At the same time, he did promote mechanization within the Army and won agreement with the Navy for the nation's coastal aerial defense to be handled by the Army Air Corps.

25. That doesn't mean he was wrong: so was Churchill; so was Patton.

26. Caesarean in demeanor, yes; but MacArthur was, in his political views, very much an American democrat, domestically at one with the moderate, limited-government conservatism of a Hoover or an Eisenhower.

27. In April 1942, he became supreme commander of the southwest Pacific. The Navy, under Admiral Chester Nimitz, took the rest.

28. General Jonathan "Skinny" Wainwright surrendered Corregidor on 7 May 1942.

29. Quoted in Perret, *Old Soldiers Never Die*, 282. As Perret notes, the field was strafed by the Japanese shortly after MacArthur boarded another B-17 and flew on to Alice Springs.

30. MacArthur, *Reminiscences*, 252.

31. Joining him in this distinction were Dwight Eisenhower, George Marshall, and Henry "Hap" Arnold.

32. Though, as Geoffrey Perret points out, MacArthur's dream of making Japan a Christian society foundered on the potential political fallout should the emperor, who was supposedly mulling conversion, choose to become a Catholic or a Protestant. See Perret, *Old Soldiers Never Die*, 520.

33. MacArthur, *Reminiscences*, 449.

34. Ibid., 459.

35.   Interestingly, he advised President Kennedy not to commit American troops to South Vietnam, seeing it as irrelevant to American interests.

36.   William Safire, ed., *Lend Me Your Ears: Great Speeches in History* (New York: W. W. Norton, 2004), 87.

CHAPTER ELEVEN: BILLY MITCHELL (1879–1936)

1.   Columbian College eventually became George Washington University.

2.   Mitchell's father was, however, very proud of his service in the Union Army in the Civil War and nurtured in his son a great love of touring battlefields, both in Europe and at home.

3.   Quoted in Alfred F. Hurley, *Billy Mitchell: Crusader for Air Power* (Bloomington: Indiana University Press, 1975), 6.

4.   He had been part of a volunteer Signals unit in Cuba and the Philippines.

5.   He also noted a widespread Japanese fascination with flying machines and advised a Chinese warlord that the best way to keep flies off his bald head was to tattoo a spider web on his skull.

6.   Quoted in Burke Davis, *The Billy Mitchell Affair* (New York: Random House, 1967), 29.

7.   Quoted in ibid., 30.

8.   He was well aware of the dangers as well as the glories of the sky. His younger brother, John, had died in a plane crash during the war.

9.   Quoted in Davis, *The Billy Mitchell Affair*, 62.

10.   Quoted in Roger G. Miller, *Billy Mitchell: "Stormy Petrel of the Air"* (Washington, DC: Office of Air Force History, 2004), 36.

11.   Quoted in Davis, *The Billy Mitchell Affair*, 127.

12.   Mitchell's wife won custody of their three children.

13.   The union produced one child, a daughter.

14.   Though it was not on his itinerary, he noted the military potential of Wake Island.

15.   Some see racism in Mitchell's depiction of "yellows" (Asiatics) versus "whites" (Europeans/Americans), but Mitchell himself derided those who said the Japanese could not fly, saying they could fly as well as any Westerner; he saw China as a reemerging giant, with a people superior to any other; and he recognized that mainland Asia offered allies against an expansionist Japan.

16.   Quoted in Douglas Waller, *A Question of Loyalty: General Billy Mitchell and the Court-Martial That Gripped the Nation* (New York: HarperCollins, 2004), 20.

17.   During a lull in the trial, one newspaper wag quipped, "If the court-martial stays off the front page another two days it's feared Col. Billy Mitchell's going to lose interest in these proceedings." Quoted in Davis, *The Billy Mitchell Affair*, 267.

CHAPTER TWELVE: JOHN A. LEJEUNE (1867-1942)

1.   At the time, cadets at the Naval Academy had four years of academic work, then two years at sea as midshipmen, before returning for final exams and commissioning. In 1912, Congress abolished the requirement of serving two years at sea and authorized graduating cadets to be commissioned as ensigns.

2.   Quoted in Merrill L. Bartlett, *Lejeune: A Marine's Life, 1967–1942* (Columbia: University of South Carolina Press, 1991), 3; see also pages 37–38 for the context and the possibility that Lejeune's assignment to the naval engineers was overturned by the secretary of the Navy.

3.   Quoted in Bartlett, *Lejeune*, 39.

4.   Allan R. Millett and Jack Shulimson, eds., *Commandants of the Marine Corps* (Annapolis, MD: Naval Institute Press, 2004), 108.

5.   Quoted in George B. Clark, *Devil Dogs: Fighting Marines of World War I* (Novato, CA: Presidio Press, 2000), 391.

6.   John A. Lejeune, *Reminiscences of a Marine* (Quantico: Marine Corps Association, 1979), 260.

7.   Pershing's appointment of Lejeune quieted Marine demands for a division of their own. On Lejeune being the first Marine officer to command a division, see Bartlett, *Lejeune*, 4.

8.   Lejeune, *Reminiscences of a Marine*, 321.

9.   The Navy secretary was Edwin Denby. His orders are quoted in Bartlett, *Lejeune*, 155.

CHAPTER THIRTEEN: GEORGE S. PATTON (1885-1945)

1.   Later, when he was serving in Mexico, he conceded to his wife that if he could not achieve greatness as a soldier, he would settle for raising horses.

2.   Quoted in Roger H. Nye, *The Patton Mind: The Professional Development of an Extraordinary Leader* (New York: Avery Publishing, 1993), 14, 16.

3.   Quoted in Martin Blumenson, *Patton: The Man behind the Legend, 1885–1945* (New York: William Morrow, 1985), 59.

4.   Quoted in Carlo D'Este, *Patton: A Genius for War* (New York: HarperCollins, 1995), 149.

5.   Quoted in ibid., 155.

6.   Quoted in Blumenson, *Patton: The Man behind the Legend*, 89, 92.

7.   Quoted in ibid., 95.

8.   Quoted in D'Este, *Patton: A Genius for War*, 204.

9.   Quoted in ibid., 205.

10.   Patton thought he saw his martial ancestors in the clouds urging him on. Biographer Carlo D'Este notes that Patton's son, George S. Patton IV, saw a similar apparition, his father in the clouds, telling him to get his "ass across the road" under shelling in the Korean War. See D'Este, *Patton: A Genius for War*, 257–58.

11.   Quoted in ibid., 263.

12.   Patton rode fiercely, not just in polo, but in hunting and racing, and like many a good horseman, endured his share of being thrown from the saddle. He was also kicked in the head by a horse. He was accident prone—whether on horseback or not—and in a car accident during World War I had his head go through the windshield. He suffered so many blows to the head that some have wondered whether this added to his emotional volatility, which became more pronounced with age.

13.   Quoted in Stanley P. Hirshson, *General Patton: A Soldier's Life* (New York: HarperCollins, 2002), 131.

14.   George S. Patton Jr., "The Obligation of Being an Officer," 1 October 1919.

15.   He sometimes paid a price for it too—and not only in later contrite apologies. It nearly cost him his role as captain of the Army polo team in Hawaii in 1935 until his opponents (whom he had cursed) demanded he be reinstated.

16.   See Alan Axelrod, *Patton: A Biography* (New York: Palgrave Macmillan, 2006), 70.

17.   Quoted in Rick Atkinson, *An Army at Dawn: The War in North Africa, 1942–1943* (New York: Henry Holt, 2002), 35.

18. Quoted in Blumenson, *The Patton Papers, 1940–1945* (Cambridge, MA: Da Capo Press, 1996), 102.

19. Quoted in Blumenson, *Patton: The Man behind the Legend*, 215.

20. Quoted in Axelrod, *Patton's Drive: The Making of America's Greatest General* (Guilford, CT: The Lyons Press, 2009), 87.

21. Quoted in Blumenson, *The Patton Papers*, 545.

22. Quoted in Axelrod, *Patton's Drive*, 107.

23. They went armed with, among things, a prayer card from Patton with Christmas greetings on one side and the now-famous prayer Patton commissioned, beseeching God for "fair weather for Battle…that armed with Thy power, we may advance from victory to victory, and crush the opposition and wickedness of our enemies and establish Thy justice among men and nations. Amen." Quoted in Blumenson, *Patton: The Man behind the Legend*, 251.

24. Quoted in Axelrod, *Patton's Drive*, 136.

25. This was Ohrdruf concentration camp.

26. Quoted in Blumenson, *Patton: The Man behind the Legend*, 264.

27. He caused an unfortunate stir in the press by more than once comparing Nazi Party membership to membership of the Republican or Democrat Party.

28. Quoted in Blumenson, *Patton: The Man behind the Legend*, 281.

29. Quoted in D'Este, *Patton: A Genius for War*, 557. D'Este also quotes "A Soldier's Prayer," written by Patton at the request of an Episcopal chaplain, pages 557–58.

CHAPTER FOURTEEN: GEORGE C. MARSHALL (1880–1959)

1. Quoted in Mark A. Stoler, *George C. Marshall: Soldier-Statesman of the American Century* (Boston: Twayne Publisher, 1989), 17.

2. H. H. Arnold, *Global Mission* (New York: Harper & Brothers, 1949), 44. Arnold himself became the "father" of the United States Air Force and its only five-star general. Arnold remained a lifelong friend of Marshall's.

3. Quoted in Stoler, *George C. Marshall*, 27–28.

4. Quoted in William Frye, *Marshall: Citizen Soldier* (Indianapolis: Bobbs-Merrill, 1947), 146.

5. Marshall thought the transfer of troops from the attack on Saint-Mihiel to the Meuse Argonne Offensive was the "hardest nut I had to crack in France."

Quoted in Ed Cray, *General of the Army: George C. Marshall, Soldier and Statesman* (New York: Cooper Square Press, 2000), 72.

6. Jim Lacey, *Pershing* (New York: Palgrave Macmillan, 2008), 160.

7. Quoted in Carlo D'Este, *Eisenhower: A Soldier's Life* (New York: Henry Holt, 2002), 198.

8. Pershing had recommended Marshall for promotion to brigadier general; instead, postwar reductions in personnel and rank meant that Marshall reverted to the rank of major in 1920. In 1923, he was promoted to lieutenant colonel.

9. Quoted in Stoler, *George C. Marshall*, 55.

10. This also gives some insight into the first Mrs. Marshall. She is quoted in ibid., 48.

11. He wanted to, but could not, add Dwight Eisenhower to his team of instructors.

12. Allen, who became an Army lieutenant, was killed in Italy in 1944.

13. Quoted in Cray, *General of the Army*, 111.

14. Quoted in Stoler, *George C. Marshall*, 70–71.

15. Quoted in ibid., 78.

16. Quoted in Eric Larrabee, *Commander in Chief: Franklin Delano Roosevelt, His Lieutenants, and Their War* (Annapolis: Naval Institute Press, 1987), 101.

17. Quoted in Edward M. Coffman, *The Regulars: The American Army, 1898–1941* (Cambridge: Harvard University Press, 2004), 419.

18. Quoted in D'Este, *Eisenhower: A Soldier's Life*, 466.

19. Quoted in Cray, *General of the Army*, 111.

20. Quoted in Edgar Puryear, *Nineteen Stars: A Study in Military Character and Leadership* (Novato, CA: Presidio Press, 2003), 321.

21. He was the first twentieth-century American general to be awarded this rank. MacArthur, Eisenhower, Hap Arnold (all given the rank in December 1944), and Omar Bradley (1950) would follow. It has not been awarded since.

22. Quoted in Stoler, *George C. Marshall*, 157.

23. Quoted in ibid., 161.

24. George C. Marshall, *The Papers of George Catlett Marshall*, eds. Larry I. Bland and Mark A. Stoler, vol. 6, *"The World Hangs in the Balance"* (Baltimore: The Johns Hopkins University Press, 2013), 484.

25. The school later (in 1978) erected a statue in his honor as well.

26.   Quoted in Cray, *General of the Army*, 731.

27.   Quoted in Larrabee, *Commander in Chief*, 99.

CHAPTER FIFTEEN: EDDIE RICKENBACKER (1890–1973)

1.   Edward V. Rickenbacker, *Rickenbacker: An Autobiography* (New York: Prentice-Hall, 1967), 6.

2.   Quoted in W. David Lewis, *Eddie Rickenbacker: An American Hero in the Twentieth Century* (Baltimore: The Johns Hopkins University Press, 2005), 81.

3.   Quoted in H. Paul Jeffers, *Ace of Aces: The Life of Captain Eddie Rickenbacker* (New York: Presidio Press, 2003), 51.

4.   Rickenbacker, *Fighting the Flying Circus* (New York: Frederick A. Stokes Company, 1919), 194–95.

5.   Rickenbacker, *Rickenbacker: An Autobiography*, 120. He was also appalled that the American Air Service stinted on parachutes because the chutes were too cumbersome for the tight cockpits and because it was feared they would give too many pilots an excuse to say "Geronimo" and abandon their planes— an attitude from the higher-ups that infuriated Rickenbacker.

6.   Penicillin as a treatment for infections, it should be remembered, had not yet been discovered. Rickenbacker underwent one bout of surgery that kept him out of action for a few days in July 1918, but lied about the continued pain in order to keep flying. A month later he couldn't keep up the charade and ended up submitting to a second surgery. He declared himself cured in time to join the Battle of Saint-Mihiel in September.

7.   Quoted in Jeffers, *Ace of Aces*, 135.

8.   They remained friends until Runyon's death, in December 1946. Rickenbacker flew over New York City and cast Runyon's cremated remains over Manhattan, as per Runyon's wish.

9.   Rickenbacker, *Rickenbacker: An Autobiography*, 144.

10.   The failure of her previous marriage to the wealthy Clifford Durant was not her fault—or such was the judgment of her former father-in-law, William C. Durant, who settled a trust fund on her as her reward for "doing her best in a lost cause." See Jeffers, *Ace of Aces*, 207–8, and for more detail, Lewis, *Eddie Rickenbacker: An American Hero*, 258.

11.   Quoted in Jeffers, *Ace of Aces*, 216.

12.   Rickenbacker, *Rickenbacker: An Autobiography*, 149.

13.   Rickenbacker voted for Roosevelt in the 1932 election because he thought he was "sound and conservative." Once in the White House, Roosevelt had, by Rickenbacker's reckoning, made "a complete 180-degree turn and taken off in the other direction toward liberalism and socialism." Quoted in James P. Duffy, *Lindbergh vs. Roosevelt: The Rivalry That Divided America* (Washington, DC: Regnery, 2010), 24.

14.   Quoted in Burton Folsom Jr., *New Deal or Raw Deal? How FDR's Economic Legacy Has Damaged America* (New York: Threshold/Simon & Schuster, 2008), 96.

15.   Rickenbacker, *Rickenbacker: An Autobiography*, 190.

16.   Ibid., 272.

17.   It remains secret, because it was never written down, but we know the gist: it was a reprimand from the secretary of war, Henry Stimson, to MacArthur for publicly criticizing President Roosevelt's war strategy. Stimson was also outraged at the tone of MacArthur's cables to Army Chief of Staff George Marshall.

18.   Quoted in Jeffers, *Ace of Aces*, 295.

19.   Quoted in Finis Farr, *Rickenbacker's Luck: An American Life* (New York: Houghton Mifflin, 1979), 332. He also judged John F. Kennedy "overrated" and Richard Nixon "a better man than people give him credit for."

CHAPTER SIXTEEN: FRANCIS P. DUFFY (1871–1932) AND ALVIN C. YORK (1887–1964)

1.   Quoted in Stephen L. Harris, *Duffy's War: Fr. Francis Duffy, Wild Bill Donovan, and the Irish Fighting 69th in World War I* (Sterling, VA: Potomac Books, 2006), 5.

2.   Some still think him a poetaster. His popular poem "Trees" ("I think that I shall never see / A poem lovely as....") is more parodied than the rest of his verse is remembered.

3.   Sergeant Kilmer was killed in action on 30 July 1918. Father Duffy led his burial detail.

4.   Francis P. Duffy, *Father Duffy's Story: A Tale of Humor and Heroism, of Life and Death with the Fighting Sixty-Ninth* (New York: George H. Doran Company, 1919), 60–61.

5.   Both quotations can be found in Harris, *Duffy's War*, 180–81.

6.   McCoy's assessment of Father Duffy can be found in ibid., 203.

7.   Duffy, *Father Duffy's Story*, 136.

8.   Donovan had told Father Duffy, "Oh, Hell, Father, I don't want to be a Colonel. As Lieutenant Colonel I can get into the fight and that's what I'm here for." Quoted in Harris, *Duffy's War*, 307.

9.   Quoted in ibid., xviii. In 1937, a statue of Duffy was erected in Times Square.

10.   Quoted in ibid., xvii.

11.   Quoted in David D. Lee, *Sergeant York: An American Hero* (Lexington: University Press of Kentucky, 1985), 7.

12.   Richard "Little Bear" Wheeler, ed., *Sergeant York and the Great War: His Own Life Story and War Diary* (San Antonio, TX: Mantle Ministries/Vision Forum, 2011), 104.

13.   Quoted in Lee, *Sergeant York: An American Hero*, 20.

14.   Wheeler, ed., *Sergeant York and the Great War*, 86–87.

15.   Quoted in Lee, *Sergeant York: An American Hero*, 26.

16.   Quoted in ibid., 43.

17.   Wheeler, ed., *Sergeant York and the Great War*, 205.

18.   Quoted in Lee, *Sergeant York: An American Hero*, 73.

19.   Still serving as a public high school, the institute was sometimes called the Alvin C. York Agricultural Institute because the state legislature had originally designated the school a center of agricultural learning.

20.   At a minimum, it won large audiences—and an Oscar for Gary Cooper.

21.   It was what we might call today a "zero-tolerance" policy. York's remarks are quoted in Lee, *Sergeant York: An American Hero*, 119.

CHAPTER SEVENTEEN: HARRY S. TRUMAN (1884–1972)

1.   Quoted in Alonzo L. Hamby, *Man of the People: A Life of Harry S. Truman* (New York: Oxford University Press, 1995), 57.

2.   Quoted in Roy Jenkins, *Truman* (London: Bloomsbury Publishing, 1986), 9.

3.   He read, among other things, Plutarch's *Lives* and the works of Cicero, Shakespeare, Tennyson, and Mark Twain.

4.   He liked to joke, "My choice early in life was either to be a piano player in a whorehouse or a politician—and to tell the truth there's hardly a difference." Quoted in Hamby, *Man of the People*, 15.

5. Quoted in D. M. Giangreco, *The Soldier from Independence: A Military Biography of Harry Truman* (Minneapolis: Zenith Press, 2009), 81.

6. Quoted in ibid., 98.

7. Quoted in ibid., 114.

8. Quoted in ibid., 166.

9. Quoted in Robert H. Ferrell, ed., *Dear Bess: The Letters from Harry Truman to Bess Truman, 1910–1959* (Columbia: University of Missouri Press, 1998), 295.

10. The couple had one daughter, Mary Margaret, born in 1924.

11. He and his fellow county judges served as government administrators rather than in courtrooms.

12. The Pendergasts were Catholic. Truman, interestingly, came to think of Catholics as a necessary part of the Democrat Party's coalition but never shook a distrust of them that was partly Protestant and partly political, viewing them as too prone to both isolationism and McCarthyism.

13. Quoted in David McCullough, *Truman* (New York: Simon and Schuster, 1992), 204.

14. This moniker, cited in Hamby, *Man of the People*, 199, came from the *New York Times*.

15. Quoted in McCullough, *Truman*, 214.

16. Quoted in ibid., 237.

17. Quoted in Robert Dalleck, *Harry S. Truman* (New York: Times Books, Henry Holt, 2008), 17; see also McCullough, *Truman*, 342.

18. Quoted in McCullough, *Truman*, 350. Truman likewise disdained Patton, writing in his diary, "Don't see how a country can produce such men as Robert E. Lee, John J. Pershing, Eisenhower, & Bradley and at the same time produce Custers, Pattons, and MacArthurs." Quoted in Ferrell, ed., *Off the Record: The Private Papers of Harry S. Truman* (Columbia: University of Missouri Press, 1997), 47.

19. Quoted in Dalleck, *Harry S. Truman*, 29.

20. Ibid., 37.

21. Quoted in Melvyn P. Leffler and Odd Arne Westad, eds., *The Cambridge History of the Cold War*, vol. 1, *Origins* (Cambridge: Cambridge University Press, 2010), 156.

22. Quoted in McCullough, *Truman*, 599; Truman disparaged all hyphenated Americans, and while a Zionist and a liberal on civil rights legislation—he issued the executive order to integrate the armed services—he was not at all inhibited about saying what he thought were the failings of various ethnic and religious groups.

23. Quoted in Dalleck, *Harry S. Truman*, 74. The Progressive Party ticket was in fact endorsed by the Communist Party USA.

24. His supporters, of course, especially among the GOP's East Coast establishment, saw his political moderation as a virtue, and viewed him as a fearless, incorruptible crime fighter as a federal prosecutor and Manhattan district attorney, a capable governor, and a spirited contender against FDR in 1944.

25. The *Chicago Daily Tribune* was published by Truman's political archenemy and fellow Great War veteran and artilleryman, Colonel Robert R. McCormick.

26. Dean Rusk, as told to Richard Rusk, *As I Saw It*, ed. Daniel S. Papp (New York: Norton, 1990), 162.

27. Quoted in John Toland, *In Mortal Combat: Korea, 1950–1953* (New York: William Morrow, 1991), 37.

28. Quoted in Dalleck, *Harry S. Truman*, 148.

29. The phrase came from a famous exchange during his 1948 whistle-stop campaign. When some enthusiast in the crowd shouted, "Give 'em hell, Harry," Truman responded winningly, "I never give anybody hell. I just tell the truth on the Republicans, and they think it's hell!" See Ferrell, *Harry S. Truman: A Life* (Columbia: University of Missouri Press, 1995), 278.

30. See Alonzo L. Hamby's introduction, pages vii–ix in Giangreco, *The Soldier from Independence*.

CHAPTER EIGHTEEN: WILLIAM J. DONOVAN (1883–1959)

1. Of his two surviving brothers, one, Timothy, went to medical school; the other, Vincent, went to the seminary and became a priest. He also had two surviving sisters, Loretta and Mary.

2. Ruth bore him two children—a son, David, and a daughter, Patricia.

3. Both quotations can be found in Stephen L. Harris, *Duffy's War: Fr. Francis Duffy, Wild Bill Donovan, and the Irish Fighting 69th in World War I* (Sterling, VA: Potomac Books, 2006), 38.

4. Quoted in ibid., 135.

5. Quoted in ibid., 351.

6. Quoted in Douglas Waller, *Wild Bill Donovan: The Spymaster Who Created the OSS and Modern American Espionage* (New York: Free Press, 2011), 31.

7. Notable on his itinerary were frequent trips to Germany, an interview with Mussolini, and two weeks investigating the Italian war in Abyssinia.

8. Quoted in Richard Dunlop, *Donovan: America's Master Spy* (New York: Rand McNally, 1982), 184.

9. Quoted in Waller, *Wild Bill Donovan*, 85.

10. Donovan was deeply worried about pro-Nazi saboteurs in the United States but thought Japanese Americans posed little, if any, threat. He argued against interning Japanese Americans as counterproductive. Roosevelt disagreed.

11. The Foreign Information Service was run by Pulitzer Prize–winning playwright turned presidential speechwriter Robert Emmet Sherwood, who had fallen out with Donovan. Sherwood was a fellow veteran of the First World War with an interesting backstory. He had been rejected by the American armed services as too lightweight for his height, about six foot seven, so he crossed the border and enlisted with the Canadian Black Watch. He saw combat and was wounded.

12. In Yugoslavia, Donovan was far more bullish on supporting, or at least maintaining relations with, the anti-Communist Chetniks than were the British, who had become convinced that the Communist-led Partisans were the more effective anti-Nazi force. In 1944, after the Allied invasion of Normandy, Donovan won the consent of Marshal Josip Tito, leader of the Partisans, for an OSS intelligence mission to the Chetniks. The mission was successful in gathering information and helping liberate Allied airmen shot down over Chetnik territory, but short-lived—from the end of August to the beginning of November—as President Roosevelt ordered it closed. In May 1945, the Communist Partisans ordered all American and British agents out of the country. In Greece Donovan's and Churchill's views were reversed: the prime minister insistent on backing the royalist anti-Communists, Donovan on sending support to the Greek Communists, regarding them as the more effective force against the Germans.

13. Quoted in Waller, *Wild Bill Donovan*, 174.

14. Quoted in Anthony Cave Brown, *Wild Bill Donovan: The Last Hero* (New York: Times Books, 1982), 471.

15. This was not just spite on Hoover's part, though Hoover and Donovan continued to loathe and spy on each other. Hoover, as head of the FBI, was better briefed than Donovan on the Soviets' extensive intelligence operations in the United States. Donovan continued to share intelligence with the Soviets and gained, he thought, valuable insights into Soviet strategy.

16. Nevertheless, at the Nuremberg war crimes trials, Donovan and Jackson became rivals and enemies over prosecution strategy, and Jackson denied him a role in examining or cross-examining witnesses.

17. Quoted in Brown, *Wild Bill Donovan: The Last Hero*, 833.

CHAPTER NINETEEN: THE ROOSEVELTS

1. Quoted in Joan Paterson Kerr, *A Bully Father: Theodore Roosevelt's Letters to His Children* (New York: Random House, 1995), 7.

2. Alice's mother, Alice Hathaway Lee, died two days after Alice's birth; the rest of TR's children were born from his second wife, Edith Kermit Carow.

3. Quoted in Kerr, *A Bully Father*, 32

4. Quoted in Edward J. Renehan Jr., *The Lion's Pride: Theodore Roosevelt and His Family in Peace and War* (New York: Oxford University Press, 1998), 65.

5. Quoted in Kerr, *A Bully Father*, 46.

6. Quoted in Renehan, *The Lion's Pride*, 10.

7. Quoted in Kerr, *A Bully Father*, 58.

8. He and his wife had four children, born between 1918 and 1926.

9. Quoted in Peter Collier with David Horowitz, *The Roosevelts: An American Saga* (New York: Simon & Schuster, 1994), 198.

10. In addition, Roosevelt—endlessly furious at the Wilson administration's lack of preparation for war and apparent laggardness in making good on shortages of weapons, ammunition, equipment, and supplies—provided money to buy necessities for his sons' troops.

11. Edward V. Rickenbacker, *Fighting the Flying Circus* (New York: Frederick A. Stokes Company, 1919), 193.

12. Quoted in Renehan, *The Lion's Pride*, 163.

13. Quoted in Edmund Morris, *Colonel Roosevelt* (New York: Random House, 2010), 528.

14. Roosevelt blamed Wilson for a regulation that barred her, as the sister of a soldier, from going to France. "It is wicked," he wrote. "She should have been

allowed to go, and to marry Quentin; then, even if he were killed, she and he would have known their white hours. It is part of the needless folly and injustice with which things have been handled." Quoted in Renehan, *The Lion's Pride*, 188.

15.   Quoted in ibid., 198, 200.

16.   Both quoted in ibid., 4–5.

CHAPTER TWENTY: IN DUBIOUS BATTLE

1.   The British were far and away the military leader against the Bolsheviks, with forty thousand British and more than five thousand imperial troops (almost all Canadians, with a small detachment of Australians). The Japanese were the most numerous, with seventy thousand troops in Siberia, but their goals were far less ideological than straightforwardly territorial. There were about thirteen thousand Americans all told and twelve thousand combined French and French imperial troops. Then there was a disparate array of Czechs (the fifty thousand– to seventy thousand–strong Czech Legion), Greeks, Poles, Estonians, Serbs, Romanians, Italians, and others.

2.   In a speech in 1949, at the outset of the Cold War, Churchill commented, "The failure to strangle Bolshevism at birth...lies heavily on us today." Speech at the Massachusetts Institute of Technology, 31 March 1949, quoted in Geoffrey Best, *Churchill: A Study in Greatness* (London: Hambledon and London, 2001), 93.

3.   The Churchill quotations are taken from William Manchester, *The Last Lion: Winston Spencer Churchill, Visions of Glory, 1874–1932* (New York: Little, Brown, 1983), 680–81.

4.   Churchill to the British cabinet ministers, February 1919, quoted in Henry Pelling, *Winston Churchill* (Ware, Hertfordshire: Wordsworth Editions, 1999), 258.

5.   Manchester, *The Last Lion*, 680.

6.   John Toland, *No Man's Land: 1918, the Last Year of the Great War* (New York: Doubleday, 1980), 308.

7.   Quotations from the *aide-mémoire* are as cited in John Toland, *No Man's Land: 1918, the Last Year of the Great War* (New York: Doubleday, 1980), 308–9 and Max Boot, *The Savage Wars of Peace: Small Wars and the Rise of American Power* (New York: Basic Books, 2002), 211.

8. Clifford Kinvig, *Churchill's Crusade: The British Invasion of Russia, 1918–1920* (London: Hambledon Continuum, 2006), 57.

9. Quoted in ibid.

10. Quoted in Byron Farwell, *Over There: The United States in the Great War, 1917–1918* (New York: W. W. Norton, 1999), 276.

11. The casualty rate—stemming from everything from influenza to Bolshevik bullets—is as estimated by E. M. Halliday in *When Hell Froze Over* (New York: ibooks/Simon & Schuster, 2000), 21.

12. Quoted in Ilya Somin, *Stillborn Crusade: The Tragic Failure of Western Intervention in the Russian Civil War, 1918–1920* (New Brunswick: Transaction Publishers, 1996), 46.

CHAPTER TWENTY-ONE: THE VICTORS AT VERSAILLES

1. Secretary of State Robert Lansing was one who recognized the dangers of "self-determination," noting in his diary, "It will raise hopes which can never be realized. It will, I fear, cost thousands of lives. In the end it is bound to be discredited, to be called the dream of an idealist who failed to realize the danger until it was too late to check those who attempt to put the principle into force. What a calamity that the phrase was ever uttered! What misery it will cause! Think of the feelings of the author when he counts the dead who died because he coined a phrase!" Quoted in Karl E. Meyer, *The Dust of Empire: The Race for Mastery of the Asia Heartland* (New York: Public Affairs, 2004), 5. Wilson himself later conceded that "When I gave utterance to those words, I said them without the knowledge that nationalities existed, which are coming to us day after day." Quoted in Margaret MacMillan, *Paris 1919: Six Months That Changed the World* (New York: Random House, 2002), 12.

2. All quotes from President Woodrow Wilson's speech to a joint session of Congress, 8 January 1918.

3. In 2004 he was beatified by the Catholic Church for his holy life, including his attempt to negotiate an end to the Great War.

4. One exception to this was Wilson's sympathy for non-czarist Russia, whose constituent nations, save for the Poles, he was inclined to sweep back under the Russian rug, if for no other reason than that he had not known that they existed.

5.   Theodore Roosevelt helpfully reminded Georges Clemenceau and British foreign secretary Arthur Balfour that in a parliamentary system, like their own, Wilson would no longer be leading the government.

6.   Quoted in H. W. Brands, *Woodrow Wilson* (New York: Times Books, 2003), 108. Wilson used this kind of language repeatedly against opponents of the League. A variation of the Whig version of history, it was and is a favorite liberal trope against conservatives.

7.   Quoted in Alexander L. George and Juliette L. George, *Woodrow Wilson and Colonel House: A Personality Study* (Mineola, NY: Dover Publications, 1964), 230.

8.   Quoted in MacMillan, *Paris 1919*, 94.

9.   Quoted in Brands, *Woodrow Wilson*, 108.

10.   Quoted in MacMillan, *Paris 1919*, 94.

11.   Winston S. Churchill, *The Second World War*, vol. 1, *The Gathering Storm* (New York: Mariner Books, 1986), 22.

12.   Germany made its final World War I reparations payment in 2010.

13.   Quoted in Keith Jeffery, *Field Marshal Sir Henry Wilson: A Political Soldier* (Oxford: Oxford University Press, 2006), 238. General, soon to be Field Marshal, Sir Henry Wilson had helped Lloyd George and his staff "war game" the memorandum by acting out the negotiating positions of France (as an aggrieved woman, a crucial part, he argued, of French public opinion) and Germany (in the more suitable role, perhaps, of a military officer).

14.   Quoted in MacMillan, *Paris 1919*, 197.

15.   More than 90 percent of the Saarlanders voting in the plebiscite voted for reunion with Germany, which was achieved in 1935.

16.   Adolf Hitler, elevated to chancellor after Germany's 1933 elections, repudiated the debt, but it was taken on by the West German government after the Second World War.

17.   Sheldon Anderson, *Condemned to Repeat It: "Lessons of History" and the Making of U.S. Cold War Containment Policy* (New York: Lexington Books, 2008), 41.

18.   Quoted in ibid., 41.

19.   Quoted in A. Scott Berg, *Wilson* (New York: G. P. Putnam's Sons, 2013), 602.

20.   Quoted in ibid., 607.

21.   Quoted in ibid., 699.

EPILOGUE

1. Walter C. Langer, *The Mind of Adolf Hitler: The Secret Wartime Report* (New York: Basic Books, 1972), 135.
2. Quoted in ibid., 37.
3. Quoted in Henry Steele Commager, *The Story of the Second World War* (Sterling, VA: Potomac Books, 2004), 50.
4. Quoted in ibid., 51.
5. Quoted in Ian Kershaw, *Hitler*, vol. 2, *1936–1945, Nemesis* (New York: W. W. Norton, 2001), 299.
6. Winston S. Churchill, *The Second World War*, vol. 1, *The Gathering Storm* (New York: Houghton Mifflin, 1948), xiv.
7. Quoted in James Langland, ed., *The Chicago Daily News Almanac and Year-Book for 1918* (Chicago: The Chicago Daily News Company, 1917), 527.
8. Similar dedications had taken place in Britain, at Westminster Abbey, and in France, at the Arc de Triomphe, in 1920, to commemorate the sacrifice of soldiers known only unto God.
9. The inscription was added ten years later.
10. David Fromkin used this phrase to title his book *In the Time of the Americans: The Generation That Changed America's Role in the World* (New York: Alfred A. Knopf, 1995). See his wonderful postscript on pages 551–52.

SELECT BIBLIOGRAPHY

Alexander, Joseph H. *The Battle History of the U.S. Marines: A Fellowship of Valor.* With Don Horan and Norman C. Stahl. New York: HarperCollins Perennial, 1999.

Anderson, Sheldon. *Condemned to Repeat It: "Lessons of History" and the Making of U.S. Cold War Containment Policy.* New York: Lexington Books, 2008.

Arnold, H. H. *Global Mission.* New York: Harper & Brothers, 1949.

Ashby, LeRoy. *William Jennings Bryan: Champion of Democracy.* Boston: Twayne Publishers, 1987.

Asprey, Robert B. *At Belleau Wood.* Denton: University of North Texas Press, 1996.

———. *The German High Command at War: Hidenburg and Ludendorff Conduct World War I.* New York, William Morrow and Company, 1991.

Astore, William J., and Dennis E. Showalter. *Hindenburg: Icon of German Militarism.* Washington, DC: Potomac Books, 2005.

Atkinson, Rick. *An Army at Dawn: The War in North Africa, 1942–1943*. New York: Henry Holt, 2002.

Auchincloss, Louis. *Woodrow Wilson*. New York: Viking, 2000.

Axelrod, Alan. *Miracle at Belleau Wood: The Birth of the Modern U.S. Marine Corps*. Guilford, CT: Lyons Press, 2010.

———. *Patton: A Biography*. New York: Palgrave Macmillan, 2006.

———. *Patton's Drive: The Making of America's Greatest General*. Guilford, CT: Lyons Press, 2009.

Barnett, Correlli. *The Great War*. London: BBC Worldwide Limited, 2003.

———. *The Swordbearers: Supreme Command in the First World War*. London: Cassell & Company, 1963.

Barr, James. *Setting the Desert on Fire: T. E. Lawrence and Britain's Secret War in Arabia, 1916–1918*. New York: W. W. Norton, 2009.

Bartlett, Merrill L. *Lejeune: A Marine's Life, 1967–1942*. Columbia: University of South Carolina Press, 1991.

Bell, H. C. F. *Woodrow Wilson and the People*. Garden City, NY: Country Life, 1945.

Berg, A. Scott. *Wilson*. New York: G. P. Putnam's Sons, 2013.

Bernhardi, Friedrich von. *Germany and the Next War*. Translated by Allen H. Powles. New York: Longmans, Green, 1912.

Berry, Henry. *Make the Kaiser Dance*. Garden City, NY: Doubleday & Company, 1978.

Best, Geoffrey. *Churchill: A Study in Greatness*. London: Hambledon and London, 2001.

Blumenson, Martin. *Patton: The Man behind the Legend, 1885–1945*. New York: William Morrow, 1985.

———. *The Patton Papers, 1940–1945*. Cambridge, MA: Da Capo, 1996.

Bond, Brian. *The Unquiet Western Front: Britain's Role in Literature and History*. Cambridge: Cambridge University Press, 2002.

Boot, Max. *The Savage Wars of Peace: Small Wars and the Rise of American Power*. New York: Basic Books, 2002.

Brands, H. W. *T. R.: The Last Romantic*. New York: Basic Books, 1997.

———. *Woodrow Wilson*. New York: Times Books, 2003.

Brown, Anthony Cave. *Wild Bill Donovan: The Last Hero*. New York: Times Books, 1982.

Bruce, Robert B. *A Fraternity of Arms: America and France in the Great War*. Lawrence: University Press of Kansas, 2003.

———. *Pétain: Verdun to Vichy*. Washington, DC: Potomac Books, 2008.

Buchan, John. *A History of the First World War*. Moffat, Scotland: Lochar Publishing, 1991.

Camp, Dick. *The Devil Dogs at Belleau Wood: U.S. Marines in World War I*. Minneapolis: Zenith Press, 2008.

Cassar, George H. *The Tragedy of Sir John French*. Cranbury, NJ: Associated University Presses, 1985.

Catlin, A. W., and Walter A. Dyer. *"With the Help of God and a Few Marines."* New York: Doubleday, Page, 1919.

Churchill, Winston S. *The Second World War*. Vol. 1, *The Gathering Storm*. New York: Mariner Books, 1986.

———. *The World Crisis*. New York: Charles Scribner's Sons, 1931.

Clark, George B. *Devil Dogs: Fighting Marines of World War I*. Novato, CA: Presidio Press, 2000.

Clayton, Anthony. *Paths of Glory: The French Army, 1914–1918*. Cassell & Company, 2005.

Coffman, Edward M. *The Hilt of the Sword: The Career of Peyton C. March*. Madison: University of Wisconsin Press, 1966.

———. *The Regulars: The American Army, 1898–1941*. Cambridge: Harvard University Press, 2004.

———. *The War to End All Wars: The American Military Experience in World War I*. Lexington: University Press of Kentucky, 1998.

Collier, Peter. *The Roosevelts: An American Saga*. With David Horowitz. New York: Simon & Schuster, 1994.

Commager, Henry Steele. *The Story of the Second World War*. Sterling, VA: Potomac Books, 2004.

Cooper, John Milton, Jr. *The Warrior and the Priest: Woodrow Wilson and Theodore Roosevelt*. Cambridge: Belknap Press of Harvard University, 1983.

———. *Woodrow Wilson: A Biography*. New York: Alfred A. Knopf, 2009.

Corrigan, Gordon. *Mud, Blood and Poppycock: Britain and the First World War*. London: Cassell Military Paperbacks, 2004.

Cray, Ed. *General of the Army: George C. Marshall, Soldier and Statesman*. New York: Cooper Square Press, 2000.

Crocker, H. W., III. *Don't Tread on Me: A 400-Year History of America at War, from Indian Fighting to Terrorist Hunting*. Crown Forum, 2006.

———. *The Politically Incorrect Guide to the British Empire*. Washington, DC: Regnery Publishing, 2011.

Dallas, Gregor. *1918: War and Peace*. New York: Overlook Press, 2001.

Dalleck, Robert. *Harry S. Truman*. New York: Times Books, Henry Holt, 2008.

Dalton, Kathleen. *Theodore Roosevelt: A Strenuous Life*. New York: Vintage, 2004.

Davis, Burke. *The Billy Mitchell Affair*. New York: Random House, 1967.

D'Este, Carlo. *Eisenhower: A Soldier's Life*. New York: Henry Holt, 2002.

———. *Patton: A Genius for War*. New York: HarperCollins, 1995.

Devlin, Patrick. *Too Proud to Fight: Woodrow Wilson's Neutrality*. New York: Oxford University Press, 1975.

Doughty, Robert A. *Pyrrhic Victory: French Strategy and Operations in the Great War*. Cambridge, Massachusetts: Belknap Press of Harvard University Press, 2005.

Duffy, Francis P. *Father Duffy's Story: A Tale of Humor and Heroism, of Life and Death with the Fighting Sixty-Ninth*. New York: George H. Doran Company, 1919.

Duffy, James P. *Lindbergh vs. Roosevelt: The Rivalry That Divided America*. Washington, DC: Regnery, 2010.

Dunlop, Richard. *Donovan: America's Master Spy*. New York: Rand McNally, 1982.

Dupuy, Trevor N. *A Genius for War: The German Army and General Staff, 1807–1945*. Garden City, NY: Military Book Club, 2002.

Eisenhower, John S. D. *Yanks: The Epic Story of the American Army in World War I*. With Joanne T. Eisenhower. New York: Touchstone, 2002.

Essame, H. *The Battle for Europe 1918*. New York: Charles Scribner's Sons, 1972.

Farr, Finis. *Rickenbacker's Luck: An American Life*. New York: Houghton Mifflin, 1979.

Farwell, Byron. *The Great War in Africa, 1914–1918*. New York: W. W. Norton & Company, 1986.

———. *Over There: The United States in the Great War, 1917–1918*. New York: W. W. Norton, 2000.

Ferguson, Niall. *The Pity of War: Explaining World War I*. New York: Basic Books, 1999.

Ferrell, Robert H., ed. *Dear Bess: The Letters from Harry Truman to Bess Truman, 1910–1959*. Columbia: University of Missouri Press, 1998.

———. *Harry S. Truman: A Life*. Columbia: University of Missouri Press, 1995.

———, ed. *Off the Record: The Private Papers of Harry S. Truman*. Columbia: University of Missouri Press, 1997.

———. *Woodrow Wilson & World War I, 1917–1921*. New York: Harper and Row Publishers, 1985.

Fleming, Thomas. *The Illusion of Victory: America in World War I*. New York: Basic Books, 2003.

Folsom, Burton, Jr. *New Deal or Raw Deal? How FDR's Economic Legacy Has Damaged America*. New York: Threshold/Simon & Schuster, 2008.

Fromkin, David. *Europe's Last Summer: Who Started the Great War in 1914*. New York: Vintage, 2005.

———. *In the Time of the Americans: The Generation That Changed America's Role in the World*. New York: Alfred A. Knopf, 1995.

———. *A Peace to End All Peace: The Fall of the Ottoman Empire and the Creation of the Modern Middle East*. New York: Avon Books, 1990.

Frye, William. *Marshall: Citizen Soldier*. Indianapolis: Bobbs-Merrill, 1947.

Fussell, Paul. *The Great War and Modern Memory*. New York: Oxford University Press, 1975.

Gallagher, Tom. *Outcast Europe: The Balkans, 1789–1989, from the Ottomans to Miloševi*. New York: Routledge, 2001.

George, Alexander L., and Juliette L. George. *Woodrow Wilson and Colonel House: A Personality Study*. Mineola, NY: Dover Publications, 1964.

Giangreco, D. M. *The Soldier from Independence: A Military Biography of Harry Truman*. Minneapolis: Zenith Press, 2009.

Gilbert, Martin. *The First World War: A Complete History*. New York: Henry Holt, 1996.

———. *A History of the Twentieth Century*. New York: William Morrow, 2002.

Girouard, Mark. *The Return to Camelot: Chivalry and the English Gentleman*. New Haven: Yale University Press, 1981.

Goldhurst, Richard. *Pipe Clay and Drill: John J. Pershing; The Classic American Soldier*. New York: Reader's Digest Press, 1977.

Goodspeed, D. J. *The German Wars, 1914–1945*. New York: Bonanza Books, 1983

———. *Ludendorff: Genius of World War I*. Boston: Houghton Mifflin Company, 1966.

Gould, Stephen Jay. *Bully for Brontosaurus: Reflections in Natural History*. New York: W. W. Norton, 1991.

Griffiths, William R. *The Great War*. Garden City Park, NY: West Point Military History Series, Square One Publishers, 2003.

Halliday, E. M. *When Hell Froze Over*. New York: ibooks/Simon & Schuster, 2000.

Hamby, Alonzo L. *Man of the People: A Life of Harry S. Truman*. New York: Oxford University Press, 1995.

Harris, Stephen L. *Duffy's War: Fr. Francis Duffy, Wild Bill Donovan, and the Irish Fighting 69th in World War I*. Sterling, VA: Potomac Books, 2006.

Hawley, Joshua David. *Theodore Roosevelt: Preacher of Righteousness*. New Haven: Yale University Press, 2008.

Hemingway, Ernest. *A Farewell to Arms*. New York: Charles Scribner's Sons, 1957.

Hendrick, Burton J. *The Life and Letters of Walter H. Page*. Vol. 1. Garden City, NY: Doubleday, Page, 1922.

Hirshson, Stanley P. *General Patton: A Soldier's Life*. New York: HarperCollins, 2002.

Hodgson, Godfrey. *Woodrow Wilson's Right Hand: The Life of Colonel Edward M. House*. New Haven: Yale University Press, 2006.

Horne, Alistair. *The Price of Glory: Verdun 1916*. New York: Penguin, 1993.

Hurley, Alfred F. *Billy Mitchell: Crusader for Air Power*. Bloomington: Indiana University Press, 1975.

Jackson, J. Hampden. *Clemenceau and the Third Republic*. New York: Collier Books, 1962.

Jeffers, H. Paul. Ace of Aces: *The Life of Captain Eddie Rickenbacker*. New York: Presidio Press, 2003.

Jeffery, Keith. *Field Marshal Sir Henry Wilson: A Political Soldier*. Oxford: Oxford University Press, 2006.

Jenkins, Roy. *Truman*. London: Bloomsbury Publishing, 1986.

Johnson, Douglas V., II, and Rolfe L. Hillman Jr. *Soissons 1918*. College Station: Texas A&M University Press, 1999.

Johnson, Thomas W., and Fletcher Pratt. *The Lost Battalion*. Lincoln: University of Nebraska Press, Bison Books, 2000.

Jones, Jerry W. *U.S. Battleship Operations in World War I*. Annapolis: Naval Institute Press, 1998.

Keegan, John. *The First World War*. New York: Alfred A. Knopf, 1999.

Kennedy, David M. *Over There: The First World War and American Society*. New York: Oxford University Press, 2004.

Kerr, Joan Paterson. *A Bully Father: Theodore Roosevelt's Letters to His Children*. New York: Random House, 1995.

Kershaw, Ian. *Hitler*. Vol. 2, *1936–1945, Nemesis*. New York: W. W. Norton, 2001.

Kinvig, Clifford. *Churchill's Crusade: The British Invasion of Russia, 1918–1920*. London: Hambledon Continuum, 2006.

Lacey, Jim. *Pershing*. New York: Palgrave Macmillan, 2008.

Langer, Walter C. *The Mind of Adolf Hitler: The Secret Wartime Report*. New York: Basic Books, 1972.

Langland, James, ed. *The Chicago Daily News Almanac and Year-Book for 1918*. Chicago: Chicago Daily News Company, 1917.

Larrabee, Eric. *Commander in Chief: Franklin Delano Roosevelt, His Lieutenants, and Their War*. Annapolis: Naval Institute Press, 1987.

Lee, David D. *Sergeant York: An American Hero*. Lexington: University Press of Kentucky, 1985.

Leffler, Melvyn P., and Odd Arne Westad, eds. *The Cambridge History of the Cold War*. Vol. 1, *Origins*. Cambridge: Cambridge University Press, 2010.

Lejeune, John A. *Reminiscences of a Marine*. Quantico: Marine Corps Association, 1979.

Lengel, Edward G. *To Conquer Hell: The Meuse Argonne, 1918, The Epic Battle That Ended the First World War*. New York: Henry Holt, 2009.

Lewis, W. David. *Eddie Rickenbacker: An American Hero in the Twentieth Century*. Baltimore: Johns Hopkins University Press, 2005.

MacArthur, Douglas. *Reminiscences*. New York: Crest Books, 1965.

Macdonald, Lyn. *1914*. New York: Atheneum, 1988.

Mackin, Elton E. *Suddenly We Didn't Want to Die: Memoirs of a World War I Marine*. Novato, CA: Presidio Press 1993.

MacMillan, Margaret. *Paris 1919: Six Months That Changed the World*. New York: Random House, 2002.

Magnus, Philip. *Kitchener: Portrait of an Imperialist*. New York: E. P. Dutton, 1959.

Manchester, William. *American Caesar: Douglas MacArthur, 1880–1964*. New York: Dell/Laurel, 1983.

———. *The Last Lion: Winston Spencer Churchill, Visions of Glory, 1874–1932*. New York: Little, Brown, 1983.

Marshall, George C. *The Papers of George Catlett Marshall*. Edited by Larry I. Bland and Mark A. Stoler. Vol. 6, *"The World Hangs in the Balance."* Baltimore: Johns Hopkins University Press, 2013.

Marshall, S. L. A. *The American Heritage History of World War I*. New York: Simon and Schuster, 1964.

Massie, Robert K. *Nicholas and Alexandra*. New York: Random House, 2011.

May, Ernest R. *The World War & American Isolation, 1914–1917*. Chicago: Quadrangle Paperbacks, 1966.

McCullough, David. *Truman*. New York: Simon and Schuster, 1992.

McMeekin, Sean. *The Russian Origins of the First World War*. Cambridge: Belknap Press of Harvard University Press, 2011.

Meyer, Karl E. *The Dust of Empire: The Race for Mastery of the Asian Heartland*. New York: Public Affairs, 2004.

Miller, Roger G. *Billy Mitchell: "Stormy Petrel of the Air."* Washington, DC: Office of Air Force History, 2004.

Millett, Allan R. *Semper Fidelis: The History of the United States Marine Corps*. New York: Macmillan, 1980.

Millett, Allan R., and Jack Shulimson, eds. *Commandants of the Marine Corps*. Annapolis, MD: Naval Institute Press, 2004.

Millett, Allan R., and Peter Maslowski. *For the Common Defense: A Military History of the United States*. New York: Free Press, 1994.

Millman, Chad. *The Detonators: The Secret Plot to Destroy America and the Epic Hunt for Justice*. New York: Little, Brown, 2006.

Morison, Samuel Eliot. *The Oxford History of the American People*. Vol. 3, *1869 to the Death of John F. Kennedy, 1963*. New York: Mentor, 1972.

Morris, Edmund. *Colonel Roosevelt*. New York: Random House, 2010.

Mosier, John. *Cross of Iron: The Rise and Fall of the German War Machine, 1914–1918*. New York: Henry Holt, 2006.

Neiberg, Michael S. *Foch: Supreme Allied Commander in the Great War*. Dulles, VA: Brassey's, 2003.

———. *The Second Battle of the Marne*. Bloomington: Indiana University Indiana Press, 2008.

Nye, Roger H. *The Patton Mind: The Professional Development of an Extraordinary Leader*. New York: Avery Publishing, 1993.

O'Connor, Richard. *Black Jack Pershing*. New York: Doubleday, 1961.

Palmer, Michael A. *The German Wars: A Concise History, 1859–1945*. Minneapolis: Zenith Press, 2010.

Pelling, Henry. *Winston Churchill*. Ware, Hertfordshire: Wordsworth Editions, 1999.

Perret, Geoffrey. *Old Soldiers Never Die: The Life of Douglas MacArthur*. Avon, MA: Adams Media, 1996.

Pershing, John J. *My Experiences in the World War*. New York: Frederick A. Stokes, 1931.

Pitt, Barrie. *1918: The Last Act*. London: Reprint Society, 1964.

Pollock, John. *Kitchener: Architect of Victory, Artisan of Peace*. New York: Carroll & Graf, 2001.

Porch, Douglas. *The French Foreign Legion: A Complete History of the Legendary Fighting Force*. New York: HarperCollins, 1991.

Porter, Bruce D. *War and the Rise of the State: The Military Foundations of Modern Politics*. New York: Free Press, 1994.

Price, Matthew C. *The Advancement of Liberty: How American Democratic Principles Transformed the Twentieth Century*. Westport, CT: Praeger, 2008.

Prior, Robin, and Trevor Wilson. *The First World War*. Washington, DC: Smithsonian Books, 2003.

Puryear, Edgar. *Nineteen Stars: A Study in Military Character and Leadership*. Novato, CA: Presidio Press, 2003.

Rainsford, W. Kerr. *From Upton to the Meuse: With the Three Hundred and Seventh Infantry*. Charleston, SC: Forgotten Books, 2012.

Ramage, James A. *Gray Ghost: The Life of Colonel John Singleton Mosby*. Lexington: University Press of Kentucky, 1999.

Renehan, Edward J., Jr. *The Lion's Pride: Theodore Roosevelt and His Family in Peace and War*. New York: Oxford University Press, 1998.

Rickenbacker, Edward V. *Fighting the Flying Circus*. New York: Frederick A. Stokes Company, 1919.

———. *Rickenbacker: An Autobiography*. New York: Prentice-Hall, 1967.

Rose, Norman. *Churchill: The Unruly Giant*. New York: Free Press, 1994.

Rusk, Dean. *As I Saw It*. Edited by Daniel S. Papp. As told to Richard Rusk. New York: Norton, 1990.

Safire, William, ed. *Lend Me Your Ears: Great Speeches in History*. New York: W. W. Norton, 2004.

Seeger, Alan. *Letters and Diary of Alan Seeger*. New York: Charles Scribner's Sons, 1917.

Sharp, Mike, Ian Westwell, and John Westwood. *History of World War One*. Vol. 1, *War and Response, 1914–1916*. Tarrytown, NY: Marshall Cavendish, 2002.

Simkins, Peter, Geoffrey Jukes, and Michael Hickey, *The First World War: The War to End All Wars*. Oxford: Osprey Publishing, 2003.

Skeyhill, Tom, and Richard Wheeler, eds. *Sergeant York and the Great War: His Own Life Story and War Diary*. San Antonio: Vision Forum, 2011.

Slotkin, Richard. *Lost Battalions: The Great War and the Crisis of American Nationality*. New York: Henry Holt, 2005.

Smythe, Donald. *Guerrilla Warrior: The Early Life of John J. Pershing*. New York: Charles Scribner's Sons, 1973.

Somin, Ilya. *Stillborn Crusade: The Tragic Failure of Western Intervention in the Russian Civil War, 1918–1920*. New Brunswick: Transaction Publishers, 1996.

Stallings, Laurence. *The Doughboys: The Story of the AEF, 1917–1918*. New York: Harper & Row, 1963.

Stevenson, David. *Cataclysm: The First World War as Political Tragedy*. New York: Basic Books, 2004.

Stokesbury, James L. *A Short History of World War I*. New York: Perennial, 2002.

Stoler, Mark A. *George C. Marshall: Soldier-Statesman of the American Century*. Boston: Twayne Publisher, 1989.

Strachan, Hew. *The First World War*. London: Penguin, 2003.

Sumner, Ian. *The First Battle of the Marne, 1914: The French "Miracle" Halts the Germans*. Oxford, England: Osprey Publishing, 2010.

Tate, James P. *The Army and Its Air Corps: Army Policy toward Aviation, 1919–1941*. Maxwell AFB, AL: Air University Press, 1998. ·

Terraine, John. *The First World War, 1914–1918*. London: Macmillan, 1984.

———. *The Great War*. Ware, Hertfordshire: Wordsworth Editions, 1998.

———. *To Win a War: 1918, the Year of Victory*. London: Cassell & Company, 1978.

Thomason, John W., Jr. *Fix Bayonets!* Naval and Military Press, no date.

Toland, John. *In Mortal Combat: Korea, 1950–1953*. New York: William Morrow, 1991.

———. *No Man's Land: 1918, The Last Year of the Great War*. Lincoln: University of Nebraska Press, Bison Books, 2002.

Tuchman, Barbara W. *The Guns of August.* New York: Ballantine Books, 1994.

Vandiver, Frank E. *Black Jack: The Life and Times of John J. Pershing.* Vol. 1. College Station: Texas A&M University Press, 1998.

Waller, Douglas. *A Question of Loyalty: General Billy Mitchell and the Court-Martial That Gripped the Nation.* New York: HarperCollins, 2004.

———. *Wild Bill Donovan: The Spymaster Who Created the OSS and Modern American Espionage.* New York: Free Press, 2011.

Walzer, Michael. *Just and Unjust Wars: A Moral Argument with Historical Illustrations.* New York: Pelican Books, 1984.

The War College Division, General Staff Corps. "A Statement of a Proper Military Policy for the United States." September 1915. Published by the Government Printing Office 1916.

Warner, Philip. *Field Marshal Earl Haig.* London: Cassell Military Paperbacks, 2001.

———. *Kitchener: The Man behind the Legend.* New York: Athenuem, 1986.

Weigley, Russell F. *The American Way of War: A History of the United States Military Strategy and Policy.* Bloomington: Indiana University Press, 1977.

Wheeler, Richard "Little Bear," ed. *Sergeant York and the Great War: His Own Life Story and War Diary.* San Antonio, TX: Mantle Ministries/Vision Forum, 2011.

INDEX